The victim in the Irish criminal process

The victim in the Irish criminal process

Shane Kilcommins, Susan Leahy, Kathleen Moore Walsh and Eimear Spain

Manchester University Press

Copyright © Shane Kilcommins, Susan Leahy, Kathleen Moore Walsh and Eimear Spain 2018

The right of Shane Kilcommins, Susan Leahy, Kathleen Moore Walsh and Eimear Spain to be identified as the authors of this work has been asserted by them in accordance with the Copyright, Designs and Patents Act 1988.

Published by Manchester University Press
Oxford Road, Manchester M13 9PL
www.manchesteruniversitypress.co.uk

British Library Cataloguing-in-Publication Data
A catalogue record for this book is available from the British Library

ISBN 978 1 5261 0638 4 paperback

First published 2018

The publisher has no responsibility for the persistence or accuracy of URLs for any external or third-party internet websites referred to in this book, and does not guarantee that any content on such websites is, or will remain, accurate or appropriate.

Typeset
by Toppan Best-set Premedia Limited

Contents

Foreword	*page* vii
Acknowledgements	xi
List of abbreviations	xiii
Introduction	1
1 The victim and the justice system: from key *personal* stakeholder to *institutional* outcast	7
2 The re-emergence of victims of crime in Ireland	28
3 The victim in law: a juridical excursus	52
4 Service provision for victims of crime in Ireland	85
5 Ongoing challenges for victims of crime and the criminal justice sector	111
Conclusion	141
Bibliography	145
Index	169

Foreword

In 2003 a European Commission report commented that: 'One of the greatest tests of the quality of a justice system is how well it treats its victims. Appropriate treatment is a demonstration of societies' solidarity with each individual victim and a recognition that such treatment is essential to the moral integrity of society.' This book adds a rich tapestry of historical information, analysis and support information for all involved with the criminal justice system in Ireland, for victims, for Gardaí, for the prosecution, for the defence and for the judiciary. The timing of this book is very important and informative as we move to transpose the European Union (EU) Directive on Victims' Rights into our legislation with the Criminal Justice (Victims of Crime) Bill 2015 making its way through the houses of the Oireachtas.

Victims of crime enter the criminal justice system by chance rather than by choice. Few would deny the often devastating effects that crime has on those upon whom it is inflicted. Victims of crime may be affected in many ways: physically, emotionally, psychologically and financially. Indeed, their participation and co-operation in the criminal justice system is essential to the prosecution of the guilty and in law enforcement's efforts to control crime in our society. This book gives us a unique insight into every aspect of the victim in the Irish context.

One of the many aspects of this book is the very important historical context it presents. It tracks the participation of the victim in the criminal justice system from the eighteenth century, when victims were the 'principal investigators of crime and the key decision-makers in the prosecution process', through to the culmination of the displacement of the victim, whose role in the twentieth century became 'confined largely to the bit-part role of reporting crime' and to being only a witness for the State as prosecutor. Not only is this historical exposé very informative and interesting but, in highlighting the process that developed over time from victim as main actor to 'bit-part role', we learn how important it is to ensure that a fair balance of rights is struck between the accused and the victim as we move to implement the EU Directive on Victims' Rights into our statute books.

For twenty-four years I worked as a psychotherapist in private practice. Many of my clients were victims of sexual abuse. Some were victims of childhood sexual abuse and others were victims of rape, mainly within intimate partner relationships. However in all that time not one of my clients reported the crimes committed against them to the Gardaí. One has to ask the question why this was the case. As a consequence of the non-reporting it is not surprising that, as research confirms, so many of these crimes are committed with impunity.

My initial training was in the early 1980s in London, where I trained as an individual psychotherapist and subsequently I trained in Ireland as a Family Therapist in the Mater Hospital and as a Group Analyst in St Vincent's Hospital. At that time the consulting room was seen to be as sacred and confidential as the confessional. There was no question of breaking that confidence. Now, on looking back one could interpret this stance as supporting all the secrecy that surrounded sexual violence and, in a way, as some kind of unconscious collusion with the status quo. But it also reflected that peripheral place that the victim came to occupy in the criminal justice system. There was never any question of my clients reporting to the Gardaí or going to court. Their expectation was that they would not be believed and they would not get justice and would possibly suffer further victimisation by the system.

From 2006 to 2016 I was the chief executive officer of the Dublin Rape Crisis Centre (DRCC). The Ferns Report had recently been published. The Centre had, in collaboration with the Royal College of Surgeons, published the SAVI (Sexual Abuse and Violence in Ireland; McGee et al.) Report in 2002. While at the time it got very little recognition, over the years it became acknowledged as the most comprehensive research on attitudes to and beliefs about sexual violence in Ireland and was the impetus for the subsequent Ryan, Murphy and Cloyne Reports. We set about lobbying Government, armed with the information from the research, to have the recommendations of SAVI implemented. As a consequence, two new SATUs (Sexual Assault Treatment Units) were set up in Mullingar and Galway, which brought the number of SATUs in the country to six. We delivered eight national annual awareness-raising campaigns supported by COSC (the National Office for the Prevention of Domestic, Sexual and Gender Based Violence, and we presented annual statistics. And yet, as is highlighted in all chapters in this book, we still have a long way to go to ensure that the needs of victims are met.

The stories from victims attending the DRCC included descriptions of their experiences of re-victimisation by the criminal justice system, from reporting to the Gardaí through to their court experiences. Not every victim's experience was a totally bad one; however, all the victims who spoke to us said that they felt that they were incidental to the criminal justice process. Many who had gone through the system and got a conviction would say that if they had the time over again they would not proceed with their case. As is further demonstrated in this book, victims decided not to proceed with their cases because of a variety of reasons, from an initial bad experience of reporting the crime through to inordinate delays and a lack of communication with the various agents of the criminal justice system. Research supported by the European Daphne Project *'Different Systems, Similar Outcomes?' Tracking Attrition in Reported Rape Cases in Eleven Countries*; Corr, M.; O'Mahony, P.; Lovett, L. and Kelly, L. (April 2009), highlighted Ireland as having the highest attrition rate in comparison to eleven other EU countries in cases of sexual crimes.

The Victim in the Irish Criminal Process brings together every aspect of the victim in the criminal justice system in the Irish context in a way that has not been done before. It will serve as a great source of information and validation of victims' experiences, not only for academics but also for those who work on a daily basis with victims of crime and who are in a position to lobby government for the many changes that are still so necessary to redress the balance of the victim and the accused in our criminal justice system. One of the additional assets of this book is that it is possible to read each chapter as a stand-alone in its own right. From the Introduction through the five chapters we learn how the criminal justice system is influenced and how changes come about as society develops and changes. However, change is a process and very often it can be too slow, which can affect the delivery of justice. The old adage 'justice delayed is justice denied' comes through as truth in many of the chapters of this book. For victims, this is not good enough!

As is highlighted particularly in the last chapter, there are still many improvements that are needed to ensure that a balance is struck between the rights of the victim and the accused in our criminal justice system so that justice is delivered. There are still big gaps that have to be bridged and significant investment is still needed in service provision, research, education and training to bring about the necessary changes. I believe this book will be a very welcome support to those who are working on the front line with victims. It gives them the necessary comprehensive research to support and enable them to lobby more effectively for victims' rights. In time, hopefully, we will see more victims coming forward to report the crimes committed against them and perpetrators will know that they will not be able to commit these crimes any more with impunity, which will go a long way to supporting the prevention of crime.

A most interesting, informative and accessible read.

Ellen O'Malley Dunlop
Adjunct Professor, School of Law, University of Limerick

Acknowledgements

It remains only for us to thank those who have assisted us in the completion of this book. Our publisher, Manchester University Press, was at all times supportive of what we were doing. We must also thank our respective families and friends. Eimear would like to thank Des for all his support and kindness during the writing of this book. From inception to completion, the experience of writing this book has been a memorable and enjoyable one; for this she thanks her friends and co-authors. Kathleen would like to thank her husband, Peter, for his unconditional support. Shane would like to thank his wife, Maria, for her patience, support and good humour in the writing of this book. He would also like to acknowledge the wonderfully distractive influence of his children, Kate, Jack, Jane and Ruth. Susan would like to thank her parents, Denis and Rita Leahy, for their support and encouragement, as well as her co-authors for their insights and collegiality throughout the writing process.

Abbreviations

All ER	*All England Law Reports*
CLR	*Commonwealth Law Reports*
COSC	National Office for the Prevention of Domestic, Sexual and Gender Based Violence
CPS	Crown Prosecution Service
CSO	Central Statistics Office
CVH	Crime Victims Helpline
Den	*Denison & Pearce's Crown Cases Reserved*
DPP	Director of Public Prosecutions
DRCC	Dublin Rape Crisis Centre
ECHR	*European Court of Human Rights, Judgments*
EHRLR	*European Human Rights Law Review*
EHRR	*European Human Rights Reports*
FRA	European Union Agency for Fundamental Rights
Frewen	*Judgments of the Court of Criminal Appeal*
IECA	*Ireland Court of Appeal*
IECCA	*Ireland Court of Criminal Appeal*
IEHC	*High Court of Ireland*
IESC	*Supreme Court of Ireland*
IHC	*Inhouse Counsel*
ILRM	*Irish Law Reports Monthly*
ILTR	*Irish Law Times Reports*
IR	*Irish Reports*
KB	*Law Reports, King's Bench Division*
LGBT	lesbian, gay, bisexual and transgender
NGO	non-governmental organisation
PULSE	Police Using Leading Systems Effectively
RCNI	Rape Crisis Network of Ireland
SATU	Sexual Assault Treatment Unit
UN Declaration	UN Declaration of Basic Principles of Justice for Victims of Crime and Abuse of Power

Introduction

This book will examine the changing role of victims of crime in the Irish criminal process. Their status has not remained static over time. Rather, it has been subject to a series of ruptures which have dramatically altered their standing. Under the pre-modern exculpatory justice system which existed in the seventeenth and eighteenth centuries, where wrongdoing was understood as a personal altercation, victims were given primacy as decision makers: they could elect to leave matters rest; settle privately; or prosecute, but decide upon the charge. They were, in essence, the principal claims-makers. Their ownership of the alleged wrongs meant that their voices – built largely upon subjective experiences – carried a powerful justificatory force. Personal referents and preferences were actively embraced as a vital currency in criminal relations, one which linked the parties most affected in the conflict to the justice network.

By the mid-nineteenth century, however, the justice system was steadfastly disassociating itself from local and personal determinants. It sought instead to become a more depersonalised, rule-governed affair with the State at the centre. Conflicts were no longer viewed as the property of the parties most directly affected. Victims of crime were increasingly required to fit in to a new architecture of criminal and penal semiotics, one which gave primacy to system relations, emphasising ideals such as rationality, liberalism, uniformity, State power and depersonalisation. Their individual experiences, which provided such a motivating impulse under the exculpatory model, were now increasingly rejected as invalid knowledge, given their personal, irrational, emotive and unconstrained tendencies. Such experiences would now be routed through the medium of the *public interest* and packaged and presented in institutional terms. New imperatives were also foregrounded within this institutional arrangement, particularly those that emphasised procedure, the ideological neutrality and rationality of the process, and its objectivated nature. The singularity of relations which ensued in the nineteenth and twentieth centuries meant that most relevant facts and phenomena were interpreted through a narrow, State/accused lens. The operational self-enclosure inherent within this logic of action confined the victim to a peripheral role, one which did not permit or endorse personal claims over the conflict.

In the last four decades, justice systems are partially being reconstructed again, as they demonstrate an increased sensitivity to the needs and concerns of victims of crime. A 'vision of the victim as Everyman' is part of a 'new cultural theme' (Garland, 2001: 12), one which is widely represented in social, political and media circles. It has been suggested that a number of factors has facilitated this increased awareness of victims in Western criminal justice systems (Maguire, 1991: 363–433). To begin with, the introduction of state compensation programmes can be viewed as an early attempt to move victims away from the periphery of the criminal process. In England and Wales, for example, Margaret Fry proposed a scheme of State compensation for the victims of violence as early as 1957. Specific victimological studies became more prominent and began to direct the criminological gaze away from its focus on offenders, towards a typology of victims' experiences of the wrongdoing. These studies, among others, were important in generating academic interest in victims of crime. They were followed up by the introduction of mass victimisation surveys, commencing in the 1970s in the United States (US) before also being employed in the early 1980s in the United Kingdom (UK), which among other things drew attention to the under-recording of crime, repeat victimisation, fear of crime and victims' experiences with various criminal justice agencies such as the police, prosecutors, trial judges and other court personnel.

In the Republic of Ireland, studies such as that undertaken by Breen and Rottman (1984), O'Connell and Whelan (1994) and Watson (2000) all began to highlight the experiences of victims (McCullagh, 1986: 13–14). However, mass crime victimisation studies had a somewhat sluggish trajectory when compared with other jurisdictions (commencing in the US in 1972 and the UK in 1982), hindered no doubt by the absence of a strong criminal justice research culture and successive governments' dismissive attitude towards policy based on crime data and crime statistics (Kilcommins et al., 2004: 72–4; Cotter, 2005: 295). Mass crime victimisation surveys commenced only in 1998, with the introduction of a crime segment into the Quarterly National Household survey.

The growth in the women's movement also, it is argued, 'raised the consciousness of women to the oppression of criminal violence' (Moore Walsh, 2013: 182–9; Young, 2006: 3). More specifically, increased self-activism also ensured that victims of crime became more visible again (Maguire, 1991: 370). The first domestic abuse shelter, for example, was established in 1974 (Moore Walsh, 2013: 188). The first Rape Crisis Centre was set up in Dublin in 1977 and Derek Nally established Victim Support in 1985. Service provision for victims of crime in the Republic of Ireland has expanded in recent decades. The Victims Charter, for example, marked an important policy development (McGovern, 2002: 393; Rogan, 2006b: 153). This Charter was produced by the Department of Justice, Equality and Law Reform in September 1999 (and was revised in 2010), reflecting the 'commitment to giving victims of crime a central place in the criminal justice system'. The needs of crime victims are also addressed by a wide variety of victims' organisations, alliances and associations. While a significant proportion are specialised in nature, dealing with specific types of victim or services, there are also some key national groups. For example, the national Crime Victims Helpline, which represents a proactive initiative to support crime victims, was launched in 2005.

Moreover, the revelations brought about as a result of inquiries over the last two decades into Church sexual abuse and institutional abuse – which occurred in the carceral archipelago that emerged post Independence – is now very much part of the *Zeitgeist* (Raftery and O'Sullivan, 1999). The Ryan Report, established to inquire into child abuse in institutions of the State from 1936 onwards, for example, noted in 2009 that: '[c]hildren with a learning disability, physical and sensory impairments and children who had no known family contact were especially vulnerable in institutional settings. They described being powerless against adults who abused them, especially when those adults were in positions of authority and trust. Impaired mobility and communication deficits made it impossible to inform others of their abuse or to resist it. Children who were unable to hear, see, speak, move or adequately express themselves were at a complete disadvantage in environments that did not recognise or facilitate their right to be heard' (Commission to Inquire in to Child Abuse, 2009: 14). Among other things, it has helped to raise experiences of victimhood in the collective conscience, and awareness of illegitimate and abusive hierarchies of dominance. This has, in part, contributed to a growing scepticism about the institutional reification of State functionaries such as the Office of the Director of Public Prosecutions (DPP) and Gardaí (Conway, 2010; Conway, 2013). Given the demands for increased accountability and transparency in decision-making structures, government agencies are no longer as free to set their own imperatives, or to claim absolute immunity from scrutiny. Nor can they so easily defend their actions on the basis of the neutrality of their activities, or hide behind a broad-based appeal to public-interest considerations or respect for institutions of State power.

Increasing concerns about rising crime rates in Western countries from the 1970s onwards, and the perceived failure of correctionalist criminal justice projects to rehabilitate offenders, have also had an impact. It is not surprising, according to commentators such as David Garland, that the 'aim of serving victims has become part of the redefined mission of all criminal justice agencies' (Garland, 2001: 121). Among other things, it has brought into vogue the question: 'What about the victim?' (Maguire, 1991: 368).

Law has also helped to steer victim reintegration, confirming participation and protection claims for victims, while also seeking to secure the fair administration of justice. Considerations of process fairness now include the victim within its conceptual framework. While previously such deliberations were housed within the more remote medium of the 'public interest', the courts are now becoming more explicit in specifically identifying victims and competing rights. Of course, the regulation of victim experiences in law necessarily involves a level of abstraction and institutionalisation that never fully captures all of the relevant exigencies. Nevertheless, and despite these shortcomings, increasing juridification of the crime conflict is helping to overcome the previous ambivalence towards victims of crime.

Juridification of this kind has also been scaffolded by a number of international legal instruments which have also promoted recognition of the needs of victims within criminal justice systems. The United Nations General Assembly, for example, adopted the Declaration of Basic Principles of Justice for Victims of Crime and Abuse of Power in 1985 (Aldana-Pindell, 2004: 618; Doak, 2003: 10; Van Dijk, 2005: 202), which include the right to be treated with respect and recognition, to be referred to adequate support services and to receive information about the progress of the case. The Council of Europe also recognised from the 1970s onwards the importance of preventing secondary victimisation. It has done this through the adoption of a series of conventions and recommendations (Muller-Rappard, 1990: 231–45). The European Union has more recently begun to focus on the area of criminal justice. In March 2001, for example, the Council adopted a Framework Decision on the Standing of Victims in Criminal Proceedings, which provides for minimum rights (including the right to be heard and furnish evidence, access to relevant information, the opportunity to participate and the right to compensation) to be ensured in all the territories of the EU. A Directive establishing minimum standards on the rights, support and protection of victims of crime – organised around the tripartite dimensions of information, participation and protection – has been adopted and member states were given until 2015 to transpose it into law. It will result in a more sustained, systematised approach, one where criminal justice agencies are required to take account of the needs and concerns of victims of crime in their decision-making processes. Through its directly binding and enforceable provisions, it will act as an emboldening juristic reference point, ensuring the better accommodation of victims of crime in all criminal processes and practices.

The European Convention of Human Rights acts as another influential normative framework that seeks to extend the reach of rights in the criminal process to include victims of crime. Though the Convention does not explicitly refer to victims of crime, the European Court of Human Rights has placed obligations on member states under Articles 2 (right to life), 3 (degrading treatment), 6 (fair trial) and 8 (private life). Such interpretations help to identify more concrete rights for victims of crime, and act as a powerful counterpoint to the hegemonic dominance of State/accused relations.

All of this impetus is largely inclusionary. The 'axis of individualisation' in the criminal justice process – which for so long was directed only at accused/offenders, the causes of their wrongdoing (including 'othering') and their right to protection from the State – has now bifurcated to embrace the multi-faceted experiences of victimhood. This of course disturbs older, hegemonic ways of doing things (an accused/offender organising logic that infused a police–public interest–prosecutions–prisons model of justice) and the reified, exclusive voices of certain actors that were central to that process (prosecution and defence lawyers, policing authorities and judges). Its recent emergence must be seen much more as a response to a previous scandalous neglect, as a justified attempt to correct an imbalance in which the victim was constituted as a 'silent abstraction, a background figure whose individuality hardly registered' (Garland, 2001: 179).

While it is clear – particularly when viewed over a long past – that victims are re-emerging as important stakeholders, it would be unwise to oversentimentalise the progress that has been made, or to take the view that there are no more challenges ahead. Many advancements, particularly in Ireland, have been piecemeal in nature, their presence often the product of fortuitous, but isolated, determinants. Sustained progress has been hampered by the absence of any unified field about the plight of victims of crime in the criminal process. This may in part be attributable to the almost inevitable lack of resources, the constant dissonance that exists between criminal justice policy and practice (Hamilton, 2014: 55), and various embedded practices and institutional ways of doing things. The importance of adversarialism, for example, became deeply ingrained from the middle of the nineteenth century as the appropriate means of resolving criminal disputes. This deep commitment to the reception and observation of unmediated *viva voce* testimony is grounded in the need to uphold the integrity of the adjudicative process and minimise the risk of misdecision. Its reification as the only way of 'doing justice', however, conceals the extent to which it is rooted in a State/accused logic of action, one which is unwilling to countenance the discriminatory assumptions and biases inherent within such an epistemic paradigm. In addition to the obstacles posed by embedded practices, progress has also been stymied by the unwillingness of the body politic, particularly since the late 1990s, to put the inclusion of victims at the centre of the criminal justice agenda, preferring instead to pursue an expressive agenda of 'governing through crime', with its micro focus on the technologies of protection and the adoption of repressive laws against the outside 'enemy' (Hamilton, 2014: 31–55; Vaughan and Kilcommins, 2010: 132–4).

There are also more specific challenges for the Irish criminal process. A lack of knowledge among criminal justice agencies and actors about the needs of victims of crime remains a central issue. There are also many reported difficulties with the provision of information to victims and with the under-reporting of crime. Other issues that cause concern to victims include: a fear of crime, intimidation by the process, attrition rates, a lack of empathy and understanding in reporting a crime, the lack of private areas in courts, difficulties with procedural rules and legal definitions and directions (e.g. consent in rape cases), delays in the system, the lack of protection and security offered by the criminal justice system, the lack of opportunity to participate fully in the criminal process, under- and over-criminalisation, overcrowded courtrooms and an inability to hear the proceedings, low levels of awareness of victim support groups, a lack of information on claiming witness expenses and inadequate support services.

The lack of recognition of vulnerable witnesses in Ireland has also been identified (Bacik et al, 2007: 10–11). Victims of crime with disabilities, for example, remain largely invisible, not least because of the difficulties in relation to information gathering and fact finding for an adversarial justice system which for the most part refuses to engage with the ontological dimensions of disability. A recent study undertaken on victims of crime with disabilities found, for example, that people with disabilities 'are not being strategically identified as a victim group, either by victim support organisations, or those engaged at a central government policy level in dealing with victims' issues' (Edwards et al., 2012: 100). The Irish court process also remains epistemically rooted in mainstream accounts of victims' needs and concerns. Such victims fit more easily within an adversarial paradigm of justice.

This book is aimed at documenting the variety of ways in which victims of crime are now being written into the criminal process discourse and practice in Ireland, while taking account of existing challenges. By being anchored initially in the monopolistic purity of State/accused relations which existed for most of the nineteenth and twentieth centuries, it takes a long view. It will seek to show how the justice system is emerging from hegemonic dominance of that kind. Although the book is about the practices and discourses which are crystallising around this re-emergence, it is not a standpoint perspective. It does not attempt to contend with the lived experiences and realities of victimhood or with the typologies of crime which occur in Ireland. It is a desk-based project which attempts initially to map the systematic exclusion of victims of crime. It then proceeds to examine the conditions which have made their re-emergence possible and the commitments, practices and strategic priorities shaping this inclusionary momentum. By focusing on broad historical changes in the assumptions and realities that have governed victim relations, our modest ambition for this book is that it will help to amplify the dynamics and principles that shape and determine our current arrangements.

1

The victim and the justice system: from key *personal* stakeholder to *institutional* outcast[1]

Introduction

The purpose of this chapter is to explain the emergence of the modern assumptions, commitments and strategic priorities that have shaped the position of the victim in the justice system. In particular, it seeks to demonstrate how the paradigm of prosecuting and investigating crime moved from an intensely local, unstructured and victim-precipitated arrangement to a structured, adversarial, State-monopolised event where the accused was largely silenced and the victim was rendered invisible. This transformation provides an important backdrop against which to query the confluence of approaches that currently shape and determine State and societal relations with victims of crime (Vaughan and Kilcommins, 2010: 41–66).

Engaging in such a wide-ranging historical analysis of how the victim has been depicted and represented over time is of course fraught with dangers, not least given the tendency of such analysis to over-generalise and over-schematise changes in social life and in the criminal legal structure. Despite the dangers, we believe that the exercise can prove valuable. In particular, it can help us to identify and consider different trends, tendencies and currents of reflection that broadly comprise patterns of action vis-à-vis victims of crime at different historical points in time.

The purpose of the chapter therefore is to trace the ways in which different justice systems have accommodated victims of crime. By highlighting the broad historical changes in the assumptions and realities that governed victim relations under pre-modern exculpatory and modern inculpatory models of justice, it will help us to focus on and amplify the dynamics and principles that shape and determine our current arrangements. This chapter will seek to demonstrate how pre-modern exculpatory justice – operating in a social and political field in which order was conceived in local terms and where criminal wrongdoing was interpreted and understood as a *personal* altercation – gave primacy to victims as decision makers. This was gradually replaced with a new architecture of criminal and penal semiotics that reified *system* relations, emphasising ideals such as rationality, liberalism, uniformity, State power and depersonalisation. The rationalisation of the crime conflict is the key anchoring point of this chapter. It represents the shift from personal to institutional relations, ensuring that subjective and emotive experiences were increasingly represented as invalid, tainted knowledge. By structuring the chapter in this way, it will be possible to sketch out the ways in which the autonomy and power of victims of crime were gradually dismantled in the course of the nineteenth century as public power colonised ownership of criminal wrongdoing. The circuitry networks of this power included a growing reliance on formal and procedural legal rules, professional lawyers, centralised State agencies and 'objective' lay participation. The 'public interest' mechanism that was constructed to fill the void acted as a new and safe conduit for the expression of citizen and political concerns. The inculpatory model which emerged also embraced a State/accused logic of action which helped to 'objectivate' the conflict and to create a 'zone of indifference' between personal experiences and the institutional process.

The victim within an exculpatory model of justice

The peculiar geometry of eighteenth-century penal relations comprised a savage penal code ameliorated by a well-established machinery of concessions in the form of judge and jury discretion and executive clemency. Hegemony was thus maintained both by the use of the theatre of execution – and the exemplary display of terror inherent therein – and the flexible employment of concessions. They could be granted for a whole variety of reasons and included the following: the guilty party was relatively young or of otherwise good character; the guilty party was pregnant (known as 'the benefit of the belly') or could read a prescribed passage from the bible (the 'benefit of clergy'); they acceded to the petitions of the victim or the local gentry; they propitiated the 'winds of public opinion'; or the jury engaged in a form of 'pious perjury', ensuring that the accused did not hang for the offences committed (Kilcommins, 1998: 1–54; Rawlings, 1999: 39–53). Such a 'lottery of justice' must be understood against a backdrop of historically specific social relations and social control. The great majority of petitions for mercy in the eighteenth century were written by the gentry and landed aristocracy on behalf of those accused of crime. Concessions ensured, to some extent, that a good many offenders left the courtroom indebted to their more 'noble' peers and convinced of the merciful nature of justice. In this way, the criminal justice system attempted to instil compliance through examples of brute terror – but not so many as to destroy the perception of justice or rupture the bonds of paternalism – and also, in a much more subtle fashion, through examples of mercy. Balancing these dyads was particularly important in an epoch where tight social control in the form of professional policing did not exist (Hay, 1977: 17–63).

Sufficient numbers of offenders were thus enmeshed in the 'punishment as spectacle' rituals which bore witness to the majesty of the law and the 'dissymmetry of power relations' between the sovereign and his or her citizens (Foucault, 1991 repr.: 49). As Paley suggested: 'by this expedient few actually suffer death, while the dread and danger of it hang over the crimes of many' (Paley, 1833: 161). At the same time, enough offenders escaped the clutches of this theatre of terror through the mercy that the system of justice offered. Such elasticity in the form of mercy was, according to Blackstone, designed to 'endear the sovereign to his subjects, and contribute more than anything to root in their hearts that filial affection, and personal loyalty, which are the sure establishment of a prince' (as quoted in Hay, 1977: 48; Fletcher and Stevenson, 1985: 1–40).

Eighteenth-century justice also emphasised at every turn the important role of communal participation. Crime was not generally perceived in terms of a transgression of nationally accepted law. The machinery of justice was by and large constructed around informal, communal networks that could not conceive of criminal behaviour in an abstract way. With no sense of abstract crime or harm, there could be little possibility of a system to prosecute such offences. In a social world which was localised in character, responsibility for order, in keeping with the consensus justice paradigm, was in large part entrusted upon ordinary citizens (Herrup, 1989; Willis, 2008: 413). Such a system, as Philips has pointed out, 'did not rest on the modern idea of catching and prosecuting all offenders, but rather on the idea of catching, prosecuting and punishing exemplarily, a sufficient number of offenders to deter others' (Philips, 1983: 160–1). Few, moreover, wished law enforcement to be more formalised, for fear of the centralised despotism which might result. With such sporadic and unpredictable enforcement, there emerged what Foucault called 'tolerated illegality': 'the non-application of the rule, the non-observance of the innumerable edicts or ordinances were a condition of the political functioning of society ... [I]llegality was so deeply rooted and so necessary to the life of each social stratum, that it had in a sense its own coherence and economy' (Foucault, 1991 repr.: 82). These spaces of discretion and freedom were essential to the maintenance of the system of social control as it operated in pre-industrial times (Shoemaker, 1987: 294).

The machinery of justice was thus by and large constructed around informal networks. It relied heavily, for example, on the provision of private and statutory rewards for information leading to the conviction of offenders (Langbein, 1983). It utilised professional 'thieftakers' who, through intelligence networks, secured evidence of guilt against those accused of crime in return for the rewards available from the courts, as well as from victims who paid to have their stolen property returned (Paley, 1989: 301–30). It also witnessed the emergence of private associations for the prosecution of felons which organised at common expense *posses* to pursue offenders, patrols to supervise localities and the prosecution in court of offences committed against members (Philips, 1989: 117–51; Shubert, 1981: 25–41). The justice system also created a hierarchy of pardons and immunity from prosecution for those who could be induced to turn against the criminal fraternity from which they operated. Pardons as an absolute right could be claimed by accomplices in return for evidence that would convict those who had committed one of a number of specified offences. Pardons could also be claimed under royal proclamation made by the government in respect of specific offences (Radzinowicz, 1956: 40–2). Accomplices also retained the hope that they might not be prosecuted, or at least might receive a lighter sentence, if they made a full and fair confession and their evidence was used to convict other offenders. In such circumstances, accomplices were not entitled as of legal right to any better treatment. They gave their evidence 'in vinculis' [in chains] and it depended on their behaviour whether or not they were entitled to an equitable claim (*R v Rudd* 1775 1 Leach 115 at 119).

In keeping with the local orientation of justice, the 'paradigm of prosecution' in the eighteenth century rested on victims of crime (Hay, 1983: 167). They were the principal investigators of crime and the key decision makers in the prosecution process (King, 1984: 27). As Bentham (1830: 427) disapprovingly noted: 'The law gives to the party injured, or rather to every prosecutor, a partial power of pardon ... in giving him the choice of the kind of action he will commence ... The lot of the offender depends not on the gravity of his offence but on ... the injured party ... The judge is a puppet in the hands of any prosecutor.' Victims could elect not to invoke the law and to let the criminal act go unpunished; they could engage in a personal settlement or private retribution; or they could prosecute but shape the severity of any criminal charge (capital or non-capital) through their interpretation of the facts. It is, as Philips suggests, a very modern idea 'to think that every discovered offence should be followed automatically by prosecution; for centuries, the English system had worked on the principle that indictment before a court was the last resort to be tried; there were all sorts of alternative informal means which the potential prosecutor might try to use short of formal prosecution' (Philips, 1983: 158). Conflicts remained the property of the parties personally affected and this often involved recourse to informal dispute settlement (Christie, 1977: 1–15; Edelstein, 1998: 364): 'formal prosecution was the exception; negotiation and informal sanction the norm. The major courts had no monopoly over punitive sanctions in the eighteenth century. Indeed, they usually had to content themselves with processing a few scraps and particularly tough morsels which those involved in informal sanctioning processes threw their way or spat out as indigestible, and as therefore requiring the tougher teeth of the criminal law' (King, 2000: 22–3). If victims did proceed with a prosecution, it was their energy, for the most part, that carried the case through the various prosecution stages. Victims engaged in the fact finding, gathered witnesses, prepared cases, presented evidence in court as examiners-in-chief and bore the costs involved (Beattie, 1986: 35).

Moreover, local and personal knowledge about the character of the accused was not confined to that narrow space between conviction and the imposition of sentence. Rather, it occupied a more central role in the determination of the accused's guilt or innocence (Green, 1988: 281; Lacey, 2001: 361–2). In addition to playing a key role at trial, character witnesses were also very influential in support of an accused's plea for mercy post-conviction. Jurors too were chosen from the locality and had a 'keen knowledge of the good and rotten apples in their barrel' (Friedman, 1993: 27). As Sir Robert Peel admitted: '[I]t might be hard to say to a man, that his life should be valued at a particular rate, depending upon local or temporary expediency. But this was the very reasoning upon which the law was founded' (as quoted in McGowen, 1983: 110–11). As King noted:

> The criminal justice system was ... about accommodation. Accommodation with victims who wanted, and gained flexibility in deciding whether to prosecute, compound or forgive, in deciding what charge to bring, in deciding whether or not to turn up on the day of the trial; accommodation with the mitigating tendencies of semi-autonomous juries ...; accommodation with the sentencing and pardoning priorities of the good mind. These compromises not only enabled a system that was heavily dependent on popular participation to work fairly effectively; they may also have done something to prevent the law from losing its broader ideological usefulness to the propertied elite. (King, 2000: 371)

Indeed, accommodation permeated social relations more generally. Community participation in the form of crowd protest and disorder, for example, was a tolerated element of eighteenth-century life. Group disturbances in relation to issues such as food prices, executions, press-gangs, wages and turnpikes were perceived by the authorities as part of a paternalist and reciprocal model of local social relations (Lacquer, 1989: 353–4 ; Thompson, 1971: 76–136).

The fact that an accused's guilt or innocence in respect of a felony charge was determined 'by the country' and men from the locality who constituted the jury was seen as a further safeguard against the intrusions of arbitrary or despotic power. Trial by jury was a 'grand bulwark' of an accused's liberties. The merciful use of partial verdicts and 'pious perjury' heightened this sense of liberty. Blackstone, for example, noted that the trial by jury was a 'barrier ... between the liberties of the people and the prerogative of the Crown' because 'the truth of each accusation ... [must] be confirmed by the unanimous suffrage of twelve of his equals and neighbours, indifferently chosen and superior to all suspicions' (Blackstone, 1765: 349–50). Juries in the eighteenth century also, unlike their present-day counterparts, played a powerful role in the mitigation of sentences (Green, 1988: 284). This was possible in an era when the guilt- and sentencing-determining functions were woven into a relatively seamless design (Langbein, 1994: 1064).

The legal landscape was dominated by the intimate interaction of two features: a criminal offences calendar that was generously peppered with the use of the death sentence, on the one hand, but which was moulded into a justice system that was highly elastic, personal and merciful, on the other hand. It was the combination of both terror and discretion that was critically important in legitimising the status quo (Hay, 1977: 26). The substantive criminal law itself was amorphous in character. This is not surprising, given the low level of reporting and recording of cases (Cornish and de N. Clark, 1989: 565; Langbein, 1983: 3). Nor was it legitimated, as it is today, on its detachment from the local and particular circumstances of the crime. Rather, guilt was determined by a much looser conception of culpability which was closely tethered to moral blameworthiness and to local knowledge of the character of the accused. The current preoccupation with structuring the criminal law in terms of voluntary conduct, responsibility and excusing conditions – the 'analytic framework of *actus reus/mens rea*/defence' (Lacey, 1998: 23; McAuley and McCutcheon, 2000: 1–32) – was notably absent in the eighteenth century. As Lacey suggested about its earlier configuration:

> This model, operating in a world in which professional policing and prosecution and an elaborate law of evidence had yet to be developed, worked on the basis of lay evaluation of normative, character based – rather than subjective or psychological – evidence and assumptions about the individual defendant. (Lacey, 2001: 361)

Criminal trials in the eighteenth century were personal altercations, involving face-to-face confrontation between victims and their alleged tormentors (May, 2003: 21). They were amateur, hasty and relatively unstructured affairs. As compared with more modern trial arrangements, the accused was compromised in many ways. To begin with, he or she could give only unsworn testimony. Defence witnesses could not be compelled to testify; when they did testify, it was received unsworn (Beattie, 1991: 221–67; Langbein, 2003: 52). Those accused of crime were also denied access to depositions, to copies of indictments (except in trials for treason) and to the names of prosecution witnesses before the trial. Their peremptory right to challenge the composition of the jury was circumvented by not being able to see the jury list until their actual trials (Baker, 1977: 36; Gatrell, 1994: 536–7). More fundamentally, they were not, for the most part, entitled to have arguments made for them by counsel in felony trials. As Hawkins observed in *Pleas of the Crown* in 1721:

> [E]very one of common understanding may as properly speak to a matter of fact as if he were the best lawyer … It requires no manner of skill to make a plain and honest defence …; the simplicity, the innocence, the artless and ingenuous

behaviour of one whose conscience acquits him, having something in it more moving and convincing than the highest eloquence of persons speaking in a cause not their own ... Whereas on the other side, the very speech, gesture and countenance, and manner of defence of those who are guilty, when they speak for themselves, may often help to disclose the truth; which probably would not so well be discovered from the artificial defense of others speaking for them. (As quoted in Langbein, 1983: 123)

Moreover, there was no explicit presumption of innocence. In 'accused speaks' trials, as they have been referred to, the onus was always on the accused to engage in self-exculpation (Allen, 1931: 260; Langbein, 1994: 1047). He or she was viewed as a vital 'testimonial resource' (Langbein, 1999: 314–64). Once the prosecution case concluded, the judge would turn to the accused and say something to the effect: 'you have heard the evidence: what do you have to say for yourself' (Beattie, 1986: 349). The implication was clear. If those accused of crime were innocent, then they were going to have to demonstrate it through an active defence where their version of events could be heard and their demeanours be observed (Cairns, 1998: 49). Indeed the right of those accused to speak – rather than the right to silence – was viewed as being the fundamental safeguard in their defence of criminal allegations under this exculpatory model of justice (Langbein, 1994: 1047–85). The theory was that the prisoner should speak 'either to clear himself or to hang himself' (Ibid.: 1053). In addition, few limitations existed over the evidence that could be adduced against an accused at trial and there was nothing in the way of a set of crystallised exclusionary rules of evidence. The burden of proof, too, was not as sharply drawn as it is today. Fact finding was thus securely linked to more general beliefs about knowledge and truth, which helped to shape a 'satisfied conscience' threshold for judgement (Shapiro, 2014).

Though those accused of crime were much more limited in the civil liberty rights that they could rely upon in the eighteenth century, some elements of equilibrium did exist in courtroom relations. First, and as we have already seen, hegemony was in part maintained though judicial discretion and mercy in the form of executive clemency and 'pious perjury'. A good many accused left courtrooms having benefited from one of the various forms of mercy that the system of justice offered. Second, trial judges, to some extent, protected the interests of those accused of crimes at trials (Beattie, 1991: 252). This was alluded to by Coke in the early seventeenth century: '[T]he court ought to be ... of counsel for the prisoner to see that nothing be urged against him contrary to law and right' (as quoted in Langbein, 1994: 1050). They would, for example, ensure that illegal procedures were not allowed to the detriment of those in the dock; they would strike out erroneous indictments; and they would on occasion cross-examine prosecution witnesses whom they suspected of giving false testimony. They could also apply a very strong formalistic logic in respect of the framing of indictments and search warrants. Formalities of this nature in indictments in the seventeenth and eighteenth centuries were described by Sir William Holdsworth as 'this extraordinary and irrational set of rules that have grown up round the wording of indictments' (Holdsworth, 1908 repr.: 618–19). This strict interpretation of procedural rules was crucial in maintaining hegemonic order. The perceived objectivity of justice fitted very neatly in the English collective consciousness with a keen awareness of its fundamental liberty rights as free-born citizens. As Hay noted: 'When the ruling class acquitted men on technicalities they helped instil a belief in the disembodied justice of law in the minds of all who watched. In short, its very inefficiency, its absurd formalism, was part of its strength as ideology' (Hay, 1977: 33; Baker, 1977: 45–7). The aphorism that a judge was 'counsel for the prisoner' should not, however, be overstated. A judge's primary duty was to ensure the legality of the various events that occurred at trial. Though a judge may have kept a watchful eye on the accused's corner, he did not help him or her to select or build a defence (Cairns, 1998: 52; McGowen, 1983: 105).

It can be said that the justice system that existed in Britain and Ireland in the period in question was exculpatory and localised in nature. It privileged the subjective experiences of victims. When formal justice was invoked, which was the exception rather than the rule, it relied heavily on victim and popular participation. Formal resolution of grievance remained very much the property of individual victims or associations of victims, who monopolised the investigative and prosecutorial functions. Victims could thus assert primacy as claims-makers. Their ownership of the alleged wrongs had a powerful justificatory force, which ensured that their subjective experiences and personal preferences were received relatively unfiltered and carried meaningful weight. The criminal trial itself was a personal, largely unregulated altercation, with the working assumption that the accused was, in the absence of exculpation, guilty. This ensured that the accused was at all times an active, participating trial actor, a vital 'testimonial resource' whose self-exculpatory narrative was closely scrutinised by the judge and local jury in determining culpability. The degree of culpability itself was heavily shaped by moral and local knowledge considerations. Moreover, few restrictions existed on what could be admitted in trial. Most evidentiary facts which had broad probative value as regards the offence committed were heard in open court and required defence rebuttal, regardless of their prejudicial effect on the accused.

Dismantling the old equipoise of power

From the late eighteenth century onwards, however, the assumptions, commitments and priorities that sustained the equilibrium between patrician and plebeian were beginning to break down. With the rise of a 'middling sort', notions of deference, discretion, dependency and paternalism increasingly gave way to an emphasis on values such as equality, certainty and proportionality. This reorientation in commitments was greatly aided by profound elite concerns with phenomena such as population increase, rapid economic change, urbanisation and developments in Ireland. The dawning of industrial capitalism, in particular, witnessed the introduction of a new economic order which centralised production, 'commodified' the labourer and emphasised task-orientated toil over time-orientated toil (Thompson, 1967: 60). In such an environment, the inefficiencies of parochial value determinants of the old criminal law system, where order was conceived of in local terms, came under attack (Stone, 1987: 248; Thompson, 1981: 189–208). Criminal law had to become more systematic, logical and regular. It had to be premised on a rationally calculating criminal – juridical man or woman – who knew in advance the certain penal consequences that would follow if he or she threatened the new forms of wealth and property that were produced during the period (Norrie, 2001: 20). This meant that many of the previously 'tolerated illegalities', such as workers picking up the residues of their labour, were now seen as prejudicial to the interests of property owners and were proscribed by law. As Lea noted: 'What is criminal is no longer the sanctity of property of this or that landowner but property in general; no longer violence against this or that person but violence in general' (Lea, 2002: 37). A new technique of criminal and penal semiotics was required which discarded the inefficient use of discretionary violence and relied instead on a 'play of representations, and signs circulating discreetly but necessarily and evidently in the minds of all' (Foucault, 1991 repr.: 101).

The growth of cities was also one of the significant consequences of the industrial revolution. In 1750, for example, there were two cities in Britain and Ireland with more than 50,000 inhabitants – London and Edinburgh; in 1801 there were eight and by 1851 there were twenty-nine, including nine with a population exceeding 100,000 (Hobsbawm, 1968: 67). The harsh conditions of dislocation generated by the concentration of transient populations in centres such as London, Birmingham, Glasgow, Liverpool and Leeds also quickly challenged the prevailing paternalistic and parochial social-control apparatus. The Gordon Riots of 1780, the impact of the French Revolution, the spread of radicalism and Jacobin ideas, the level of disturbance in Ireland and the violent industrial discord associated with the Luddite movement all, in varying degrees, confronted the settled polity and resulted in increased calls – predominantly from the newly emergent industrial bourgeoisie – for a system of justice that was more certain than that espoused under the prevailing hegemonic order (Thompson, 1963: 484). For example, with the dawning of industrial capitalism, plebeians were no longer permitted to utilise collective violence as a means of equalising power relations. As a consequence of the changing social, political and economic order, the old equipoise could no longer be sustained. A new set of social relations evinced itself in which the propertied classes were increasingly indisposed to mediate with the moral economy of the crowd and the threat of perennial rioting which it posed. In its place a new governing consensus was emerging which demanded that disorder and illegality would not be tolerated in a growing industrialised and rationalised society (Brewer, 1980: 18–27; Storch, 1980: 32–7).

The rationalising and centralising features of modernity also acted as a 'common matrix' of change, helping *inter alia* to reify certain relations (State/accused) and alienate others (victims). The momentum of this rationalising impulse in the late eighteenth and early nineteenth centuries is evident, for example, in the desire to have a fixed code of penalties proportioned to the offence and administered with certainty, in contrast to the prevailing model, which was too extreme and abounded with anomalies (Bentham, 1970 repr.; McGowen, 1988). It is also evident in the growing embrace of a 'free will' perception of offending (Saleilles, 1968: 43); in attempts at combating disease, particularly in the military, through the utilisation of techniques such as quarantine systems, and new hygienic regimes including delousing, whitewashing of walls, dispensaries and medical inspections (Dobson, 1987: 17); in the desire to create a uniform prison system (Ignatieff, 1978; McGowen, 1986); in the need to establish work rhythms and systematise production in factories (McKendrick, 1961); in the reform of policing (Silver, 1967: 7–8; Storch,1975: 66); and in the reorganisation of the workhouse system (Driver, 1993: 65). This increasing 'rationalisation of social life' resulted in a growing 'emancipation from prejudice' (Habermas, 2004 repr.: 147) by, in part, the devaluation of all local, subjective and personal experiences and knowledge. This, as we shall see later in the chapter, had far-reaching consequences for the epistemic primacy of the victim in the criminal process.

More broadly, this rationalising impulse is also evident in Cesare Beccaria's text in 1764, *On Crimes and Punishment*, which was very influential in drawing attention to the arbitrariness and ineffectiveness of a justice system that relied heavily on discretionary gross exemplarity. Criminal justice, according to Beccaria, had to become a more rational instrument of government. Adopting a Hobbesian view of the social contract, he argued that the Rule of Law was the framework under which free and independent citizens united to form a society. Each individual negotiated away some of his or her liberty rights to secure peace and safety under the protection of the sovereign. The individual, however, gave up no more liberty 'than suffices to induce others to defend it'. Obedience to authority was, through this analytic social-contractarian construct, grounded in the proper exercise of authority. The sum of all these sacrificed portions of liberty legitimated the sovereign right to punish – 'all that exceeds it is abuse and not justice' (Beccaria, 1995 repr.: 120–1). To secure effective order, punishment had to be certain, calibrated in accordance with the offence committed and designed to prevent the commission of crime. The certainty of punishment, according to Beccaria, 'will always make a stronger impression than the fear of another which is more terrible but combined with the hope of impunity: even the least evils, when they are certain, always terrify men's minds' (Beccaria, 1995 repr.: 130). In concluding his treatise, which he originally published anonymously, he also suggested: 'In order for punishment not to be, in every instance, an act of violence of one or of many against a private citizen, it must be essentially public, prompt, necessary the lest possible in the given circumstances, proportionate to the crimes, dictated by the laws.'

This notion of the social contract, where individuals cede part of their freedom to a sovereign in return for security and freedom, is one of the cornerstones of the modern liberalist agenda. It is premised on a Rule of Law framework which restrains the arbitrary or coercive exercise of executive authority, where a strong State must have respect for and indeed, in some instances, yield to a weak enemy. Though each citizen acceded some freedom to the sovereign in the interests of self-preservation, and the protection of liberty rights and human entitlements, the *quid pro quo* nature of the arrangement ensured, through a rhetoric and logic of liberal legalism, that the sovereign guaranteed to respect the liberty, equality and freedom of each citizen. The sum of power ceded could not be employed arbitrarily to usurp freedom or liberty. Thus the old hierarchical order of patronage was increasingly being undermined by a classical liberalist and utilitarian belief in the free individual who possessed 'negative' rights which could be construed as freedoms from government (Bellamy, 1992; Berlin, 1969; Gray, 1986). The ascriptive status of individuals under the old hierarchical model of authority, where individuality was to some extent subsumed into a person's attachment to a particular location, grouping and placement within that grouping, was overtaken by a new horizontal vision which emphasised rationalism, liberalism, egalitarianism and freedom (Shapiro, 1986: 80–150). The primacy of the individual and his or her self-determining and self-realising capabilities was now taking centre stage. In contrast to the fixed identities fashioned by pre-modern status relationships, modern progressive societies were viewed as oscillating more towards relations that recognised the importance of individualism and individual autonomy. Anchored to a Cartesian subject, the self-determining tendencies of *contract* now replaced *status* as one of the organising principles of society (Habermas, 2010: 77; Kilcommins, 2004: 144–67; Maine, 1927: 100). Lea refers to this process of 'criminalising abstraction' – 'abstracting an accused's criminality from the complex of other characteristics which make him what he is' – as one of the foundation stones of modern criminal law and criminal justice (Lea, 2002: 1–3).

There were also more specific concerns about the justice system. Though the idea of a centralised police force was seen as anathema to English sensibilities on liberty in the eighteenth and early nineteenth centuries, it was also apparent that the old system of law enforcement, which was heavily reliant on rewards, thieftaking and accomplice-driven prosecutions, was not working in a more urbanised and industrial setting. Too much had been conceded to localism and heterogeneity, resulting in a 'badly regulated distribution of power' (Foucault, 1991 repr.: 79). The system of private prosecutions and prosecutors was also increasingly called into question. In many instances the actions of victims were seen as vengeful, capricious and open to intimidation and blackmail, 'resulting in the shameful perversion of the criminal trial for private ends' (as quoted in Rock, 2004b: 338). The enactment of the Dublin Police Act in 1786, which was rejected the year previously in London, also helped to focus the political elite's attention on new methods of law enforcement (Boyle, 1972: 115–37; Palmer, 2003: 98–112). Once centralist authority in Dublin Castle had won out over personal liberty, and was seen to work, it provided subtle energy for reform of policing in England. This, as Lea suggests, helped to mark a transition from sovereignty to government, 'from a world in which crime was simply a wrong, a personal interaction between individuals or individuals and their superiors, to one in which crime was disruption, in which an offence against the criminal law was a disruption of the public peace and of the effective working of society' (Lea, 2004: 6).

The justice system was also influenced by the increased lawyerisation of the criminal trial process in the late eighteenth and early nineteenth centuries. This helped to reconfigure courtroom relations along more adversarial lines that tipped the scales of justice in the direction of the accused (Landsman, 1990: 539). The gradual influx of criminal lawyers – culminating in the introduction of the Prisoner's Counsel Act of 1836 – altered the dynamic of proceedings in a number of ways: it subjected the evidence adduced against an accused to much closer scrutiny; it shifted the burden of proof to the prosecution; it helped to clarify and develop the rules of evidence (the rule of hearsay, for example); it ensured that the accused knew in advance the precise charges laid against him or her, thereby allowing a better defence to be prepared; and it permitted a more thorough cross-examination of all prosecution witnesses, including thieftakers, accomplices and reward seekers after 'blood money' (Beattie, 1991: 221–67).

Events in Ireland also tested to the limits the old paternalistic and localised model of justice and were an influential impetus in its change. This is not surprising, given that the ideology of law did not transfer as smoothly, or permeate as deeply, between the ruling and poorer classes. Its foreign and repressive components ensured that the task of unmasking its 'false consciousness' was made a good deal easier. Ireland was a colonial society and deference to elite hegemony was not as forthcoming. The perceived tradition and heritage of the liberty of free-born citizens in England, which helped to maintain the status quo between rulers and ruled, worked in the opposite direction in Ireland. The defeated, dispossessed, disenfranchised Catholic lives of many Irish acted as a point of solidarity around which they could protest against maintaining the status quo with the ruling elite. As a result, a more 'uneasy governance' – which oscillated more towards order being secured through repression rather than through consensus – existed in Ireland in the eighteenth and early nineteenth centuries (Boyle, 1972: 125–6; Carroll Burke, 2000: 27–36; Henry, 1994; Palmer, 1988: 35–56). Although disorder also existed in England and was to some extent tolerated, the nature of illegality in Ireland was perceived by the administration as being more collective, permanent and threatening. Furthermore, and although Ireland similarly employed the private prosecution procedure of England in the eighteenth century, it was not anything as successful. No doubt many criminals in England escaped the clutches of the law during this period through intimidation of victims. The scale of intimidation, however, was far more widespread and organised in Ireland and was tied in to the political situation that endured there. This ensured that the victim's task was, in many instances, at worst 'perilous and at best extremely difficult' (McEldowney, 1980: 21; McEldowney, 1989: 430). This was especially so if the criminal acts were perceived to be 'political'. The communal participation which formed such an integral constituent of social control in England was, not surprisingly, also less in evidence in Ireland. Spurred on by a variety of 'dimensions of difference' and a psychology of dispossession and colonisation, agrarian violence and militant nationalism were never very far from the foreground of social and political relations. The 'Irish question' therefore also raised further concerns about the employment of a local, victim-orientated model of justice, and it provided the authorities, as we have noted above, with an opportunity for the introduction of a new network of policing and prosecution practices.

The victim within an inculpatory model of justice

The criminal complex was gradually redrawn in the nineteenth century as a new statist administrative machinery emerged for investigating, prosecuting and punishing crime. The penal field increasingly dissociated itself from the local, personal and arbitrary confrontations that governed criminal relations in the eighteenth century and became a more depersonalised, rule-governed affair with the State at the centre. Private disputes and vendettas were gradually monopolised by the State apparatus and rerouted into the courtroom. A society in which 'the law operates more and more as the norm' (Foucault, 1979 repr.: 144) slowly emerged – reflecting the 'public interest' and the 'will of the people' – in which the temptation to commit crime would no longer be countered by a sovereign will to command and a display of terror (McGowen, 1986: 313–17). When this process was completed, 'sovereign power was transformed into a public power' (Garland, 2001: 30). Within such a society, executive arbitrariness and discretionary power abuses were constrained, egalitarianism was advocated and procedural justice was increasingly promoted in addition to substantive justice. In distilling the criminal process into a more privatised, State/accused event, an 'equality of arms' framework was created as part of a broader Rule of Law value system. This addressed the problem of the previously 'bad economy of power' which 'vested too much ... on the side of the prosecution ... while the accused opposed it virtually unarmed' (Foucault, 1991 repr.: 79). Redistributing this economy of power meant an expansion in the exclusionary rules of evidence that could be employed by the defence against the prosecution case; clearer and greater obligations imposed on the State to prove its case against the accused; better opportunities afforded to the defence to prepare its case and test the prosecution case; and the removal of any obligation of self-exculpation on the accused. Even when the case was proved against the accused, he or she was subjected to a new power to punish in which 'an economy of continuity and permanence ... replace[d] that of expenditure and excess' (Foucault, 1991 repr.: 87).

There are a number of principal features of this new model of justice, although it should be borne in mind that a concrete framework of justice does not simply emerge as a fully unified functioning entity with crisp lines of division between it and the model it replaces; nor does it break down into sharp, discontinuous forms. The various strands that comprise a model develop at different paces and are embedded to different degrees. This ensures that the lines of demarcation between one model and another are often blurred, contested affairs. To begin with, and very much in keeping with the rationalising impulse of the age, the personal knowledge and benevolence of the exculpatory model of justice seemed increasingly arbitrary and overly discretionary. The goal became to 'rout the personal from the courtroom' (McGowen, 1983: 116) through establishing a new administrative machinery for investigating, prosecuting, trying and sentencing for criminal wrongdoing. Gradually the trial shifted from an intense local 'kind of morality play' (Green, 1988: 363) to a more structured affair which relied on ideals such as proportionality, reason, equality and uniformity, where the focus was on the actions rather than the character of the accused. Thus, over the course of the nineteenth century the criminal trial jettisoned its amateur, local, personal and unstructured tendencies. As Wiener (1990: 66) suggested:

> [R]emoving the personal element from the workings of the law would, it was hoped, lower the emotional intensity of the subject's relationship to the law. In the place of the metaphors of the family, which encouraged both unpredictability and excessive release of the passions by plaintiffs and accused, the law and its courts were to be imbued with the character of a market, a meeting place of self-contained, self-disciplining individuals rationally pursuing their own interests under the impersonal arbitration and discipline of the unvarying rules of law. Passionate contest was to be placed in the professional hands of lawyers, for whom passion was an instrument of calculation, and confined by the rules of law, presenting no danger to society. Out of their contest, as out of a noisy but rule-governed marketplace or stock exchange, justice would emerge.

The trial thus evolved from an 'expressive theatre' that sought the discovery of truth via an 'accused speaks' forum to a more reflective, categorised process which sought the determination of justice through testing the prosecution case (Langbein, 1994: 1048). For Wiener, this was part of a broader trend: 'during the first half of the nineteenth century criminal justice was pressed to move from a series of expressive semipersonal confrontations ... to a more restrained, rule governed, predictable, depersonalised process'(Wiener, 1990: 65; Christie, 2010: 116).

The logic of adversarialism that unfolded had a number of important consequences. To begin with, the evidential case presented against the accused began to be defined by more explicitly formulated evidentiary rules of law in the late eighteenth and early nineteenth centuries. The beyond reasonable doubt standard of proof, for example, crystallised into a legal formula and it became recognised as a 'maxim of ... law that ten guilty men should escape rather than one innocent man should suffer' (*R v Hobson* (1823) 1 Lew CC 261). As Foucault suggested, the system of proof under the old inquisitorial model was giving way to a new logic, supposedly premised on science and common reason, that demanded that the 'truth of the crime will be accepted only when it is completely proven' (Foucault, repr. 1991: 97). Facilitated by the lawyerisation of the trial process, exclusionary rules of evidence were also formulated as rules of law. These rules increasingly acted as filtering devices that examined prosecution evidence through the lens of its possible prejudicial effect on the accused. They included: the inadmissibility of hearsay evidence; greater scrutiny over the voluntariness and fairness of confessions; the introduction of corroboration warnings in respect of accomplice testimony; more rigorous examination of the competence of prosecution witnesses; and the exclusion of bad-character evidence to raise a presumption of guilt against an accused (Beattie, 1986: 363–77; King, 2000: 225–8; Landsman, 1989–90; Langbein, 2003: 180–251). As a result, the criminal trial process gradually became a search for justice, not truth.

This meant that the 'ordinary' adversarial criminal trial – involving 'a contest morphology' that included oral presentation of evidence, lawyer-led questioning, cross-examination by counsel, relative 'judicial passivity' during the guilt-determining phase of the trial and informational sources secured by both the prosecution and defence – became deeply ingrained throughout the twentieth century as the appropriate means of resolving criminal disputes (Damaska, 1986: 88). The observation of direct, unmediated responses to questions is often crucial in this regard. Consistency of account, clear and rational recollection, accuracy as to detail, appearance and deportment, and poised expressions and body language are all important indicators of a witness's truthfulness and credibility in relation to determinations of fact. A failure along any or all of these lines either at reporting or trial stages could cast fatal doubt on the truthfulness of a witness's account, which ultimately impacted on decisions to prosecute and determinations of guilt. This deep commitment to the reception and observation of unmediated *viva voce* testimony is grounded in the need to uphold the integrity of the adjudicative process and minimise the risk of misdecision (Doak, 2005: 294–316; Goodpaster, 1987: 135). Under this adversarial model, the criminal system came to resemble an 'obstacle course' where 'each of its successive stages is designed to present formidable impediments to carrying the accused any further along in the process' (Packer, 1968: 163). In addition to the embracement of adversarialism, the common law and statutory rules that were introduced to safeguard those accused of crime also increasingly became fused with constitutional jurisprudence and, more recently, with human rights jurisprudence. Active judicial review, especially since the 1960s, has permitted the development of a great corpus of jurisprudence – constructing a 'meta-Constitution' – on the constitutional role in protecting the rights of the accused and on restricting State power. Logical consistency regarding rules (rule formalism or a 'rulebook' conception of the Rule of Law) was now further buttressed by rights and principles – implemented through a constitutional structure – which commanded that 'rules in the rule book capture and enforce moral rights' ('a rights-based' conception of the Rule of Law) (Dworkin, 1985: 11–12).

In line with these changes, there was also a dramatic reconfiguration in courtroom relations. Where previously the accused, judge and jury had played pivotal roles in the pursuit of truth, now it was the lawyers that monopolised the gatekeeping function that determined what constituted truth (McGowen, 1983: 89–125). As a result, the focus came increasingly to bear on the prosecution case and 'away from the objective that had preoccupied the old altercation trial which was to see how the defendant responded to the prosecution case' (Langbein, 2003: 271). The accused was thus freed from the burden of self-exculpation and was no longer an informational resource for the prosecution. In addition to silencing the accused, the reconfiguration in relations also significantly reduced the role of the judge in adducing fact evidence. Under this new inculpatory model of justice the trial judge did not actively examine and cross-examine witnesses, or engage in the protective benevolence of the accused's interests. The judge's function now became much more impartial and less active – to secure justice through enabling the adversarial contest to take place (Langbein,1994: 1071; Langbein, 2003: 312). Juries also became more tightly controlled. Their role, as self-informing, 'semi-autonomous institutions' (Green, 1988: 310) that engaged in mitigation of sanctions, could not be sustained under a *Zeitgeist* that recoiled from personalism, localism, discretionary accommodations and anti-Rule of Law practices. Although jury mitigation of sanctions would continue, it would be on a greatly reduced basis as the jury 'slowly ceased to be viewed as a discretionary body' (Green, 1987: 72).

The State also very gradually began to monopolise the prosecutorial function as the view emerged that the security of society could not be left at the whim of individual victims. Sir Robert Peel, for example, had argued in 1826:

> [I]f we were legislating de novo, without reference to previous customs and formed habits, I for one should not hesitate to relieve private individuals from the charge of prosecution in the case of criminal offences justly called by writers upon law – public wrongs. I would have a public prosecutor acting in each case upon principal, and not on the heated and vindictive feelings of the individual sufferer, on which we mainly rely at present for the due execution of justice ... and I would by the appointment of a public prosecutor guard against malicious or frivolous prosecutions on the one hand, and on the other, I would ensure prosecution in cases in which justice might require it. (As quoted in May, 2003: 194)

The 'formed habits' referred to by Peel, particularly the fear of centralised despotism, remained steadfastly apparent in nineteenth-century England. Nonetheless, centrally organised schemes of prosecution were also operating on an extempore basis in the first half of the century in parts of Durham and Northumberland (Rock, 2004b: 331–54). Scotland, India and Ireland had also made the task of prosecution an executive function. In Ireland, for example, Crown solicitors were appointed to prosecute criminal cases in each of the circuits in 1801, and by the mid-nineteenth century sessional Crown solicitors were appointed in each of the counties (Bridgeman, 2003: 113–41; Delaney, 1979: 43–4; McEldowney, 1989: 435–6). Jospeh Napier, a former Attorney General for Ireland, noted in 1855 that prosecution was 'founded on the principle ... that the Executive Government is properly ... charged with the security of society: that the security of life and property belongs peculiarly to the Executive Government, and that all prosecutions ought to be conducted by responsible public officers' (as quoted in Rock, 2004b: 339–40). In England, a statute passed in 1879 created the Office of the Director of Public Prosecutions, thus facilitating the gradual emasculation of the victim's previously pivotal role in initiating and carrying on criminal proceedings (Hay, 1983: 165–86; Langbein, 1973: 313–75). By now, the duties of investigation, prosecution, sentencing and punishment – all of which had previously been premised to a large degree on popular participation – had become more privatised, focused and discreet State/accused events.

Violence and justice were now to a greater extent monopolised by the central authorities. The era of victim justice as 'accommodation' and theatre was at an end. Conflicts were no longer viewed as the property of the parties most directly affected. Previously strong stakeholder interests such as victims and the local community were gradually colonised in the course of the nineteenth century by a State apparatus which acted for rather than with the public. Subjects increasingly ceded 'their authorisations to use coercion to a legal authority that monopolises the means of legitimate coercion and if necessary employs these means on their behalf' (Habermas, 2008 repr.: 12). In monopolising the investigative and prosecutorial functions, the State obviously imbalanced the equilibrium in power relations. Although constituted as a rational being, the accused in such circumstances was now seen as vulnerable in that he or she was pitted against the unlimited resources of the State. In this context, it is not surprising that a whole corpus of exclusionary rules and fairness-of-procedure rights emerged to ensure that the accused was afforded the best possible defence against unfair prosecution and punishment. Since, and to paraphrase Stephen, the State was so much stronger than the individual citizen, and was capable of inflicting so very much more harm on the individual than the individual could inflict upon society, it could afford 'to be generous' (Stephen, 1883: 354). The local victim justice system thus increasingly yielded to a Leviathan criminal justice system that was governed by a new set of commitments, priorities and policy choices.

This new institutional pattern quickly transcended the victim's interaction with the crime conflict and re-shaped how it was presented, addressed, legitimated and concluded. Within such a depersonalised, bureaucratised system, the victim was displaced, confined largely to the bit-part role of reporting crime and of adducing evidence in court as a witness, if needed at all. The victim's space for negotiation and participation in pursuing his or her own interests was thus dismantled by an increasingly State/accused-centred logic of action which sought to institutionalise the politics of pain and disturbing events within an 'iron cage'. Bureaucracy, as Weber informs us, 'develops the more perfectly, the more it is dehumanized, the more completely it succeeds in eliminating from official business love, hatred, all purely personal, irrational, and emotional elements' (Weber, 1978 repr.: 975). The functional and impersonal imperatives of a modern criminal justice apparatus did not require the establishment of 'contextual' relations with either the accused or the victim. Instead it was increasingly organised around a constitutional state and the 'institutionalised fiction' of the 'public sphere as the central principle of its organisation' (Habermas, 2010: 125), both of which helped to promote the sense of 'civilized association' and an 'objectivated' (Habermas, 2004: 148) criminal process.

From being a cornerstone in the regulation of relations concerning the conflict, victims increasingly found their individual experiences (such a vital currency in the pursuit of justice in the pre-modern era) assimilated into general group will – the public interest. The latter was validated through the institutional architecture of a criminal justice system, whereas the former was increasingly viewed as invalid knowledge, given its partiality, subjectivity, emotiveness and unconstrained dimensions, all of which were filtered out by the operations of a justice system. In the course of the nineteenth century, the individual victim's experience was increasingly rendered as part of the fiction of the collective public interest and packaged and presented in institutional terms. This marked the shift from victim-mediated justice to bureaucratised, State/accused mediated justice. Crime therefore was no longer viewed as a personal altercation, but as a phenomenon that required an institutional response demarcated from emotive, subjective and personal references. In creating this 'buffer zone between *system* and *person* [by establishing a] zone of indifference' (Habermas, 2006: 308) between the lived ontological experiences of the crime conflict and its effective administration, new imperatives could be foregrounded, particularly those that emphasised procedure, the ideological neutrality and rationality of the process and its objectivated nature.

Criminal law also underwent reform to become a more rigid and impartial set of prescriptions that purportedly bound all members in the same manner (Norrie, 2001: 21). The rationalising zeal of authorities in the nineteenth century included a strong commitment to positive law and its densification, a growing emphasis on procedural rationality, and the processing of crime through State agencies and specialised officials. Increasingly the focus of criminal law moved away from the notion of 'manifest criminality' based on the disposition of the accused, to a more formalised conception of criminal liability. Hierarchy, status, patronage, absolute sovereignty and moral and discretionary imperatives had no place under this Rule of Law vista which advocated certainty, permanency, coherency, systematic application and a 'strictly professional legal logic' (Habermas, 2010 repr,: 53; Weber, 1978 repr.: 885; Wiener, 1999: 472): *veritas non auctoritas facit legem* (truth not authority makes law) became the driving impulse. The private, personal and negotiable elements of the exculpatory process were thus increasingly dismantled by more bureaucratic, rational impulses (King, 1984: 25). As Habermas noted: '[t]he positivization, legalization, and formalization of law meant that the validity of law can no longer feed of the taken-for-granted authority of moral traditions' (Habermas, 2004 repr.: 260). Instead, its validity would be based on the 'systematisation of doctrinal propositions and the emphasis on legal formalism and professional juridical input' (Ibid.: 256). The positivization and densification of law also helped to steer the conflict away from local and lay participation. The initial anchoring point of this more rationalised approach to criminal law was the 'reasonable man', a responsible, rational, self-disciplining subject who, it was thought, was capable of being deterred by a properly prescribed system of criminal laws and a tariff of enforced sanctions (Farmer, 1996: 66; Lacey, 1998: 9–49; Wiener, 1999: 482). This more codified approach to law also impacted on the image of the human subject who increasingly came to be constituted as a rational, autonomous and self-governing being. This is brilliantly captured by Wiener (1990: 54–5), who noted:

> The ideal of the responsible individual came to stand ever more at the centre of the law. Its administration was overhauled to better embody the assumption that the members of the general public were to be considered more rational and responsible than they had been hitherto ... A crucial supposition underlying early Victorian law reform was that the most urgent need was to make people self-governing and that the best way to do so was to hold them, sternly and unblinkingly, responsible for the consequences of their actions.

Thus, in the course of the early to mid-nineteenth century the accused was gradually constructed as an abstract juridical subject who was free and equal, and capable of logically determining what was in his or her best interests. It was accordingly his or her *constitution* – rather than *situation* – that became a key legal battleground (Wiener, 1999: 504).

This drift towards the creation of an asocial subject also had important consequences in terms of the penal disposal of convicted offenders. In keeping with the ideology of individualism, rationality and self-governance, judicial sentencing in the nineteenth century increasingly embodied a policy of deterrence and retribution, the former 'to deny the utility of crime, the latter to reconstitute the social contract after breach' (Garland, 1981: 19–45). The discourse of individualism and moralisation held that criminal acts – like actions in any other realm where the ideology of economic liberalism could permeate – were the outcome of rational choice, calculation and volition. Such an archetype of sentencing is premised on presumed rationality: 'thus conceived, criminal law becomes a wholly abstract construction, taking cognisance only of the crime, while ignoring the criminal ... Crime becomes a legal abstraction, after the manner of a geometrical construction or an algebraic formula' (Saleilles, 1968: 43). In effect, the system of sentencing created in the mid-nineteenth century focused on the materiality of the crime 'where the subjective criminality of the agent was determined by the objective criminality of the deed', and where the system of disposal for the judiciary rested on 'crystallised' and mechanical punishments (Ibid.: 43). Garland (1985: 18) neatly encapsulated the asocial juridical framework which emerged in the nineteenth century when he suggested:

> The offender is defined as a legal subject, a citizen inscribed with rights and duties, entitled to equal treatment before the law. The State which punishes does so by contractual right in accordance with the terms of a political agreement. Its power to punish has its source in the offender's action – it is the agreed consequences of a contractual breach. The State has here no intrinsic or superior right. It meets the citizen on terms of equality and must not encroach upon his or her rights, person or liberty except in circumstances which are rigorously and politically determined in advance – *nulla poena sine lege*. In this penal vision we meet the ideology of the minimal legal state, the liberal dream, guardian of the free market and the social contract.

The prison, which came to dominate the penal landscape in the mid-nineteenth century, fitted ideally with this algebraic conception of offending behaviour.

Conclusion

The purpose of this chapter has been to highlight the characteristics and strategy choices that gave a distinctive shape to the modern system of justice. Criminal wrongdoing was increasingly reconstituted as a public matter to be resolved almost exclusively through the prosecution process. Localism and heterogeneity, elements cherished under the old order, were actively jettisoned under this modern arrangement. This must be seen as part of a drive to institutionalise interpersonal conflicts, uncoupling them from everyday practices in lifeworld contexts. A State/accused logic of action thus came to constitute and demarcate the modern criminal process, mediating all validity claims in respect of the conflict. Criminal wrongdoing became a rationalised domain of action, measured in part by its capacity to filter out non-objective truth claims. Victims who participated in the modern inculpatory process did so as legal subjects, with little or no power to make decisions about outcomes.

The State could draw upon a centralised police force and a public prosecutor's office which would gather and present evidence in the public interest. As a consequence, in part, of this process of State monopolisation, a discourse and practice of liberal legalism emerged (emphasising the universality, liberty and sameness of the individual person) to rebalance power relations in the justice arena. For the accused, this meant that the justice network was restructured to incorporate a clearer and more substantive body of due process rights that would guarantee, as far as practicable, both substantive and procedural justice. This ensured that the dynamic of the courtroom altered so that the trial gaze reorientated itself to focus almost exclusively on the prosecution case. Even when convicted of the crime, the offender was still protected from the State – exercising the will of the people – through the entitlement of having a proportionate punishment imposed, one that accorded both with the crime committed and, in time, any relevant individual circumstances.

The reification of these State/accused relations had the effect of excluding the victim, his or her absentee status quickly acquiring a relative permanence, 'fixity' and immovability. His or her experiences were rooted exclusively through this new institutional framework, ensuring that they were interpreted and understood around an axis that focused on the State, the law, the public interest and the accused. The inculpatory model of justice that emerged zealously neutralised any emotive or personal dimensions to the crime by distilling them into a single, rationally knowable, closed worldview – the public interest. The victim increasingly therefore became a 'non-person in a Kafka play' (Christie, 1977: 8), unable to raise claims about the validity of his or her ontological experiences as the unstable 'I' was subsumed within this objectivated 'public interest'. His or her voice was not heard – and was not capable of being understood – given the commitments, value choices and governing principles of this new institutional arrangement.

Note

1 An earlier version of this chapter appeared in *Terrorism, Rights and the Rule of Law: Negotiating Justice in Ireland* (Willan Publishing, 2008).

2

The re-emergence of victims of crime in Ireland

Introduction

During the majority of the twentieth century the crime victim in the criminal justice systems in most common law jurisdictions was afforded no meaningful role or voice. Criminal justice systems were built on the notion that the state was the injured party. The crime victim was merely the complainant who activated the criminal justice system by notifying the police of the crime suffered. If an arrest was made, the victim was then a witness for the prosecution and treated like any other piece of evidence for the prosecution. While the prevailing theory was that the state was on the side of the crime victim and seeking to punish the offender, often crime victims found themselves at odds with the representatives of the state within the system: the police and prosecutor.

In Ireland in the last two decades of the twentieth century the plight of crime victims became recognised and various legal and service related accommodating measures were put in place. The trickle of change eventually reached a watershed. In 2006, then Tánaiste (Deputy Prime Minister) and Minister for Justice, Michael McDowell, announced the formation of a small group to address the fact that 'it seems that we may now have arrived at a situation where on occasions the scales of justice are tilted too heavily to one side. Unfortunately when that occurs, that imbalance is likely to favour the criminal rather than the innocent victim' (Department of Justice, 2006). The following year McDowell's Balance in the Criminal Law Review Group recommended sweeping changes to some of the rights afforded to the accused (Balance Group, 2007), and many of these recommendations found expression in legislation such as the Criminal Procedure Act 2010.

It is submitted that the re-emergence of the crime victim in Ireland was due to four principal influences that created pressure on the Irish government to alter the status of crime victims. These principal influences were: (1) victimology research; (2) the victims' movement; (3) the recognition and expansion of human rights; and (4) crime became a national election issue, with a contemporaneous decrease in public satisfaction with the criminal justice system. The first three influences were international in character and the fourth influence was domestic. This chapter will outline these four principal influences that transformed the victim of crime in Ireland from a piece of evidence to a stakeholder in the criminal justice system worthy of consideration, requiring the scales of justice to be balanced. In doing so, the chapter will highlight an apparent paradox: many of the activities that transformed victims of crime into recognised criminal justice stakeholders were the result of initiatives and efforts meant to aid offenders.

Victimology research

Criminology is a discipline that gathers and analyses empirical data in order to explain violations of the criminal law and societal reactions to the violations. Modern criminology traces its roots back to the late nineteenth century. The growth of criminology in Britain as a discipline was slow (Radzinowicz, 1994), and British criminology consolidated itself only in the middle years of the twentieth century (Bowling and Ross, 2006: 12; Garland, 1988). This reluctance to embrace criminology in academic circles flows from the resistance of British universities toward the social sciences in the early part of the twentieth century. Ireland, after achieving independence, deliberately adopted British attitudes concerning the nature and purpose of the university, including a general resistance toward the social sciences (Lee, 1989: 584).

It is generally accepted that good policy requires good information. The best policy-making approach is one that is based upon factual information and evidence. This is particularly true in the area of public policy, as it is more complex, diverse and interconnected (Collins and Menton, 2006: 65). In 1974 the lack of research on the criminal justice system was lamented in the Oireachtas (Parliament) (Kilcommins et al., 2004: 82), yet successive Ministers for Justice rejected or ignored calls for academic studies or research into crime, often citing lack of resources or claiming to have a firm grasp or understanding of the problem. For example, in 1992 Padraig Flynn, the then Minister for Justice, noted that there may be value in academically based and structured surveys of the public attitude to crime, but his priority was to use all resources on more practical and effective measures to prevent and detect crime. He believed that he had a firm grasp on the public's attitude to crime because he had an open-door policy and participated in various forums on crime-related issues, such as appearing on a chat show devoted to discussing crime (Flynn, 1992). Just four years later two high-profile killings caused moral panic. It was finally acknowledged by a Minister for Justice when establishing the Crime Council in 1999 that '[o]ne of the obstacles to effective policy making in the area of crime and crime prevention is the scarcity of research' (O'Donoghue, 1999).

Victimology, or the science of studying crime victims, began in Europe after the end of the Second World War (Young, 1997: 195). Criminology is credited with siring victimology despite itself (Rock, 1994: xvi). Thus, victimology began as a sub-discipline of criminology and did not become a field of scientific endeavour as a separate discipline until around 1970 (Drapkin and Viano, 1974; Karmen, 2004: 9). Although victimology commenced in Europe, it flourished in the US, where the social sciences were supported. Victimology did not flourish in Britain, due to the slow growth of criminology, and the situation in Ireland was worse. Notwithstanding the acknowledgement that effective policy making in the area of crime requires research, just one year before Minister McDowell announced the formation of the Balance Group, criminology was described in Ireland as an 'absentee discipline' (O'Donnell, 2005: 99).

The European criminologists undertaking the earliest victimology studies were concerned primarily with victim precipitation or the part the victim played in causing the crime. In 1937 Benjamin Mendelsohn, a criminal defence lawyer in Romania, published his system (Dussich, 2006; Mendelsohn, 1937; Wemmers, 1998: 5) of criminal defence premised upon the contribution of the victim to the criminal act (Schafer, 1974: 17). Mendelsohn is credited with being the first to deal scientifically with the personality of the victim (Wemmers, 1998: 5). He viewed the victim as one factor among many in the criminal case. He corresponded with Sigmund Freud and it is believed that he may have endorsed the Freudian notion that victims unwittingly seek their victimisation as a means of abating feelings of guilt over sexual feelings (Hoffman, 1988: 89). By 1956 Mendelsohn had abandoned his earlier works and advocated the development of general victimology as a discipline in its own right, independent of criminology or criminal law. The human rights abuses during the Second World War, of which Mendelsohn was a victim, are credited with the new direction in his work (Dijk, 1999: 2).

Notwithstanding Mendolsohn's early work, Hans von Hentig is often identified as the founder of victimology (Mawby and Walklate, 1994; Spalek, 2006; Zedner, 1994) and credited with laying the basis for academic research regarding victims of crime (Wemmers, 2005: 121). He published *The Criminal and His Victim* in 1948, and this work is widely regarded as the seminal text in developing victim studies (Zedner, 2002: 420). Hentig criticised the static, single-dimensioned study of the offender and insisted that many crime victims contributed to their own victimisation by inciting or provoking the criminal or by creating or fostering a situation likely to lead to the commission of the crime (Fattah, 2000: 72; Hentig, 1948: 436). Hentig's work has been criticised for being based on anecdotal observation rather than empirical evidence (Spalek, 2006: 34).

Academic papers began to appear in some jurisdictions in 1958, and in 1959 an American publication entitled the *Journal of Public Law* ran the first of several symposia and special issues on victimology (Elias, 1986: 18). In 1958 Marvin Wolfgang published his classic homicide study, *Patterns of Criminal Homicide*. This work systematically and empirically tested von Hentig's theories. Wolfgang defined victim-precipitated offences as those in which the victim is a direct, positive precipitator in the crime (Wolfgang, 1958: 252). His victim-precipitation theory caused controversy, particularly as he alleged that some homicides were caused by the unconscious desire of the victim to commit suicide (Wolfgang, 1958: 213). The most controversial application of Wolfgang's model of victim precipitation concerned forcible rape. Menachem Amir was Wolfgang's student and published *Patterns in Forcible Rape* in 1971 (Amir, 1971). The controversy generated by the victim-precipitation studies almost scuttled the discipline before it obtained a foothold in academia (Doerner and Lab, 2002: 13).

In 1968 Stephen Schafer published *The Victim and His Criminal* (Schafer, 1968), a reversal of von Hentig's title. This book is viewed as a correction to von Hentig's work and traced the status of the victim within criminal justice systems throughout what Schafer classified as the Golden Age,[1] the Dark Age[2] and the re-emergence of the victim[3] in the US in the late 1960s. Research turned from attempting to blame the victim to determining the true extent of criminal victimisation. The first National Crime Victimisation Survey in the US was performed in 1972 (Whyte, 2007: 452) to determine the dark figures of crime, or crimes not reported to the authorities, and to record the experiences of victims of crime (Baumer and Lauritsen, 2010: 132; UN, Office on Drugs and Crime and Economic Commission for Europe Task Force, 2010: 3).

Several academic milestones quickly occurred. The first international symposium on victimology was held in Jerusalem in 1973 (Dussich, 2006: 116). In 1976, Emilio Viano founded *Victimology: An International Journal* in Washington, DC. In the 1980s surveys of crime victims became prominent in Britain (Goodey, 2005: 51) because academics and politicians had become interested in crime victims (Walklate, 2000: 183). Enthusiasm for these surveys 'spilled over into the 1990s with many towns and cities replicating the format to produce their own survey on victimisation and fear of crime' (Goodey, 2005: 51). The Home Office undertook the first national British Crime Survey in 1982 (Hough and Mayhew, 1983). In 2001 it was estimated, based on the British Crime Survey, that only one out of four crimes committed in Ireland were represented in official Gardaí statistics (Young et al., 2001).

The first International Crime Victimisation Survey was conducted in the late 1980s when twenty industrialised countries were surveyed. Ireland participated in the European Survey on Crime and Safety (ESCS) in 2005. The ESCS 2005 in turn became part of the 2004–6 International Crime Survey. Ireland has not participated in subsequent International Crime Victimisation Surveys.

The earliest victimology studies in Ireland were crime victimisation surveys. The first such study was carried out on behalf of the Economic and Social Research Institute in 1982–83 and was published in 1984 (Breen and Rottman, 1984). Ten years later, the Dublin Crime Survey was conducted to determine the unreported crime in Dublin (O'Connell and Whelan, 1994). In 1999 the Central Statistics Office (CSO), within its Quarterly National Household Survey (QNHS), for the first time inserted questions concerning crime and victimisation (CSO, 1999). Information was also sought concerning attitudes to the risk and fear of crime. The CSO continues to gather information via the QNHS.

The QNHSs have certain drawbacks and limitations. Certain offences such as sexual offences are excluded from the surveys. Also, these surveys are sent to households, thus many groups of people such as the homeless are automatically excluded from the surveys, notwithstanding the fact that homeless persons may be in the highest risk category for crime and have the lowest reporting rate to police (Kilcommins et al., 2004: 103). In order to draw attention to, or to discover the extent of offences excluded from, the QNHS, organisations began to sponsor studies. For example, in 1995 Women's Aid conducted a national survey on domestic abuse and found that the rate of reported violence in the home underestimated the true level of the problem (Kelleher et al., 1995). Similarly, the Health Service Research Centre examined for the first time the underlying level of sexual abuse and violence in Ireland and issued the *SAVI Report* in 2002 (McGee et al., 2002).

Following international trends, Irish researchers expanded their research beyond determining the amount of unreported crimes and began to highlight the experiences or plight of different types of crime victims. In 1998 comparative research was conducted on the different legal principles and practices in rape laws across the EU and the impact of the legal principles and practices on the victims of rape (Bacik et al., 1998). The following year a further study on domestic abuse made recommendations aimed at improving the experiences of victims in court (Kelleher et al., 1999). In 2000 Dorothy Watson published a survey on victims of recorded crimes. Police records from October 1994 to September 1995 were used and the study explored the experiences of these general victims of crime (Watson, 2000). In 2002 Victim Support Ireland commissioned the Tourism Research Centre at the Dublin Institute of Technology to conduct a survey crime against tourists (Campbell, 2002).

When the establishment of the Balance Group was announced in 2006, victimology studies in Ireland had progressed beyond discovering the extent of unreported crime and had commenced examining the experience of crime victims in the Irish criminal justice system. Two independent studies were commissioned by the Commission for the Support of Victims of Crime, which was established by Minister McDowell in 2005. The first study was completed in late 2007 (Bacik et al, 2007) and two of the findings were that legislation on victim supports did not meet EU and international requirements and there was a need for an enforceable Victims Charter. The second study was published in 2010 (Kilcommins et al., 2010) and highlighted that crime victims were satisfied with the voluntary organisations providing services, but were were not satisfied with their treatment by some of the criminal justice agencies (Ibid.: 180). Other victimology studies published after 2006 often have been directed toward specific types or groups of victims. For example, a study reflecting the attrition of rape cases in Ireland and the experiences of rape victims within the criminal justice system was published (Hanly et al., 2009). The needs and concerns of family members of homicide victims featured in two studies (Cooper, 2008; McGrath, 2009), and disabled victims of crime in another (Edwards et al., 2012).

To summarise, notwithstanding the slow pace of the development of criminology in Ireland, and the fact that successive Ministers for Justice rejected or ignored calls for academic studies or research into crime, victimology studies began to be undertaken in Ireland from the early 1980s. Following international trends, the studies commenced with attempting to discover the amount of crime not reported to the Gardaí. By the time the Balance Group was announced in 2006 victimology studies had progressed to examining the experience of crime victims within the criminal justice system, thus creating pressure on the government to address issues raised.

The victims' movement

At the same time that victimology was struggling to establish itself as an academic subject, various social movements concerned with victims of crime began to form, including: the feminist victims' movement, the human rights movement and the international victims' movement (Elias, 1993: 48–9). All of the various movements concerned with crime victims can be divided into the official victims' movement and the unofficial victims' movement (Elias, 1993: 53). An official victims' movement is one that focuses mainly upon state-defined victimisation, with initiatives funded largely by the state. In essence, the groups in the official victims' movement have the ear of State policy makers. On the other, hand, an unofficial victims' movement would include groups that challenge state-defined victimisation and may include radicalising strategies to alter or change the criminal justice system. Groups of the unofficial victims' movement are often marginalised by State officials in terms of funding and voice because they are perceived as threatening. The official victims' movement is less threatening to State officials because it does not tend to openly criticise government policy or the criminal justice system (Elias, 1993: 54).

In the US a victims' rights movement[4] emerged in the 1960s as a national reform movement consisting of a large collection of diverse pressure groups intent upon influencing the political system (Weed, 1995: 1). The US movement sprang from other grassroots contemporary social movements: the civil rights and women's movements (Viano, 1992). The successes of the civil rights movement galvanised other groups to seek an end to disparate treatment through both the courts and legislation. One of the greatest beneficiaries of the US civil rights movement was the women's movement.

During the 1960s one of the main concerns of the women's movement was the sexual exploitation of women, particularly in the context of rape. Radical feminists believed that it was necessary to go outside the existing male-dominant structures and began to engage in large self-help projects such as the establishment and maintenance of rape crisis centres and shelters for battered women (Bevocqua, 2000: 29–31). These feminists put their efforts into creating help outside the criminal justice system rather than trying to change the existing system. The earliest shelter for battered women was established in Pasadena in 1964 (Weed, 1995: 15), and one of the first rape crisis centres was established in Washington, DC in 1972 (Bevocqua, 2000: 29–31). The domestic abuse shelters and rape crisis centres represent the first victims' rights activities with a dynamic interaction between service provision and demands for legal and institutional changes (Williams and Goodman, 2007: 240–1). The radical feminists, by establishing the rape crisis and domestic abuse shelters, established an unofficial victims' movement. With a conscious desire, they chose to remain as independent as possible of governmental funding in order to remain independent of interference.

During the 1960s feminists were organising in the US and Britain. However, it was the radical shift in the US women's movement that is credited with leading to the establishment of the first rape crisis centres and domestic abuse shelters. Both the US and Britain experienced preceding civil rights movements, although this was not the case in Ireland. Notwithstanding the lack of a preceding civil rights movement, many of the founders of the women's movement in Ireland were active or were connected to the republican and civil rights movements in Northern Ireland (Smyth, 1993: 247).

The Irish Women's Liberation Movement was founded in early 1970 (Smyth, 1993: 247), at the same time that Ireland began the process of entering the EU. The Irish Women's Liberation Movement immediately began to challenge the unique position of the Catholic Church in Irish society (Mahon, 1996: 187). Although granted the vote six years before British women (Burke, 1999: 24), Irish women were relegated to a subordinate position both in public and in private life after Independence.[5] The State, by allowing the Church to provide social services, allowed women to be abused[6] and exploited.[7]

Notwithstanding the difficulties encountered in challenging the unique position of the Church, the Irish Women's Liberation Movement was quick to embrace the radical feminist approach. The first rape crisis centre in Ireland was established in Dublin in 1977 (Hunt, 2001), while the first rape crisis centre in

Britain opened in London a few months earlier in 1976 (Zedner, 2002: 434). The first refuge was established in Britain in Chiswick in 1972, making it the first refuge in Europe (Williams and Goodman, 2007: 241), and the first refuge in Dublin was established in 1974 on Harcourt Street, when a group of women squatted in a vacant house (IILE, 2011: 24). The issue of rape and battered women was placed firmly on the political map in Britain (Mawby and Gill, 1987: 76) and it is submitted in Ireland.

Developments in this field were not always pioneered by Britain, and the clearest example of Ireland leading Britain is in relation to the introduction of victim impact statements. Victim impact statements were introduced in California in 1974 (Wemmers, 2005: 121–2). They were in use and introduced into Irish law in 1993, almost a decade before similar legislation was introduced in Britain. This is surprising, because the organisation credited with the introduction into Ireland, the Irish Association of Victim Support (Victim Support Ireland), was a direct transplant from the UK.

Victim Support,[8] which began as a local initiative in Bristol in 1974, grew tremendously (Zedner, 2002: 432), becoming the fastest-growing voluntary organisation in the UK by the 1990s (Walklate, 2007: 10), and is usually identified as the victims' rights movement. Victim Support was founded at about the same time that radical feminists in Britain established rape crisis centres and domestic abuse refuges. It was founded by members of the National Association for the Care and Resettlement of Offenders as a means of helping criminal offenders rather than as a means of helping crime victims. The goal was the rehabilitation of the crime victim 'to get people who have suffered in that way to become ordinary citizens again' (Longford, 1991: 110). Only in the mid-1990s did Victim Support begin to allow victims to participate in its management and began lobbying government, behind the scenes, for services for crime victims (Rock, 1990: 51; Zedner, 2002: 433). Victim Support in Britain quickly became the official victims' movement and became so successful in influencing government policy that other groups such as Rape Crisis, which was engaged in lobbying for rights for victims of sexual offences, were marginalised (Crawford, 2000). Thus, the official victims' movement in Britain did not come about from a recognisable pressure group with a victims' policy but, rather, from a group seeking to reform penal policy (Newburn, 2003: 241).

When Victim Support Ireland was established in 1985 the only national victims' movement in Ireland was the women's movement, which was primarily concerned with victims of sexual offences and domestic abuse. Victim Support Ireland was the first voluntary group in Ireland to attempt to provide services to all crime victims rather than just victims of specific types of crimes such as rape. Derek Nally, the founder, was introduced in 1983 to Victim Support UK when he attended a policing conference in the UK. Nally believed that such an organisation was needed in Ireland and, in addition to helping crime victims, it would make the jobs of Gardaí easier (Moore Walsh, 2013: 186). At the conference the attendees were never told of the penal reform origins of Victim Support UK. Nally believed that Victim Support developed in the UK from American influences to help victims (Moore Walsh, 2013: 186). In reality, the US and UK victims' movements were completely different. The US movement was strongly rights based, comprised of diverse grassroots groups formed by victims or family, friends or supporters of victims that engaged extensively in lobbying legislators for change to the criminal justice system. The slightly later-occurring UK movement focused exclusively on the provision of services to victims. Initially the UK movement did not engage in lobbying and it did not allow crime victims to be represented in the management of the organisation.

While it has been stated that initially Victim Support Ireland was treated with 'caution and suspicion by the establishment' (Cotter, 1999: 300) this does not appear to be the case. In fact it was a member of An Garda Síochána that brought about Victim Support Ireland's establishment, and the organisation was immediately funded by the Department of Justice, receiving £10,000 in 1984 (Moore Walsh, 2013: 187). By 1994 this funding had increased to over £100,000 (Farrell et al., 2002) and by 2003 Victim Support Ireland was receiving €1.2 million in funding from the Department of Justice (McDowell, 2004). Notwithstanding the state financial support received, at all times Victim Support Ireland operated independently from all government and statutory bodies (Farrell et al., 2002). This is not surprising because most voluntary organisations in Ireland complement the work of statutory agencies (Curry, 2003: 197).

From its establishment, similar to the British experience, Victim Support Ireland grew from a couple of volunteers to having branches and volunteers in almost every major city. Nally attributed the huge growth of Victim Support Ireland to Garda Commissioner Culligan, who introduced automatic police referrals to the organisation in 1992 (Moore Walsh, 2013: 187–8). In 1993 the then Minister for Justice, Maire Geoghegan-Quinn, opined that 'voluntary bodies such as the [Victim Support Ireland] which have experience and a good record in the provision of victims services are best placed to promote the case for establishing victims rights' (Geoghegan-Quinn, 1993). Similarly in the 2002 joint request for tender for Policy Research Relating to Victim Support, the Department of Justice described Victim Support Ireland as the cornerstone of government policy on victim care (Farrell et al., 2002: Appendix A). It further stated that it supported Victim Support Ireland in relation to matters of policy and political support (Farrell et al., 2002: 10). The government's support of Victim Support Ireland was in line with the ethos of the White Paper on a Framework for Supporting Voluntary Activity and Developing a Relationship between the State and the Community and Voluntary Sector (Department of Social Community and Family Affairs, 2000). Thus Victim Support Ireland appeared to be the official victims' rights movement in Ireland.

Although Victim Support Ireland took its name from Victim Support UK it did not limit itself to reforming crime victims. Victim Support Ireland identified its functions as including: support, advocacy, representation, liaison, lobbying and promotion. The organisation acted as an advocate or voice for the concerns of crime victims in dealing with the criminal justice system and as a representative of victims' interests at local, national and international levels. It had representatives on the National Crime Council, the Parole Board and Garda Quality Service Panels, and provided advice in restorative justice projects in Dublin and Tipperary and was a member of the Victim Support Europe (Farrell et al., 2002: 26). In fact, in 1990 Victim Support Ireland was one of the founding members of Victim Support Europe.[9] Over the years, Victim Support Europe has been acknowledged as a European wide non-governmental organisation (NGO) that has consultative status with the Council of Europe and the United Nations (UN). It was involved in advocating for the binding 2001 EU Framework Decision.

Domestically, Victim Support Ireland increased awareness among the legislature and judiciary concerning the needs of victims and issues affecting them (Fitzgerald, 1995). It also liaised with statutory and other voluntary organisations concerned with the criminal justice system and the welfare of victims (Burke, 1991). Lobbying was performed through networking with other agencies, and it sought legislative changes and improvement in services for victims (Farrell et al., 2002: 9). Some of the initiatives it sought were not controversial, such as altering the manner in which identification parades were conducted which required a witness to physically touch an alleged offender by way of identification (Haughey, 1995). Victim Support was the first organisation in Ireland to publish a victims charter in 1991. It issued an updated version in 1995 (Brienen and Hoegen, 2000: 471) and assisted and advised the Department of Justice regarding its first Victims Charter in 1997 (Owen, 1996; Owen 1997a). Other initiatives resulted in controversy, such as the introduction of victim impact statements into Irish law.

Although Victim Support Ireland is credited with lobbying for the use of victim impact statements (Farrell et al., 2002: 10; Fitzgerald, 1995; McGovern, 2002: 399), their introduction has been described as a 'knee jerk reaction to public pressure, an exercise in public window dressing' (McGrath, 2008: 81). It is more accurate to state that the introduction of victim impact statements came about through the exposure of some members of the Irish judiciary to the court practices and law of New Zealand. This exposure or education came about at a dinner party arranged by Barrister Donal Egan, the then Chairman of the Board of Directors of Victim Support Ireland, for members of the Irish judiciary to listen to and speak with a visiting judge regarding New Zealand's court practices and victim impact statements (Moore Walsh, 2013: 189). Subsequently, victim impact statements were adopted as a court practice in Ireland. The biggest issue that initially arose concerned who would prepare the victim impact statements

(Moore Walsh, 2013: 190). Eventually the court practice was placed on a statutory footing in the Criminal Justice Act 1993.

In June 2002 a review of Victim Support Ireland was jointly commissioned by the Department of Justice and Victim Support Ireland, due primarily to the collapse of the automatic referral system (Farrell et al., 2002: 1). Although no complaint was made regarding the referral of crime victims to Victim Support Ireland, in 2001 the Data Protection Commissioner indicated that he would likely rule against An Garda Síochána for incompatible disclosure of personal data and asked for the automatic referral system to be reviewed (Data Protection Commission, 2001). Besides identifying the problem of the referral system as life threatening, the report found that the specialist services were in keeping with international best practice, but these specialist services were straying too far from the community-based services. The over-diversification and over-specialisation posed a potential threat to the organisation (Farrell et al., 2002: 3). Concerns were raised that its advocacy role was diluted by its identification with official policies and its campaigning edge was blunted by over-reliance on state funding (Farrell et al., 2002: 44). The review concluded that, despite the sustained efforts of volunteers, staff and directors, Victim Support represented poor value for the State's investment and would continue to do so until the referral base was substantially increased (Farrell et al., 2002: 10). What was not addressed in the report was the fact that the State could have moved to amend the data protection law to exclude referrals by the Gardaí to support organisations from data protection legislation, but no amendments were forthcoming.

McDowell reduced funding to Victim Support Ireland in 2003 and 2004 to allow extra resources to go to the Gardaí (McDowell, 2004). The internal divisions within Victim Support Ireland deepened and became public (Breslin, 2004; Dundon, 2004). It is not known what effect the demise of the referral system had on the internal divisions. In April 2005 all funding to Victim Support was removed (Kehoe, 2005; O Siocháin and Dunphy, 2005) in the middle of a funding cycle, leaving general crime victims in Ireland without any services. Thus on the eve of Minister McDowell announcing that it was time to balance the criminal justice system, the official status of Victim Support Ireland was withdrawn, and its independent voice was silenced.

After the withdrawal of all government funding Victim Support Ireland fractured. Many volunteers formed themselves into new associations competing for government funding from McDowell's newly established Commission for the Support of Victims of Crime. In contrast the unofficial victims' movement, the women's movement, with its more limited focus on victims of sexual offences and domestic abuse, has continued to represent a sustained, nationwide victims' movement in Ireland that lobbies for reform, conducts research on behalf of victims and openly aims to achieve international best practice.

The recognition and expansion of human rights

When commentators speak about rights they often refer to 'first wave' and 'second wave' rights (Kennedy, 2004: 308). The first wave refers to the time of the American and French revolutions in the late eighteenth century. In the US the Founding Fathers articulated that one of the purposes of government was to protect the individual and his rights from the State. Liberty meant that citizens were to be free of any undue influences of the State and State-sanctioned churches. Thus the emphasis was on preventing states from oppressing individuals. These rights became known as natural rights, which imply that the rights pre-exist human society. However, as Kennedy has pointed out, '[r]ights are clearly not natural and different concepts of rights emerge from different societies' (Kennedy, 2004: 308).

The second wave of rights arose after the Second World War in response to the Holocaust. The challenge was to create a set of principles which would act as a safety net within every legal system. Civil rights may be vested in citizens, but human rights would be vested in humanity. Therefore, even where civil and political rights are abridged an individual should be able to seek protection on the basis of his or her rights simply as a human being (Kennedy, 2004: 308–9). The second-wave rights activists realised that what was required was more than the standard guarantee of liberty by placing restraints on states not to oppress. The proponents advocated the introduction of positive duties on states which would require a state to act to prevent oppression of an individual from other sources. In 1948 the newly formed UN adopted the Universal Declaration of Human Rights and spawned a new generation of rights based on the values of liberty and justice, dignity and equality, community and responsibility. These second-wave rights have become known as 'human rights'. It is often stated that '[t]he extent to which human rights are respected and protected within the context of the criminal proceedings is an important measure of a society's civilisation' (Andrews, 1982: 8).

Commencing in the 1980s a human rights approach for crime victims was advocated. On the international stage victimology and human rights law were mutually expanding and were also converging (Doak, 2003: 5). The recognition that the plight of crime victims has much in common with the plight of victims of state crime or abuse of state power was a novel and radical concept (Doak, 2003: 5; Elias, 1986). This expansive shift led to human rights being described as having a paradoxical 'shield and sword' function in the application of criminal law. The primary, traditional role of human rights was to provide protection from the criminal law and thus was a defensive weapon for an individual against state power. With the recognition that victims have human rights that must be protected by the state, the criminal law has become an offensive weapon that may now require states to act on behalf of an individual such as a victim of crime (Tulkens, 2011: 579).

The UN, Council of Europe and EU were all formed in the wake of the Second World War. The UN and Council of Europe were primarily human rights focused. Both produced valuable but generally non-binding victim-centred instruments. Despite the fact that the EU was primarily economically focused (Ryan and Hamilton, 2016: 468–9), and was the last of the institutions to enter into producing instruments on behalf of victims of crime, it has produced a number of binding instruments since 2001 in the form of Framework Decisions and Directives (Ryan and Hamilton, 2016: 477–8). Ireland is a member of all three of these international organisations which all have recognised that crime victims have human rights that must be protected by member states.

The recognition that crime victims have human rights was first reflected in the seminal 1985 UN Declaration of Basic Principles of Justice for Victims of Crime and Abuse of Power. The Declaration was a continuation of the Sixth UN Congress on the Prevention of Crime and the Treatment of Offenders, which recommended that the UN continue to work on the development of guidelines and standards regarding the abuse of economic and political power. In the Preamble the General Assembly noted that victims of crime and their families, as well as witnesses, are unjustly subjected to loss, damage or injury and they may also suffer hardship when assisting in the prosecution of an offender. The Declaration, through its resolutions, sets forth specific rights for victims of crime that all member states should aim to protect in their national laws, and these rights can be categorised into four groupings: (1) access to justice and fair treatment; (2) restitution; (3) compensation; and (4) assistance. Importantly, the General Assembly noted that this was to be done without prejudicing the rights of suspects or offenders (UN, 1985).

Notwithstanding the long standing of the Declaration, and efforts to expand its influence, it has a very low profile in Ireland and references to it in law journal articles, texts, government reports and studies are scant (Moore Walsh, 2013: 217). Where the Declaration is acknowledged or referenced it is presented as not particularly significant. For example, in 2011 the Committee for Judicial Studies, published with EU funding a book entitled *The Equal Treatment of Persons in Court: Guidance for the Judiciary*. This twelve-chapter book was designed to guide the Irish judiciary in the equal treatment of persons in court, yet it contains only one reference to the Declaration in a footnote. The footnote contains three sentences concerning the Declaration and the fact that it 'sets out a number of entitlements for victims' (Committee for Judicial Studies, 2011: 166).

After the UN, the second and smaller human rights-based organisation to form in the wake of the Second World War, in 1949, was the Council of Europe. Since its formation it has contributed to building a common legal area based on respect for human rights, democracy and the rule of law. The most important instrument to come from this forum is the *European Convention for the Protection of Human Rights and Fundamental Freedoms* (Council of Europe, 1953). Ironically the *European Convention on Human Rights* does not express any rights for crime victims, but it has become the champion of recognition of victims' rights in Europe. In 2003, in an attempt to bolster the influence of the *Convention*, the Oireachtas enacted the European Convention on Human Rights Act 2003. This Act places a general obligation on the Irish courts to interpret Irish law in a manner which is compatible with the *Convention*, so far as possible, and to take account of the decisions of the European Court of Human Rights. The jurisprudence flowing from the Convention requires states to put in place effective, real measures and remedies to ensure that the rights of crime victims are protected. The jurisprudence of the Convention is discussed in detail in Chapter 4.

In addition to the jurisprudence of the European Court of Human Rights, the Council of Europe has developed a large corpus of work on behalf of crime victims in the guise of conventions and recommendations. Predating the UN Declaration, the Council of Europe in 1983 adopted the first Recommendation recognising that policies such as the prevention of crime, alternatives to prison sentences and the social reintegration of offenders would not be effective without a favourable public attitude and the provision of assistance to victims (Council of Europe, 1983). Although Recommendations are not binding, they have played an important role in raising awareness of the plight of crime victims. They have systematically tested the waters and introduced debate and discussion for change to the status quo of victims and served as a model for 'hard law' Conventions and EU Framework Decisions and Directives. A review of the Recommendations for victims of crime reveals a steady progression of standards and guidelines to rights with new Recommendations building upon past Recommendations. Notwithstanding the fact that the 1985 UN Declaration stated that victims have human rights, it was not until 2000 that a Recommendation referred to victims having rights rather than interests (Council of Europe, 2000).

At the time when the Balance Group was established, Recommendation (2006)8 (Council of Europe, 2006) was published. Recommendation (2006)8 built upon previous Recommendations, but it also placed an onus on member states to take positive actions to discover and combat victimisation before it occurs. Importantly, it defined secondary victimisation as occurring not as a direct result of the criminal act but through the response of institutions and individuals to the victim (Council of Europe, 2006).

Although the Council of Europe has produced a large body of work on behalf of victims in its Recommendations, very little has been written or acknowledged about this work in Ireland, notwithstanding the influence Recommendations have had on binding instruments. Recommendations do not feature in Irish law journal articles and texts, or government reports and publications (Moore

Walsh, 2013: 234). Lawmakers also appear unaware of the Recommendations. For example, section 17(b) of the Garda Síochána Act 2005 provides that the Garda Commissioner will prepare a code of ethics having regard to any Recommendation of the Council of Europe. However, in the Explanatory Memorandum for the Bill it provides that the purpose of the Code of Ethics is to lay down standards of conduct and make officers aware of obligations under the *European Convention on Human Rights*. Absolutely no reference is made to any other work of the Council of Europe, thus giving the appearance that the only recommendation of the Council of Europe is the *European Convention on Human Rights*.

The first Council of Europe convention to directly address the issue of victims was the 1983 *Convention on Compensation* (Council of Europe, 1983). Ireland has neither signed nor ratified the 1983 Convention. This is surprising, given the fact that Ireland has in place a non-statutory state-funded scheme for compensating victims of selected crimes. Ireland signed the 2005 *Convention on the Prevention of Terrorism* (Council of Europe, 2005a) in October 2008, but has not ratified the *Convention*. The 2005 *Convention on Prevention of Terrorism* requires member states to adopt necessary financial assistance and compensation measures to protect and support the victims of terrorism committed within the member state. Ireland signed the 2005 *Convention on Action against Trafficking in Human Beings* (Council of Europe, 2005b) and ratified it in 2010. Thus, in 2006, when the Balance Group was formed, three Conventions had been negotiated by the members of the Council of Europe recognising and advancing the human rights of crime victims. Currently Ireland has only ratified one of these Conventions.

The real surprise has to be the involvement of the EU in advancing the rights of crime victims. The EU's roots go back to the formation of the European Coal and Steel Community in 1951 in the wake of the Second World War to limit the ability of a European nation to produce weapons of war. Although the European Communities came into being in 1957 it was not until 1993 that the Maastricht Treaty became effective, giving birth to the EU. Unlike the Council of Europe, which had an interest in crime from its inception, the EU first began to develop a competence in criminal law and justice in 1976 to counter terrorism (Ryan and Hamilton, 2016: 468; Walsh, 2002b: 7). The first formal recognition of EU interest in criminal justice came in Title VI of the Maastricht Treaty. Since 1969 the general human rights principles have been introduced by the European Court of Justice to avoid clashes with national constitutional rights when making decisions, and the Maastricht Treaty incorporated the Council of Europe's *European Convention for Human Rights*.

The work of the EU regarding crime victims is not as extensive as the work of the Council of Europe. As a general overview, in 1999 the European Commission issued a communication to the European Parliament to improve the plight of crime victims in the EU (EU, 1999). This communication contains seventeen proposals under five main headings: (1) prevention of victimisation; (2) assistance to victims; (3) standing of victims in criminal procedures; (4) compensation; and (5) general issues regarding information, languages and training. Member states were called upon to implement both fair and effective legislation in the areas outlined in the communication. Shortly thereafter the EU began to adopt binding legal instruments in the form of Framework Decisions and, later, Directives.

On 15 March 2001 the Council adopted the Framework Decision on the Standing of Victims in Criminal Proceedings (EU, 2001/220/JHA). The 2001 Framework Decision has been replaced by Directive 2012/29/EU; both are discussed in detail in Chapter 4. Two other framework decisions were adopted prior to the 2006 Balance Group being established, namely: the Framework Decision on Preventing and Combatting Trafficking in Human Beings and Protecting Victims (EU, 2002/29/JHA) and the Framework Decision on Combating the Sexual Abuse and Sexual Exploitation of Children and Child Pornography (EU, 2004/68/JHA). On 29 April 2004 Council Directive 2004/80/EC,[10] relating to compensation to crime victims, was adopted after terrorist attacks in Madrid in March 2004.

The catalyst for driving the 2001 Framework Decision and the 2004 Directive is said to have been the issue of cross-border victims. It was believed that persons victimised in a state other than where resident had a different fate than if victimisation had occurred in the state of residence (Rock, 2004a: 513). Problems encountered by cross-border victims were linked with the European freedoms, and in particular with the freedom of persons to travel without restrictions within the EU. If the EU limited itself to cross-border victims it could have resulted in the ridiculous situation whereby cross-border victims would have more rights than victims resident in the country where victimised (Groehuijsen and Pembertono, 2009: 44).

Today it is recognised generally that crime victims have human rights (Duffy, 2008: 9). The extent and enforcement of these human rights is still being determined. This evolution of the conception of human rights has 'inevitably had an influence on the victim's relationship with the criminal law' (Tulkens, 2011: 594). Since the year 2000, not only has the victim been accorded an increasingly important role in criminal proceedings, but the aim of the law has shifted from 'the right to civil redress to the right to satisfaction in criminal proceedings' (Tulkens: 2011: 595). Unfortunately, due to the lack of transparency in the Irish legislative process it is not always easy to determine the influences fostering change. However, Ireland's membership in the UN, Council of Europe and EU will continue to raise awareness of the rights of crime victims and more, importantly, awareness of the binding instruments of the EU and the jurisprudence of the European Court of Human Rights will force beneficial change.

Crime became a national election issue

In the 1960s in the US, social unrest was at a level not seen since the Civil War. By the mid-1960s an unanticipated by-product of the post-war baby boom became apparent. The unprecedented increase the number in teenagers was accompanied by a corresponding increase in the volume of crime (McCormack, 1999: 248). The civil rights and anti-war protests, coupled with social liberalisation and the rising crime rate, left many citizens fearful. At the same time the US Supreme Court under Chief Justice Earl Warren abandoned precedents and the notion of *stare decisis* and engaged in what has become known as judicial activism (Irons, 1999). The emphasis of the Warren Court concerned the recognition and protection of personal rights (Schwartz: 1993: 276). This activism resulted in a profound enhancement of the rights of persons accused of crimes, but left the public fearful. While many applauded the Warren Court, it is now almost conventional wisdom that the controversial cases were especially harmful to the criminal justice system because of the public disrespect and cynicism they generated (Steiker, 1997). This disrespect and cynicism helped to fuel the grassroots victims' rights movement in the US.

Politically, crime became a national political campaign issue for the first time in the 1964 presidential campaign (Friedman, 2002: 205; Gest, 2001: 5), and was amplified in the 1968 campaign. Prior to 1965 the murder rate had held fairly steady at five murders per 100,000 people, but it began to increase steadily until it doubled in 1970, and remained at that level for the next twenty years (Blumstein and Wallman, 2000: 3). All violent crimes followed the spiralling murder-rate trend, thereby placing crime prominently in the news (Blumstein and Wallman, 2000: 3).

During the 1968 presidential election, Nixon is said to have run against Warren and his Court as much as he ran against his Democratic opponent, Hubert Humphrey (Schwartz, 1993: 329). Nixon accused the Supreme Court of seriously weakening the police forces and strengthening the criminal forces in American society. In an effort to help local law enforcement in 1968 the Law Enforcement Assistance Administration was created as a federal agency to fund state and local law enforcement agencies. The war on crime was launched, and '[s]ince then crime has never left the national stage and the national agenda' (Friedman, 2002: 205). However, well into the 1980s the legacy of the Warren Court's rulings on criminal procedure was still generating political debate (Meese, 1986).

At approximately the same time that the Warren Court in the US was generating controversy, Britain began wrestling with the dilemma of whether the traditional constitutional civil liberties approach afforded sufficient protections to the accused. The traditional constitutional position is that the British recognise civil liberties and not civil rights. Since 1974 there have been increasing calls for a Bill of Rights (Street, 1982: 315). It took two decades, from the establishment of the Council of Europe in 1949 and enactment of the European Convention of Human Rights, for the idea of a Bill of Rights to be taken seriously in British political and legal circles. In the 1950s and early 1960s the idea was ridiculed by virtually all respectable lawyers and politicians as being eccentric, un-British and unnecessary (Blackburn, 1999: 6).

The Conservative years from 1979 to 1997 were marked by the attempts of outside bodies such as the European Court of Justice and the European Court of Human Rights to protect liberties in the UK (Fenwick, 2000: 6). More complaints were made against the UK than against any other member state (Street, 1982: 308). It was noted that civil liberties were receiving more protection from international courts and under international documents rather than as the result of decisions of the judiciary applying the common law (Fenwick, 2000: 6).

Law and order has loomed large in Britain's domestic politics since the 1960s (Pearson, 1987: 13). During the 1970s recorded rates of common crime dramatically increased, the prison population soared and the public expressed fear and demanded more police actions. Crime became a national issue for the first time in the 1979 election that brought Margaret Thatcher to power as prime minister. Then, shortly after the 1979 election, due to what has been characterised as 'American style riots,' the trust that the British people had in their police was undermined. Traditionally, the public were proud of their police, but from 1981 on the police were to figure in the debate on crime as much as the criminals (Sked and Cook, 1984: 353). A report in 1983 condemned the Metropolitan Police as bigoted, racist, sexist, bored, dishonest and often drunk (Ibid.: 353). Investigation of police complaints by the force itself, introduced in 1977, was seen as a failure and it was reported that the conviction rate in London was only 17% (Ibid.: 354). A bitter, long miners' strike exposed the police as active participants in a political struggle rather than the neutral upholders of the law (Peele, 1988: 168). The miners' strike and the riots introduced the public in mainland Britain to television images of the British police in riot gear battling with British rioters and protestors (Downes and Morgan, 2002: 290). The government came under increasing pressure to protect the public from the police as much as from criminals (Sked and Cook, 1984: 354).

The winds of change of the 1960s that caused law and order to become a political issue in both the US and Britain, and stimulated in the US the radical growth of the victims' rights movement, did not sweep across Ireland until much later. Prior to the 1960s there were few constitutional cases. By the middle 1960s it was noted that judicial interpretation had become increasingly bold (Chubb, 1991: 65). While many heralded the appointment of Cearbhall Ó Dálaigh to the role of Chief Justice in 1961 as the beginning of the new era in Irish jurisprudence, likening the court to the Warren Court, Chubb has asserted that '[n]o one would suggest that the Irish courts have come anywhere near emulating the Supreme Court of the US as policy makers or reformers' (Ibid.: 75).

Just as there were few constitutional cases, up until the mid-1960s there was very little criticism of the Constitution (Coakley, 1996: 62). It has been alleged that the greatest judicial breakthrough in the 1960s occurred in a High Court opinion in 1965[11] when 'undisclosed human rights' were found in the Irish Constitution and thus started a rights revolution (Chubb, 1991: 68). Since the discovery of implied fundamental rights in the Constitution, a variety of interest groups have sought to have their grievances redressed in the context of constitutional litigation (Whyte, 2002: 9). From the middle 1960s the term 'constitutional justice' began to be used by some Irish lawyers to describe this area of human rights (Chubb, 1991: 68). However, unlike the situation in the US following the Warren years, the Irish Supreme Court decisions did not harm the criminal justice system because these decisions did not generate public disrespect and cynicism. Unlike the situation in Britain, Ireland was seldom brought before outside bodies such as the European Court of Justice and the European Court of Human Rights.

It was not until the 1990s that scandals shook the Irish political system and brought law and order into public debate. Due to the close relationship between the Catholic Church and the State, scandals that should not have impacted on the political system did.[12] The social legacies of the 1950s and 1960s were exposed. The public became outraged over the abuse and cover-up of abuses by the State and the Catholic Church (Keenan, 2016: 529–31). The controversy generated by the 1994 conviction of Father Brendan Smyth for sexually abusing children over four decades brought down the government (Holt and Devaney, 2016: 81). The existence of incest[13] and the cruel and inhumane treatment of child victims[14] sparked demands for reform (Geoghegan-Quinn, 1996; Holt and Devaney, 2016: 81). Legal commentators correctly pointed out that the criminal justice system was being radically altered without much discussion or debate (Fennell, 1993). However, it is questionable how much informed discussion or debate would have been possible, given the lack of research or studies on the impact that various measures might have had on the system, the rights of the accused, victims and witnesses. As discussed above, successive Ministers for Justice denigrated the need for research on crime.

By the mid-1990s the economy was flourishing and the so-called Celtic Tiger economy was born. However, at a time when the country was beginning to flourish economically, fear began to seize the public. The year 1996 was a defining year in the debate on law and order in Ireland. In 1996 three publicised rural killings of elderly residents alarmed the public as it now appeared apparent that 'killing had come to the countryside, the repository of the "real" Ireland' (McCullagh, 1999: 29). The high-profile killings of Detective Garda Jerry McCabe and journalist Veronica Guerin also occurred in 1996 within two weeks of each other. It was as if 'a state of national emergency had been declared' (Kilcommins et al., 2004: 137), leading to a 'textbook case' of moral panic (Black, 2016: 402–4;

Kilcommins et al., 2004: 137; Meade, 2000; O'Donnell, 2011: 78). These killings resulted in a public outcry, triggered debates on law and order and served as a catalyst for crime to become a national issue for the first time. Many citizens began to believe that Irish society was becoming increasingly violent. Prior to this time criminal justice policy was 'where inertia and apathy were occasionally punctured by crises and bouts of hysteria' (O'Donnell, 2005: 107). A task force on security for the elderly was established by the Minister for Social Welfare (Owen, 1997b). The Dáil was recalled for a special debate after the killings. In the following two years an unprecedented barrage of legislation was introduced that fundamentally changed the shape and direction of the criminal justice process with little public consultation or debate (Walsh, 1999: 113).

Although crime levels started to increase in the 1960s and peaked in 1983 (Parsons, 2016: 19), these increases were not reflected in public opinion polls, which continued to rank unemployment, emigration and the situation in Northern Ireland as much more important than crime (Kilcommins et al., 2004). In the early 1980s, Independent Newspapers, which made up a large proportion of the print media, decided to place crime at the centre of news content (Black, 2016: 402). During the general election in 1997, law and order issues for the first time took centre stage in the opinion polls (Kilcommins et al., 2004: 136). Fianna Fáil was experiencing a rare period in opposition, where it redefined itself as the party of law and order. John O'Donoghue, the Fianna Fáil justice spokesman, alleged that the country was under threat, requiring extreme measures. During the 1997 general election campaign '[p]oliticians engaged in a bidding war, promising more Gardaí, more prisons and less tolerance', with Fianna Fáil promising to give the streets back to the Irish people (O'Donnell, 2005: 107). Fianna Fáil was returned to power in 1997, 2002 and 2007, never abandoning its law and order platform.

After 1996 police powers were greatly enhanced, including the powers of arrest, entry, search and seizure; the basic principles relating to bail were revised; the burden of proof on the prosecution was eased; the right to silence was curtailed and special procedures were introduced relating to organised crime (Walsh, 1999: 113). While legal commentators continued to point out that the crime rate in Ireland was lower than in most Western developed nations for most of the twentieth century, despite the violence in Northern Ireland (O'Donnell and O'Sullivan, 2001; Parsons, 2016), the public continued to demand that something be done. It has been suggested that it is more accurate to state that the levels of violent crime in Ireland prior to 1995 had been very low (Parsons, 2016; O'Mahony, 1999). It has also been argued that, regardless of the crime rates, many people were more concerned about the growth in violent crime. A 50% increase in homicides took place from 1995 to 1998 when general crime levels were in decline (O'Connell, 2002: 117). As Kilcommins et al. (2004: 36) observed, '[c]oncern about crime was relatively muted when recorded crime rates peaked. Paradoxically, when recorded crime began to fall in the mid-1990s, concern surged, and while it has abated somewhat it remained a prominent political issue.'

At the same time when crime was becoming a national election issue confidence in the police began to erode. The Gardaí traditionally operated in complete independence, with no supervision by the prosecuting authorities or members of the judiciary (Conway, 2013). Members of the public began to make complaints about how they were treated by the Gardaí. The self-investigation of Gardaí complaints was introduced in 1986 and was not successful (Conway, 2010; Griffin, 2007). In 1987, a study revealed that the Gardaí still enjoyed high levels of confidence among the public. However, this finding was not shared by all social groups (Bohan and Yorke, 1987: 72). Confidence in the Gardaí began to wane when a number of perceived innocent people, who were not criminals or subversives, were abused in police custody[15] or prosecuted on false confessions.[16] The issue of confidence in the Gardaí became a scandal when the Morris Tribunal[17] concluded that Gardaí corruption in Donegal was evident and Gardaí had set up a breakaway republic where many members engaged in criminal activity (Conway, 2010; Morris Tribunal, 2008). The moral outrage which had rocked the Catholic Church over revelations of the cover-up of sexual offences by the clergy against children was now directed toward the Gardaí (O'Donnell, 2005: 127). Eventually the scandals took their toll and in a 2004 newspaper survey for the first time a sizable proportion of the public expressed a lack of confidence in the police (Mulcahy and O'Mahony, 2005: 5). Thus, at a time when a sizable proportion of the public expressed a lack of confidence in the Garda Síochána, the Minister for Justice placed all funding for victim support groups under the control of the Commission for Victims of Crime, which was chaired by retired Garda Assistant Commissioners.

Public distrust was not limited to the Gardaí. The 1999 Phillip Sheedy controversy[18] confirmed the public's belief that justice in Ireland is skewed in favour of those with access to the judiciary and politicians (Carey, 1999: 283). The Office of the DPP was criticised by the public for failing or refusing to disclose reasons for decisions. For example, in 2000 the DPP created a public controversy when he would not disclose why he had decided not to proceed with the retrial of Dermot Laide on manslaughter charges in the beating death of Brian Murphy by a group of affluent young men. Legislators caused public alarm by their failure to update the laws on statutory rape[19] and insanity.[20] In the case of Judge Brian Curtin public criticism was heaped upon the police, the DPP, as well as the legislators for having no mechanism in place for impeaching a sitting judge.[21] In 2003 Justice Hardiman blamed the lack of specialist legal journalists for the judiciary's bad press (*Law Society Gazette* 2003: 6). Black, on the other hand, has noted that media coverage in Ireland is a double-edged sword. While it is often problematic and one-dimensional it has been instrumental in raising awareness about hidden issues (Black, 2016: 404) such as the treatment of crime victims within the criminal justice system.

Crime first became a national political issue in 1997 and shortly thereafter public satisfaction with the criminal justice system decreased, with public distrust of the Gardaí, judiciary, legislators and DPP being generated by several public controversies. By 2004 a sizable proportion of the public expressed a lack of confidence in the Gardaí. In contrast to the experiences of the US, these events did not produce a radical growth in the victims' movement. However, they did undoubtedly influence the Minister for Justice to follow the British example in 2006 and form the Balance Group to address the imbalance in the scales of justice.

Conclusion

The re-emergence of the crime victim in Ireland was due primarily to four principal influences that created pressure on the Irish government to alter the status of crime victims, transforming the victim from a piece of evidence to a stakeholder in the criminal justice system worthy of a consideration requiring the scales of justice to be balanced. Three of the four principal influences were international in character, having flourished elsewhere before featuring in Ireland. Victimology research began in Europe at the end of the Second World War and became a separate discipline from criminology around 1970, and in 1984 Ireland's first crime victimisation survey was published. At the same time as victimology was struggling to establish itself, various social movements concerned with crime victims began to form. The first national victims' movement in Ireland was the women's movement, and in 1985 Victim Support Ireland was founded, becoming the first voluntary group to attempt to provide service to all crime victims. The recognition and expansion of human rights to include victims of crime by the UN, Council of Europe and EU began in the 1980s when victimology and human rights law were mutually expanding and converging. The extent and enforcement of these human rights is still evolving today. The fourth principal influence, crime becoming a national election issue with a contemporaneous decrease in public satisfaction with the criminal justice system, was domestic in character and undoubtedly was the catalyst for the formation of the Balance Group which recommended sweeping change to some of the rights afforded to the accused.

Notes

1 The Golden Age was the time when the victim was the central character of the justice system and performed the role of police, prosecutor and judge.
2 During the Middle Ages, with the introduction of the feudal system, restitution to the victim was replaced with fines paid to the state. The victim still had to capture the offender and often had to pay to have the offender prosecuted.

3   In the late 1960s, with the emergence of the individual rights movement and the questioning of the government's power and authority, the crime victim slowly began to assume a role of importance in some criminal justice systems.
4   For a concise overview of the US victims' rights movement, see Mastrocinqe (2010).
5   The Conditions of Employment Act 1935 allowed the ban on married women being gainfully employed, which was not removed until 1973. The 1937 Constitution endorsed a patriarchal system in which the male is considered the breadwinner and the woman is confined to the home. Art. 41 provides: 'The State recognises that by her life within the home woman gives to the State a support without which the common good cannot be achieved. The State shall, therefore, endeavour to ensure that mothers shall not be obliged by economic necessity to engage in labour to the neglect of their duties in the home.'
6   Henry (2006) noted that the mixture of religious beliefs and human reproduction sometimes leads to serious situations, often not beneficial to patients who may not share the religious convictions. She highlighted symphysitomy, or the sawing in half the pelvic bone, which left many women disabled and was preferred to caesarean section and which limited future pregnancies; compassionate hysterectomies as a form of birth control; and the incidence of death from deep vein thrombosis among older women due to many pregnancies.
7   Finnegan (2001) highlighted the use of the Magdalen Asylums as a means of social control of women and girls deemed to be wayward, where they were forced to live and work without trial in walled convents.
8   For a detailed history of Victim Support see Rock (1990: 114).
9   For a concise history of Victim Support Europe (formerly the European Forum for Victim Services) see Domenech (2003).
10 In *EU Commission v Italy* (11 October 2016) (C-601/14) the Grand Chamber of the European Court of Justice ruled that Italy had failed to fulfil its obligations under Council Directive 2004/80/EC. The Italian national scheme for crime victims was found not to cover all intentional violent crimes committed in Italy.
11 *Ryan v Attorney General* [1965] IR 294.
12 In 1992 Bishop Eamonn Casey resigned amid a scandal that he had had an affair with an American divorcee in 1973 and fathered a child (Murphy and de Rosa, 1993). Similarly, in 1994 a scandal occurred when it became known that a deceased famous singing priest, Father Cleary, had fathered two sons with his housekeeper (Hamilton and Williams, 1995).
13 The Kilkenny Incest case involved the continued physical and sexual abuse of a girl by her father from 1976 to 1991, notwithstanding the fact that the family was known to a number of child protection professionals (McGuiness, 1993).
14 Kelly Fitzgerald died in 1993 at the age of 12, following years of neglect by her parents. The child first came to the attention of authorities at the age of five months and was placed on an 'at risk' register at age 11 (Geoghegan-Quinn, 1996).
15 In 1984 after a prolonged interrogation Joanne Hayes confessed to the murder of a baby. The case became known as the Kerry Babies case. Other members of her family corroborated her confession with details not publicly known. Scientific evidence revealed that Hayes was not the mother of the baby. Criminal charges were dropped eventually (Inglis, 2003; Mulcahy, 2016: 269).
16 In 1997 Dean Lyons, an addict with a mild mental disability, confessed while in custody to two brutal murders (Birmingham, 2006). In 1999 mentally ill Paul McCabe and ex-nun

Nora Wall were convicted of raping a 12-year-old in 1990 based upon an alleged confession by McCabe, among other things. McCabe was sentenced to 12 years and Wall to life imprisonment. After serving only four days they were released, their convictions were quashed and in 2005 a miscarriage of justice was declared. It was found that no notes of the McCabe interview had been taken while he was in custody and he had not dictated the statement, as originally suggested by Gardaí (O'Brien, 2006; O'Sullivan, 2008).

17 The Morris Tribunal was established in 2002. In total five reports were made by the Tribunal from 2002 to 2006. The final report was issued in 2008. It investigated a range of allegations against the Gardaí in Donegal between 1993 and 1999. A litany of police corruption and negligence was highlighted (Morris Tribunal, 2008).

18 The Sheedy Affair caused the resignation of High Court Justice Cyril Kelly, Supreme Court Justice Hugh O'Flaherty and a court registrar. Sheedy was sentenced to four years' imprisonment for dangerous driving while under the influence of alcohol causing the death of a woman and injuring her husband and children. He was an accountant and found prison difficult. A member of his family contacted a judge. Another member of his family, who was employed by the State, contacted the Taoiseach. On 14 Oct. 1998 Sheedy was visited by the Taoiseach's friend Joe Burke. The non-sentencing judge judicially reviewed Sheedy's case and released him from prison four weeks after Burke's visit and within the first year of his sentence. When the surviving victims learned that Sheedy had been released they went public and a public outcry occurred. An official inquiry followed, the judicial resignations occurred and Sheedy voluntarily returned to prison. (Ahern, 1999).

19 During the summer of 2006 the Supreme Court struck down provisions of the Criminal Law (Amendment) Act 1935 in *CC v Ireland* [2006] IESC 33. For years the Court had hinted that in an appropriate case the provisions would be struck down. However, the legislators failed to amend or replace the 1935 Act. Immediately after the decision, men convicted and serving sentences under the provision sought release from prison. The public was alarmed and enraged (Haynes, 2007).

20 In Aug. 2002 John Gallagher, a double killer, absconded from the Dundrum Central Mental Hospital after being found guilty but insane under the Trial of Lunatics Act 1883. During his 13 years in Dundrum, Gallagher held a part time job, enjoyed unsupervised weekend release and was allowed to purchase a computer and motorbike which facilitated his escape. In *Gallagher v DPP* [1991] IR 31, the Supreme Court held that Gallagher's verdict was a finding of acquittal, which meant that little could be done to the escaped Gallagher. This controversy led to the Criminal Law (Insanity) Act 2006.

21 *Curtin v Dáil Eirean* [2006] IESC 14. Prior to Curtin applying for a judgeship, the Federal Bureau of Investigation notified an Garda Siochana that Curtin was a customer of a paedophile website in Texas. Allegedly due to the fact that Curtin was not convicted of any crime, the Gardaí did not inform the Judicial Board that Curtin was accused of a serious crime. After he was appointed to the Bench a warrant was issued to search Curtin's home and computer. Ultimately child pornography was found on his computer, but due to the fact that the search warrant had expired before it was served he could not be prosecuted. He was allowed to retire on medical grounds (Dwyer, 2008).

3

The victim in law: a juridical excursus

There has been growing recognition of the interests and needs of victims in the law arena, where previous emphasis had been predominantly on the rights of the accused and the offender (Christie, 1977; O'Hara, 2005). The result, in Ireland and in other jurisdictions, has been a series of developments which seek to enhance victims' status in relation to the alleged wrongdoing. Via the deliberative capacity of domestic and EU legislatures drawing upon the (admittedly imperfect) opinion and will formation of their citizens (Habermas, 1996: 135–50; Waldron, 1999), together with expansive judicial interpretation of constitutional and convention texts, we are slowly discovering that rights in the criminal process are not confined to an exclusive caste, anchored to a fixed date in history.

Although we may disagree about the extent to which victims should be conferred with a juridical status in the criminal arena, it seems beyond argument that it is occurring. That is the sole purpose of this chapter, to document the variety of ways in which interpersonal criminal conflict is being adjusted to accommodate victims. Much of this chapter therefore is concerned with modest legal details, 'with little territories of the everyday' (Rose, 2008: 280). It will examine issues such as the expansion in the use of video-link testimony; the use of intermediaries to contend with the somewhat harsh effects of adversarialism; the provision of legal assistance and legal representation; the use of out-of-court statements to reduce the need to give *viva voce* evidence; the reliance on prior statements to deal with the spectre of witness intimidation; the socialisation of law through victim impact statements; the development of more relaxed requirements regarding the competence of a witness to testify; greater recognition of the independence of married spouses; an increased awareness of the exclusionary assumptions that exist in relation to the reliability of certain witnesses; a less mechanical (and rigidly temporal) approach to the doctrine of recent complaint; legislative acceptance that the absence of resistance by a victim in a rape case does not equate with consent; tighter restrictions that offer victims better protection against unnecessary and distressing information being raised about their sexual histories; greater protection of the identity of victims and witnesses in criminal cases; curtailment of unjustified imputations at trial against the character of a deceased or incapacitated victim or witness; support for a complainant's right to privacy despite the requirements of disclosure; the increased willingness of courts to accommodate complainants' reasons for delays in reporting; and increased interventions in harmful contexts.

Victims of crime also have recourse to the civil jurisdiction of the courts. Indeed such a pathway is viewed as a necessary pillar in the vindication of an individual's rights. The Irish courts have been expanding jurisprudence in this field in recent years, particularly in relation to appropriate damages, delays in taking actions, new torts and the admissibility of convictions. International and EU legal instruments, along with the determinations of the European Court of Human Rights, act as another emboldening reference points. In addition to juridification along the lines outlined above, the process is also witnessing growing scepticism about the institutional reification of State functionaries such as the Office of the DPP and Gardaí. They are no longer as free to set their own imperatives, or to rely with immunity upon the ideological neutrality of their activities, given the demands for increased accountability and transparency in decision-making structures. The significance of all this detail – much of which has developed piecemeal and according to different causal forces – will be in how it connects together in the coming years.

Justice as accommodation

Before documenting the black-letter, technocratic details of how victims have been juridically provided for since the late 1980s in Ireland, it is worth noting that their status as stakeholders is becoming more and more visible in the reasoning of the courts. The criminal process is gradually becoming more sensitive to their needs and concerns as it demonstrates an increased willingness to engage with competing standpoints and principles. Such accommodation and inclusion stands in marked contrast to the long shadow cast by monolithic State/accused conceptions of fairness. This subtle restructuring of the crime conflict is evident, for example, in *Casey v DPP, Ireland and the AG*,[1] where Humphreys J. noted that 'the criminal trial is a mechanism to vindicate the legal, constitutional, EU and ECHR rights *of a victim of crime*' (our emphasis). Increasingly, considerations of process fairness include the victim as a relevant determinant within its paradigm of reference. While previously such deliberations were housed within the more remote, anodyne medium of the 'public interest', the courts are now becoming more explicit in specifically identifying victims and competing rights. In countenancing rights and principles such as bodily integrity, life, privacy, participation and protection within this standard, a more accommodating – albeit challenging and contested – interpretation of fairness is developing, one that is not exclusively dominated by accused considerations. An illustrative example of this more inclusionary interpretation of fairness is to be found in *DPP v Gerald McNeill*,[2] where Denham J. noted in the context of a sexual abuse prosecution: 'Facing into these types of prosecutions, which were becoming more common, the courts sought to achieve *a fair trial with justice for all concerned. Those concerned include the people of Ireland for whom the prosecution is brought, the accused who has the fundamental right of a fair trial, and the victims'* (our emphasis).[3]

This severance of the victim class from more public interest considerations is, it is submitted, more than mere rhetoric.[4] It signifies an important turn in the re-inclusion of the victim, a clear demarcation and express acknowledgement of her autonomous standing as a rights-holder. In addition to providing more significant normative protection, such a phenomenon is also breathing fresh life into aged criminal legal frameworks. Although oversimplified, the distinction between positive and negative rights is a useful heuristic in mapping the evolving journey of victims' inclusion. Negative rights against the state are primarily vertical – 'to fend off dangers that can arise in the government–citizen dimension ... that is, in the relationships between the administrative apparatus with its monopoly on the means of legitimate violence, and unarmed private persons' (Habermas, 2008 repr: 245). Traditional interpretive patterns emphasised the ideological primacy of negative rights in the criminal process by focusing exclusively on the accused's relationship with the conflict. This relationship was presented as fixed and unalterable, not least because of the immunities granted in constitutional and convention texts. Positive rights, on the other hand, which are both vertical and horizontal, ground affirmative claims to action – such as autonomy, life, bodily integrity, privacy and participation – by an 'interventionist state that provides infrastructures and wards off risks' (Ibid.: 247). The culture of negative rights against the State is thus gradually coming into contact with a newer culture of positive rights. The latter increasingly challenges the interest positions that the former narrowly protects, demanding recognition of the inter-subjective dimensions of the conflict by both the State and the accused.

This burgeoning influence of victims as claims-makers is also to be found in a myriad of disparate issues that arise in criminal law and criminal process jurisprudence, including leave for judicial review,[5] the defence of provocation,[6] the inclusion of evidence potentially probative of guilt,[7] delay in sexual abuse cases,[8] trial prohibition on the grounds of delay[9] and the right to have recourse to a criminal trial where there is reasonable evidence and the trial can be conducted fairly.[10] Juridification of this kind will undoubtedly impact upon State/accused relations. Synthesising sometimes competing rights and principles in ways that will ensure just and fair decisions will be a challenge. It will require an ongoing constructive interpretation of fresh cases that come before the courts. Such interpretation demands both fidelity to existing legal precedents ('formal' style reasoning) as well as an acceptance of the innovative possibilities of law and rights ('grand' style reasoning), given their evaluative aspects and potential for alteration through rules of change (Hart, 1961: 63).[11] In interpreting cases, judges will be guided by the gravitational pull of earlier decisions as part of a process for adjudicating and certifying truth claims. This will often be infused with visions of fairness, welfare and respect for human dignity which will often operate principles or justifications underpinning various precedents. As Dworkin notes, judges are often required – like interpretation within a chain novel – to make their decisions, in part, from an interpretation that both fits and justifies the institutional constitutional history of their society. This not only relates to a narrow, rule-based understanding of the rights and duties that flow from past collective decisions in the relevant disputed area, but also incorporates, more broadly, 'the scheme of principles' that justify them (Dworkin, 1998 repr: 227). They can identify unenumerated rights, expand existing rights to incorporate unforeseen issues, revise them in the light 'of fresh moral insight' and re-examine common law and legislative provisions in the light of the Constitution and the European Convention on Human Rights, striking down anything which is not compatible (Kilcommins, 2016: 326–41).[12]

Writing victims in to the criminal justice story necessarily creates disturbances and establishes competing tensions (Kilcommins et al., 2004: 150). Most commentators would accept that these tensions and disturbances are necessary so as to create a more communicative process, one which permits victims to recover, to some extent, their centrality in 'the conflict'. Some, however, urge caution, pointing to the power inherent in the image of the 'suffering victim' and its potential to embrace punitiveness (Fennell, 2001: 54; O'Flaherty 2002, 375). As McCullagh has noted, 'victim discourse in Ireland has achieved the status of being both unchallenged and unchallengeable' (McCullagh, 2014). These concerns about the coercive potential of victim discourse are, of course, real. We should be wary of the possibility of political or media manipulation, or the depiction of the criminal justice system as a 'zero-sum game' where gains for victims must be at the expense of those accused of crime.

What must be guarded against in the juridical accommodation of victims is any constructive interpretation of process fairness which unites the public interest with victims and against those accused of crime. Bifurcation of this kind presents arguments in Manichean terms, with the forces of light of the community (which incorporates victims, but not those accused of crime) set up in opposition to the forces of darkness of suspects and offenders. Such reasoning has the potential to create a false dichotomy in which the accused is increasingly alienated, and forced to face a 'moral authority of grief' as expressed both by the victim and by the public (Garland, 2001: 144; Vaughan and Kilcommins, 2008: 128–34). It also replaces one set of exclusionary practices (victim as outsider) with another (accused as other). There are two reasons why we should be wary of such reasoning, one self-interested, the other motivated by concern for the equality of others. First, reasoning via the logic of 'us' (community) versus 'them' (those accused of crime) tends to ignore the fact that the rights of the accused are actually *our* rights. There is potential for all of us, in the course of our lives, to have the finger of suspicion or criminal blame pointed in our direction. Given the potential violence that the criminal law can legitimately inflict upon us – stigmatisation, handcuffing, deprivation of liberty and ancillary punishments, such as loss of career (actual or potential), removal of good name and travel rights – it is in all of our interests to ensure that the system is as fair as possible, designed to minimise the 'risk of misdecision'. The safeguards that we provide for those accused of crime are the same safeguards that we will call upon for ourselves should the criminal laws of the state be invoked against us. Second, it is also possible to argue that it is precisely because of the potential alignment of victims' needs with society's majoritarian demand for social order that a strong scheme of rights is required for 'others', those accused of crime who are excluded from the community's definition or perception of itself (Campbell, Kilcommins and O'Sullivan, 2010: 381).

In welcoming the 'rights revolution' in the criminal process, and in accepting that this disturbs older ways of doing things and the reified voices of certain stakeholders central to that process, it is important that the justice system seeks to accommodate *all* stakeholder rights, including the claim-rights of the accused. In easy cases, this may require nothing more than the syllogistic application of the relevant individual right. In harder cases, where competing rights may be at issue, more reflexive consideration will be required, which will focus on the principles and justifications underpinning the rights at stake, and where parties will be encouraged to 'frame and test hypotheses about what these rights are' (Dworkin, 2005: 338) and what weightings should attach. The remainder of this chapter will document the variety of ways in which victims of crime are being accommodated via legal provisions.

The use of video-link evidence

Ordinarily the adversarial nature of the Irish criminal process requires that witnesses are examined *viva voce* in open court. In recognition, however, of the trauma that this may impose on victims of specified sexual or violent offences (LRC, 1989: 120–1) the legislature enacted section 13 of the Criminal Evidence Act 1992 which provides that victims, among other witnesses, can give evidence in such cases *via* a live television link. Evidence given by a television link must be video-recorded. In the case of victims of such offences who are under the age of 18[13] or are persons suffering from a 'mental handicap'(section 19), there is a presumption in favour of giving evidence via television link (section 13(1)(a)).[14] They are entitled to do so 'unless the court sees good reason to the contrary'. In all other cases, the court will exercise its discretion whether or not to permit television-link evidence.[15] The use of such a provision was contested in the Irish courts in the cases of both *Donnelly v Ireland*[16] and *White v Ireland*[17] on the grounds that it constituted an unlawful interference with an accused person's right to fairness of procedures. In neither case was the challenge successful (Connolly 2015: 24–7; Heffernan and Ni Raifteartaigh, 2014: 64–71; McGrath, 2014: 153; O'Malley, 2009: 106–10).

The courts have used their discretion to permit applications for the use of video-link facilities.[18] In the *DPP v McManus*[19] the applicant had been convicted of manslaughter of a teenager. Objections were raised in relation to the court allowing the accused's daughter, who was older than 18, to give her evidence by way of video link. It was submitted that where a witness gives evidence in the ordinary course of events, the jury has the greatest possible opportunity to assess the demeanour, deportment and reaction of such a witness in examination and cross-examination. It was argued that fair procedures dictate that the witness should be required to give evidence on oath, physically, in the presence, and under the scrutiny, of the judge and jury. It was also argued that any departure from this default positon should occur only if there was 'strong evidence' to support the application. The fact that a witness might 'freeze', be unable to answer questions when giving evidence, not want to confront her father face to face or not wish to give evidence in front of a crowd was, it was argued, insufficient grounds. These arguments were rejected by the appeal court, which noted that the witness had been the subject of lengthy cross-examination. The court went on to state that there was no evidence adduced on behalf of the defence 'upon which it could be found that there was a real or serious risk of an unfair trial, by reason of the learned trial judge exercising his discretion to permit the witness in question to give her evidence by means of live video link'.

More recently, section 39 of the Criminal Justice Act 1999 provides that where a witness is in fear or subject to intimidation in any proceedings on indictment for an offence, that person may, with leave of the court, give evidence through a live television link. Section 29(1) of the Criminal Evidence Act 1992, as substituted by section 24 of the Extradition (European Union Conventions) Act 2001, also attempts to accommodate witnesses who are outside the state from having to attend to give evidence at trial. It provides that in any criminal proceedings a witness other than the accused may, with leave of the court, give evidence through a live television link.[20]

Intermediaries

Under section 14(1) of the Criminal Evidence Act 1992, witnesses may, on application by the prosecution or the defence, also be permitted to give evidence in court through an intermediary in circumstances where they are using the live television link and are under 18 years of age or are persons with a 'mental handicap' who have reached that age in relation to a relevant offence. The trial judge can grant such an application if he or she believes that the interests of justice require that any questions to be put to the witness be put through an intermediary. Questions put to a witness in this manner shall be either in the words used by the questioner or so as to convey to the witness in a way which is appropriate to her or his age and mental condition the meaning of the questions being asked. While evidence is being given through a live television link pursuant to section 13(1) of the Criminal Evidence Act 1992, neither the judge, nor the barrister or solicitor concerned in the examination of the witness, shall wear a wig or gown. Moreover, if a child or a person with a mental disorder is giving evidence *via* a television link in respect of a victim impact statement, the same rule applies.[21]

Admission of pre-trial statements

Given the emphasis placed by our adversarial system on the orality of the proceedings, pre-trial statements are not generally permitted in the criminal process. The rationale underpinning the exclusion of such statements is that they constitute hearsay and ordinarily are excluded because the court is deprived of the normal methods of testing the credibility of the witness. A pre-trial statement, for example, is not given on oath; the demeanour of the witness making the statement cannot be observed by the trier of fact; and the defence has no opportunity to cross-examine the witness. The absence of this latter safeguard is of particular importance. More recently, however, it has been recognised that an overly rigid application of the hearsay rule can lead to injustice. Provision has accordingly been made for the admission of video-recordings, depositions and out-of-court statements in certain circumstances. Under section 16(1) of the Criminal Evidence Act 1992, for example, it provides that a video-recording of any evidence given by a person under 18 years of age or a person with an intellectual disability through a live television link at the preliminary examination of a sexual offence or an offence involving violence shall be admissible at trial. It also renders admissible at trial a video-recording of any statement – made by a person under 14 years of age or a person with an intellectual disability, being a person in respect of whom such a sexual offence or an offence involving violence is alleged to have been committed, or a person under 18 years of age in relation to a specified offence involving human trafficking or child trafficking and pornography – during an interview with a member of the Garda Síochána or any other person who is competent for the purpose, provided the witness is available at trial for cross-examination.

The person's age, if relevant, is to be calculated by reference to the date of the video-recording, not the date of trial. This provision is, as Delahunt notes, 'undoubtedly a practical step towards making the testimony of child witnesses and witnesses with an intellectual disability more easily heard within the criminal justice system' (Delahunt, 2011: 6). In either case the video-recording shall not be admitted in evidence if the court is of opinion that it is not in the interests of justice to do so. In *The People (DPP) v XY*, for example, the accused was charged with section 4 of the Criminal Law (Rape) (Amendment) Act 1990 after it was alleged that he had forced a woman with an intellectual disability into performing the act of oral sex with him. In the case, the trial judge admitted as evidence a DVD recording of an interview with the complainant. This pre-trial recording was admitted as examination-in-chief testimony (Delahunt 2011; Delahunt, 2015: 46–9; LRC CP 63 -2011: 191–2;).

The use of section 16 has been challenged on the basis that it constitutes 'a significant departure from the requirements of orality' and was potentially discriminatory.[22] This argument was firmly rejected by Humphreys J., who noted, with characteristic acuity, that 'the forensic gamesmanship of the criminal process means that an argument does not have to have a great deal of merit in order to have an influence on how a trial is conducted, or what form of resolution of the proceedings might be acceptable either to the prosecution or to the court'.[23] He also pointed out that section 16 protects rights conferred by the new EU Directive on Victims' Rights, and noted that significant safeguards attached, including the requirement that the witness must be available at the trial for cross-examination, and the proviso that the court has a discretion not to admit the evidence in the interests of justice.

More general provision for the admission of depositions (and video-recordings) at the pre-trial stage are now made under section 4 of the Criminal Procedure Act 1967, as amended. The trial court retains a discretion to exclude such evidence if it is of the opinion that it is necessary in the interests of justice. Moreover, under section 255 of the Children Act 2001, a judge of the District Court, when satisfied on the evidence of a registered medical practitioner that the attendance before a court of any child would involve serious danger to the safety, health or wellbeing of the child, may take the evidence of the child concerned by way of sworn deposition or through a live television link in any case where the evidence is to be given through such a link. This relates to certain specified offences including cruelty against children, causing or procuring a child to engage in begging, allowing a child to be in a brothel and causing or encouraging a sexual offence on a child, the murder or manslaughter of a child, any offence involving bodily injury to a child and most sexual offences (Walsh, 2005: 21).[24]

Following the high-profile collapse of a gangland murder trial in 2003 as a result of witness intimidation (Heffernan and Ni Raifertaigh, 2014: 200), section 16 of the Criminal Justice Act 2006 was enacted. It makes provision for the admission of a statement made by a witness in any criminal proceedings relating to an arrestable offence and can be employed where a witness is too frightened to give direct evidence against a potentially dangerous criminal (Donagh, 2014: 118–21; Fitzgerald, 2008: 126–9). It can be invoked either by the prosecution or the defence. It can occur in circumstances where the witness, although available for cross-examination, refuses to give evidence, denies making the statement or gives evidence which is materially inconsistent with it.[25] The statement can then be admitted if it is proved that the witness made it, it is reliable, was made voluntarily and direct oral evidence of the fact concerned would be admissible.[26] The provision represents a 'fundamental departure from traditional common law principles which for good reason, have always placed such high regard on sworn evidence given directly, immediately, and spontaneously before the fact adjudicator'.[27] In addition to reliability and voluntariness requirements, certain other safeguards also apply. The statement must be given on oath or affirmation or contain a declaration by the witness that the statement is true to the best of his knowledge or belief, or, the court is otherwise satisfied that when the statement was made the witness understood the requirement to tell the truth. In determining whether the statement is reliable, the court will have regard to whether or not it was given on oath or affirmation or was video-recorded, if there is other evidence to support its reliability, and the explanations of the witness, if any, in refusing to give evidence. The court must also be satisfied that the admission of the statement would not be contrary to the interests of justice.

Identification

In some instances eye-witness identification of the perpetrators of crime will be required at the pre-trial and trial stages of criminal process. This can be very traumatic for witnesses, particularly those who are the alleged victims. There are no one-way mirror identification systems in Garda stations, and very often the victim may find himself or herself in the same room as the accused. Moreover, at a pre-trial identification parade the witness will, according to the Garda Siochana *Criminal Investigation Manual*, generally be asked to 'place his/her hand on the identified person's shoulder', although fortunately it is now that case that this practice has been relaxed and the witness can, if he or she requests, make the identification by pointing and describing the person in question (Walsh, 2002a: para 6.55). Making an identification in court can also be difficult for a witness. More recently efforts have been made to alleviate this trauma. Persons giving evidence via television link under section 13 of the Criminal Evidence Act 1992 and section 39 of the Criminal Justice Act 1999, as referred to above, shall not now be required to identify the accused at the trial of the offence if the accused is known to them (unless the court in the interests of justice directs otherwise). Moreover, evidence by a person other than the witness that the witness identified the accused at an identification parade as being the offender shall be admissible as evidence that the accused was so identified.[28]

Victim impact statements

The reduction of victim alienation has also occurred through the use of victim impact statements (Guiry, 2006: 2–9; McGrath, 2008: 71–99; O'Malley, 1993: 40–60). Section 5 of the Criminal Justice Act 1993 made provision for the court to receive evidence or submissions concerning any effect of specified offences on the person in respect of whom an offence was committed. These offences relate to most sexual offences, genital mutilation and offences involving violence or the threat of violence to a person. Section 5 initially presupposed that the victims of these offences were capable themselves of giving evidence of the impact that the crime had on them (O'Malley, 2009: 885). To combat the narrowness of this presumption, the Irish courts began as a practice to admit the evidence of family members of homicide victims.[29] As a result of the introduction of section 4 of the Criminal Procedure Act 2010, a 'person in respect of whom the offence was committed' now includes a family member of that person when that person has died, is ill or is otherwise incapacitated as a result of the commission of the offence. A family member may also give evidence under section 5(3)(b)(ii) of the Criminal Justice Act 1993, as amended, where the victim of the specified offence suffers from a mental disorder (not related to the commission of the offence). Under section 5A of the Act, a child or a person with a mental disorder may give evidence of the impact of the crime through a live television link unless the court sees good reason to the contrary.[30] Moreover, where a child or a person with a mental disorder is giving evidence through a live television link pursuant to section 5A, the court may, on the application of the prosecution or the accused, direct that any questions be put to the witness through an intermediary (provided it is in the interests of justice to do so).[31]

The only purpose for which a victim impact statement can be received at sentencing stage is to describe the impact of the offence on the victim (or on the family members if the victim has died as a result of the offence). It cannot be used to adduce further evidence, to suggest the evidence that should be imposed, or to make fresh allegations. The prosecution bears the responsibility of ensuring that the statement restricts itself in this regard. The prosecution and defence may also examine the victim on any evidence given in respect of the impact of the crime.[32] Legal participation for victims can also occur in ways other than commenting on the impact of the crime. Section 23 of the Children Act 2001, for example, provides that any views expressed by a victim in relation to a child's criminal behaviour 'shall be given due consideration' in relation to the admission of the child onto a Garda Diversion programme, and the new Bail Bill makes provision for victim submissions.[33]

Competence to testify

The Irish criminal process works off the assumption that all witnesses are competent to testify in court. If a dispute arises as to the competence of a particular witness, the party calling that witness bears the legal burden of proving that he or she is in fact competent. At common law, a witness demonstrates competence by showing that he or she understands the nature of an oath and is capable of giving an intelligent account.[34] Testimony in civil and criminal proceedings normally requires that the evidence has to be given on oath or affirmation. As was noted in *Mapp v Gilhooley*,[35] 'the broad purpose of the rule is to ensure as far as possible that such *viva voce* evidence shall be true by the provision of a moral or religious and legal sanction against deliberate untruth'.

Issues of competence primarily arise in respect of witnesses who are children or who are persons with an intellectual disability. The law relating to both categories has become more accommodating in recent years. Traditionally, for example, a child could give only sworn evidence.[36] Such evidence could be given only if, in addition to satisfying the intelligibility criterion, the child also could demonstrate that he or she understood 'both the nature and consequences of an oath'.[37] A more secular common law approach, however, began to emerge in the 1970s in relation to sworn evidence; the determining factor was 'whether the child has a sufficient appreciation of the solemnity of the occasion and the added responsibility to tell the truth, which is involved in taking an oath, over and above the duty to tell the truth which is an ordinary duty of normal social conduct'.[38] More recently, section 27 of the Criminal Evidence Act 1992 was enacted which provides that in any criminal proceedings the evidence of a person under 14 years of age may be received otherwise than on oath or affirmation if the court is satisfied that he or she is capable of giving an intelligible account of events which are relevant to those proceedings. Significantly, and as we shall see later, section 28(1) abolishes the mandatory requirement that the unsworn evidence of a child be corroborated; a trial judge now has a discretion whether a jury should be given a warning about the dangers of convicting on the unsworn evidence of a child.

Persons suffering from an intellectual disability were traditionally excluded from giving evidence at trial. The common law, however, then altered, and permitted such a witness to testify, provided that he or she was capable of understanding the nature and consequences of an oath, was capable of giving an intelligible account and the disorder did not impede her or his ability to give evidence at trial.[39] If a witness has communicative difficulties, an interpreter may be provided to aid with the giving of evidence. In *People (DPP) v Gillane*,[40] for example, it was held that it was permissible for a witness to give identification evidence for the prosecution in a case despite the fact that he believed that staff at the Mater Hospital had inserted a microchip into his head. As the court noted, although the witness 'had very strange ideas about what was done to him when he had an operation on his head some twenty years before in the Mater Hospital, [this] does not mean that he was incapable of giving evidence'.

If, however, a person with an intellectual disability was not able or permitted to give sworn evidence, there was previously no means by which unsworn evidence could be given. In *DPP v JS*,[41] for example, a moderately mentally impaired complainant could not answer questions as to the nature of the oath or the nature of a lie at trial. She made no response when asked by the judge what the moral and legal consequences of telling a lie were. In the result, she could not be sworn and, as there was no independent evidence in the case, a *nolle prosequi* was entered (Law Reform Commission, 1990: 10). Similarly, in *DPP v MW*[42] a moderately impaired complainant alleged that she was raped in a car. The accused was charged with two counts, rape and unlawful carnal knowledge of a mentally impaired person. At the rape trial, the trial judge ruled that she was competent to take the oath. Her testimony at trial, however, was held to be contradictory and the judge directed an acquittal. Subsequently the accused was tried with the second count, unlawful carnal knowledge of a mentally impaired person. On this occasion, however, her preliminary answers on questions pertaining to the nature of an oath were less satisfactory and the trial judge declined to have her sworn. As there was no independent evidence in the case, the prosecution was compelled to enter a *nolle prosequi* (Law Reform Commission, 1990: 10).

Fortunately, section 27(3) of the Criminal Evidence Act 1992 now provides that the evidence of a person with a 'mental handicap' may be received otherwise than on oath or affirmation if the court is satisfied that the person is capable of giving an intelligible account of events which are relevant to the proceedings. In *O'Sullivan v Hamill*,[43] O'Higgins CJ noted:

> Unsworn evidence is provided for from a person with a mental handicap 'if the court is satisfied that he is capable of giving an intelligible account of events which are relevant to those proceedings'. In my view, before that section comes into play there are two requirements on which the court has to be satisfied – (1) that the person has a mental handicap, and (2) that he is capable of giving an intelligible account of events which are relevant to the proceedings. Clearly there must be an inquiry.

Determining the answers to these questions in that inquiry at trial may require expert medical opinion evidence. A corroborative warning may need to be given to the jury in respect of the testimony of a witness suffering from a mental disability (*People (DPP) v Molloy*).[44]

The spouse of an accused

Traditionally, too, the spouse of an accused was not competent to give evidence for the prosecution in a case, except in the case of rape or violence perpetrated on that spouse.[45] This was justified on the basis of marital unity (the law made no distinction between the accused and the spouse) and the importance of preserving marital harmony. The constitutionality of this rule was challenged in *People DPP v JT*,[46] a case which Charleton has described as laying 'the foundation stone of a victim's charter in Ireland' (Charleton, 1990: 143). The complainant was a 20-year-old woman who had Downs Syndrome who alleged that she had been sexually abused by her father. At trial the spouse of the accused and the complainant's mother gave evidence that at the end of a television programme concerning child sexual abuse, her daughter expressed delight that the wrongdoer in the programme was eventually brought to justice. As a result of questioning her daughter on the issue, it emerged that the complainant's father had allegedly perpetrated similar abuses as those illustrated in the programme. The accused was convicted but appealed on the basis, *inter alia*, that his spouse was incompetent to testify for the prosecution. In upholding the conviction, Walsh J. examined the common law rule and declared that its application on the facts of the case would be in violation of Article 41 of the Constitution, which protected family rights. He also noted (referring to p. 161):

> It could be strongly argued that this rule should no longer be sustained because of the fact that in the modern age with the independence of women, married or otherwise, and the recognition of the equality of men and women, both within and out of marriage, such a distinction could only be regarded as outmoded and unreal.

Section 21 of the Criminal Evidence Act 1992, as amended, now provides that in any criminal proceedings a spouse of the accused is competent to give evidence for the prosecution. Such a spouse, however, is compellable to give evidence at the instance of the prosecution only in the case of an offence which involves violence or the threat of violence to the spouse, a child of the spouse or of the accused, or any person who was at the material time under the age of 18 years, or which is a sexual offence alleged to have been committed in relation to a child of the spouse or the accused, or any person who was at the material time under the age of 18 years (Jackson, 1993: 202). More extensive compellability requirements for the prosecution exist for former spouses under section 22(2) of the same Act.[47]

Corroboration

Over the years the common law also devised particular corroboration rules in respect of certain categories of 'suspect' witnesses such as sexual complainants, children, accomplices and so on. Ordinarily, an accused person in a criminal trial can be convicted on the testimony of one witness alone. However, for suspect witnesses such as those cited above, a warning of the dangers of convicting on such evidence in the absence of corroboration had to be given to the jury. The previously fossilised exclusionary assumptions underpinning the perception of some victims/witnesses in the Irish criminal justice system is evident, for example, in the law on the corroboration of sexual complaints. In the past the evidence of a complainant in a sexual offences case required a mandatory warning to the jury on the dangers of acting on such evidence alone. This rule was justified 'by the fear that complaints of sexual offences may sometimes be the product of spite, jealousy, psychological denial of having consented, or a reaction to having been jilted; that women with nothing to lose might seek to subject a man of high social standing to blackmail; and that the accusation of rape is easily made, but difficult to defend' (Healy, 2004: 157; Leahy, 2008: 203–12; Leahy, 2013: 102–7). More recently, however, these essentialised notions about the traits and motives of sexual complainants have largely been abandoned and the trial judge now has discretion whether or not to give such a warning to the jury.[48]

In respect of the unsworn testimony of child witnesses, corroboration by some other material evidence was also required to obtain a conviction against an accused party. This could not be the unsworn evidence of another child. In *Attorney General (Kelly) v Kearns*,[49] for example, the defendant was charged with attempted carnal knowledge of a girl aged 9 (RB), indecent assault of the same girl, and indecent assault of two other girls also aged 9 (AH and MC, respectively). Two of the girls gave evidence that they were in the defendant's house together and that each saw the unpleasant acts being perpetrated against the other (RB and AH). The other girl (MC) gave evidence that on a different date she was also in the defendant's house and that he also indecently assaulted her. Playmates of the three complainants also gave unsworn testimony that the three complainants went into the defendant's house.

Molony J. held:

> It will be remembered that the children R. B. and A. H. both said they were together in [the defendant's] room, and each witnessed the assault upon the other. I am clear that R. B.'s story does not, in law, corroborate A. H.'s story, nor does A. H.'s story corroborate R. B.'s story – nor do any of the little girls, other than those alleged to be injured afford corroboration – simply because, in my opinion, they are incapable of giving corroboration. The same remarks apply in respect to the charge in connection with M. C.

Since there was no other evidence in the case, the prosecution failed, demonstrating the harshness of the rules on corroboration. For the sworn evidence of children, a mandatory warning had to be given of the dangers of convicting on such evidence in the absence of corroboration. More recently, the legislature has moved away from the operating assumption that the evidence of children was inherently flawed or unreliable. Section 28(1) of the Criminal Evidence Act 1992 abolished the requirement that the unsworn evidence of children had to be corroborated and section 28(2)(a) abolished the mandatory warning about the dangers of convicting on the sworn evidence of children in the absence of corroboration. Section 28(3) of the same Act also provides that the unsworn evidence of a child may corroborate unsworn evidence given by any other person,[50] ensuring that the decision in *Kearns* will not reoccur.

In respect of witnesses with an intellectual disability, there is no statutory law requiring corroboration or that a corroboration warning be given. However, there is some case law support for the view that in the case of such witnesses a warning should be given of the dangers of convicting on the testimony of such witnesses in the absence of corroborative evidence.[51] In Ireland, in *The People (Director of Public Prosecutions) v M.J.M*,[52] in a sexual offences case, a trial judge invoked his discretion to give a warning in a sexual offences case in part based on the mental status of the complainant, and in particular the fact that she had a childlike mind.[53]

Reasons for decisions

Traditionally, the DPP was under no obligation to give reasons in respect of a decision not to prosecute, as established in cases such as *The State (McCormack) v Curran*.[54] More recently, however, this 'special protection' has been diluted.[55] A 'Reasons for Decisions' pilot project, for example, commenced in Ireland in October 2008. In homicide offences such as murder, manslaughter, infanticide, fatalities in the workplace, and vehicular manslaughter reasons for decisions not to prosecute, or to discontinue a prosecution, are given by the Office of the DPP on request to parties closely connected with the deceased, such as members of the deceased's family or household, their legal or medical advisers or social workers acting on their behalf. Such reasons, however, would be given only where it was possible to do so without creating an injustice.

Miscellaneous

In more recent years the system has also witnessed a greater awareness of the reasons why a complainant may not have made a complaint of a sexual offence at the first reasonable opportunity but still avail of the doctrine of recent complaint;[56] a relaxation of the exclusionary rule on opinion evidence in certain circumstances;[57] the introduction of a provision which makes it clear that the absence of resistance by a victim in a rape case does not equate with consent;[58] tighter restrictions that offer victims better protection against unnecessary and distressing information being raised about their sexual histories;[59] separate legal representation for sexual offence complainants where an application is made to admit previous sexual history;[60] greater protection of the identity of victims[61] and witnesses[62] in criminal cases; the introduction of measures to restrict unjustified imputations at trial against the character of a deceased or incapacitated victim or witness;[63] the exclusion of persons guilty of murder, attempted murder or manslaughter from taking a share in the estate of the victim;[64] the introduction of an exception to the rule against double jeopardy when new and compelling evidence becomes available;[65] the construction of a more 'contextualised' understanding of fairness in historic child sexual abuse cases by, *inter alia*, no longer aligning delays in prosecuting with presumptive prejudice (Ring 2009; Ring, 2013); the introduction of bail conditions requiring a bail applicant to refrain from going to specific locations or to meet specified persons; attempts to regulate the disclosure of counselling records (Leahy, 2012: 34–9; LRC, 112 -2014: 53–4); the ability of the DPP to appeal unduly lenient sentences;[66] and provisions for the payment of compensation to victims through a non-statutory scheme introduced in 1974, and a statutory scheme introduced under section 6 of the Criminal Justice Act 1993 (Coen, 2014: 371–86; Fennell, 2010: 250–60; Rogan, 2006c: 202–8; Vaughan and Kilcommins, 2010: 59–75).

The courts are now also willing to admit background evidence in criminal cases, often to render comprehensible the relationship between the accused and the complainant. Such evidence can now be admitted if it is so relevant to facts to be proved by the prosecution or defence and to be determined by the jury that it is necessary to render comprehensible such fact or facts. If a complainant of sexual abuse in the past referred to incidents other than those indicated in the indictment, it raised the strong possibility of a defence application being made to discharge the jury on the grounds that evidence prejudicial to the accused had been introduced. The law therefore did not align with the social reality of prolonged sexual abuse in that a complainant would often be able to give an account of the repeated and persistent abuse, but would rarely be able to clearly distinguish separate incidents of that abuse. Strict rules on prejudicial effect had, as O'Donnell J. noted, 'the potential to become a particularly cruel catch-22 for genuine victims of prolonged abuse.[67] The admissibility of relevant background evidence mediates such concerns.

Legal Aid

Legal Aid is not generally available to victims of crime in Ireland. An exception has, however, been created for victims of sexual crime and human trafficking. Section 26(3A) of the Civil Legal Aid Act 1995 provides that a complainant in a sexual offence case[68] qualifies for legal advice free of any contribution. Potential victims of human trafficking are also entitled to legal advice from the Legal Aid Board in relation to any matter connected with the commission of a human trafficking offence and/or in relation to any offence of which the person is alleged to be a victim of what is alleged to have been committed in the course of, or otherwise in connection with, the human trafficking offence.[69] Victims of certain sexual offences are also entitled to legal representation if it is proposed that evidence of their sexual history will be adduced during the trial.[70] Victims of crime can also apply to the Legal Aid Board for legal representation in civil cases, including applications for safety and barring orders (Quinn O'Flaherty, 2016: 114–29).

New offences and interventions

Moreover, the boundaries of criminalisation are continually being extended to officially censure forms of conduct that can cause serious harm. These include offences such as harassment,[71] coercion,[72] intimidation,[73] human trafficking,[74] child trafficking and pornography,[75] threats to kill or cause serious injury,[76] threats by phone or text message,[77] endangerment,[78] abduction,[79] stalking and revenge porn,[80] withholding information on certain offences against vulnerable persons,[81] reckless endangerment of a child[82] and the introduction of post-conviction orders to protect victims from harassment by offenders.[83] The labelling of misconduct has also been expanded by the abolition of common law defences such as reasonable chastisement[84] and the marital exemption in relation to rape.[85] There has also been legislative and judicial clarification of what constitutes reasonable self-defence in the home.[86] In addition to a broadening spectrum of criminalisation, mechanisms of intervention in harmful contexts have also been provided for in law. These include provisions in relation to child[87] and adult safety[88] in emergency situations; the possibility of using a portfolio of care and supervision orders for children; the availability of protection, safety and barring orders under the Domestic Violence Act 1996; child safeguarding and child harm reporting requirements;[89] broader disclosure requirements;[90] the provision of health services to women who worked in the Magdalen Laundries or similar institutions;[91] the payment of compensation to the victims of uninsured and unidentified motorists as a result of agreements between motor insurance companies and the Minister of Local Government; and protected disclosure of child abuse[92] and wrongdoing in health care settings.[93]

International Legal Instruments

A number of key developments in Europe have also promoted recognition of the needs of victims within criminal justice systems. The impetus provided by the UN, the Council of Europe and the EU has been outlined in an earlier chapter. While the new EU Directive is discussed in detail below, it is worth noting that the European Convention on Human Rights, which Ireland incorporated at a sub-constitutional level in 2003, has also been interpreted in ways that afford rights to victims of crime. It therefore acts as another influential normative framework that seeks to extend the reach of rights in the criminal process to include victims of crime. Although the Convention does not explicitly refer to victims of crime, the jurisprudence of the European Court of Human Rights has placed obligations on member states to criminalise wrongdoing, to take preventive operational measures, to protect society from potential dangers, to provide appropriate civil remedies, to investigate and give reasons and to adequately protect victims and witnesses at various stages in the criminal process. These obligations arise under Articles 2 (right to life), 3 (degrading treatment), 6 (fair trial) and 8 (private life) and have been analysed in a variety of cases.[94] In 1996, for example, the Court in *Doorson v The Netherlands*[95] expanded its interpretation of Article 6, primarily concerned with the rights of defendants in criminal proceedings, to take account of the rights of vulnerable witnesses and defendants. It noted:

> It is true that Article 6 does not explicitly require the interests of witnesses in general, and those of victims called upon to testify in particular, to be taken into consideration. However their life, liberty or security of person may be at stake, as may interests coming generally with in the ambit of Article 8 [right to a private life]. Such interests of witnesses and victims are in principle protected by other, substantive provisions of the Convention, which imply that Contracting States should organise their criminal proceedings in such a way that those interests are not unjustifiably imperilled. Against this background, principles of fair trial also require that in appropriate cases the interests of the defence are balanced against those *of witnesses or victims called upon to testify*. (Our emphasis)

A series of other obligations and safeguards have been interpreted through the provisions. They include, for example, the requirement that states carry out effective investigations of crime. Effectiveness in this context requires public scrutiny to ensure accountability in practice;[96] an efficient and independent judicial system;[97] the hierarchical and institutional independence of those responsible for the investigation of a crime from those implicated in the events;[98] prompt responses by the authorities;[99] the effective implementation of court orders to protect victims;[100] and a legal and administrative framework that adequately protects rights such as bodily integrity and privacy.[101]

The European Court of Human Rights has also held that the accused's right to disclosure of relevant evidence is not absolute and may need to be weighed against competing interests, including the protection of witnesses and the need to uphold individual fundamental rights.[102] It has also held that personal cross-examinations by defendants should be subject 'to a most careful assessment', given their potential to breach the rights of complainants under Article 8,[103] and that out-of-court statements may be admitted having regard to the need to 'weigh in the balance the competing interests of the defence, the victim, and witnesses, and the public interest in the effective administration of justice'.[104] The Court has also repeatedly emphasised the positive requirement that states take appropriate steps to safeguard the lives of those within their jurisdictions.[105]

This jurisprudence has been referred to in the Irish courts. For example, Charleton J. in examining the exclusionary rule in *People (DPP) v Cash*[106] noted: 'the entire focus is on the accused and his rights; the rights of the community to live safely has receded out of view'. He drew attention to the European Convention on Human Rights, and particularly the decision in *X and Y v The Netherlands*,[107] which suggests that rules which hinder a fair prosecution may be incompatible with the Convention. He then emphasised the following principle: 'Criminal trials are about the rights and obligations of the entire community; of which the accused and the victim are members ... The cases of *J.T.* [discussed above] and ... *X. and Y.* make it clear that the victim, being the subject of a crime, can have interests which should be weighed in the balance as well of those of the accused.'[108]

The European Court of Human Rights has also addressed the issue of vulnerability and victimhood in Ireland. Jurisprudence from the Court indicates that there is an enhanced state responsibility to protect children and vulnerable adults that are in the purview of the state and to ensure that the investigation and trial processes for such witnesses are as efficient and protective as possible. In *O'Keeffe v Ireland*[109] the applicant attended a national school in west Cork where she was sexually assaulted on twenty occasions by the principal in a six-month period commencing in 1973. An earlier complaint by a third party relating to the sexual misconduct of the principal had been made to a local parish priest, who acted as the manager of the school, in 1971. This complaint was not reported to the Gardaí, the Department of Education and Science or to any other state authority and was not acted upon by the parish priest. The applicant instituted civil proceedings against the principal and the Irish State, claiming damages for personal injuries suffered as a result of the sexual abuse. In relation to the hearing against the State, the High Court in Ireland held that the State was not vicariously liable for the sexual assaults of the principal. This was upheld on appeal to the Supreme Court. The applicant then took a case to the European Court of Human Rights, arguing that there had been a violation of Article 3 regarding the State's failure to fulfil its obligation to protect the applicant. The applicant also argued that there was a lack of an effective remedy regarding the State's failure in this regard.

Given the fundamental nature of the rights guaranteed by Article 3 and the vulnerable nature of children, the Court accepted that the Irish Government had an inherent obligation to ensure the protection of children from ill-treatment in a primary education context. The key issue was whether the State's framework of laws, including its methods of detection and reporting, provided effective protection for children attending a national school against the risk of sexual abuse, a risk of which the authorities had or ought to have had knowledge at the relevant time. The Court held that the Irish State was in breach of Article 3 in not adopting appropriate measures and safeguards to protect vulnerable individuals. These measures should have included effective mechanisms for the detection and reporting of any ill-treatment by and to a state-controlled body. The Court also held that the applicant did not have an effective domestic remedy available to her as regards her complaints under Article 3, which resulted in a violation of Article 13 of the Convention.

All of this jurisprudence demonstrates that a literal, formalistic approach to the Convention has been rejected in favour of a broader reading that encompasses principles which command that 'rules in the rule book capture and enforce moral rights' (Dworkin, 1985: 11–12). Such an expansionary interpretation acts as a counterpoint to the hegemonic dominance of State/accused relations and the exclusiveness, in particular, of accused rights as 'trump cards'. Facilitated by this human rights jurisprudence, we are thus witnessing a very gradual concretisation of the rights of victims of crime (De Than, 2003; Doak 2009; Emmerson et al., 2007, 741–84), which governments are required to respect 'case by case, decision by decision' (Dworkin, 1998: 223).

EU Directive on Victims' Rights

This concretisation of the rights of the victim found expression at EU level with the introduction of Directive 2012/29/EU. The improvement of the 'rights, support, protection and participation of victims' in criminal proceedings has long been identified as a priority for the EU,[110] with the Directive 2012/29/EU establishing minimum standards in this regard.[111] The EU Directive on Victims' Rights forms part of a horizontal package of measures launched in May 2011 by the Commission, aimed at ensuring that a minimum standard of rights apply to victims of crime irrespective of their nationality or the location within the EU in which the crime takes place. It is clear that crime within the EU is both extensive and costly, with both domestic and cross-border elements. It is estimated that the cost of crime within the EU is €233 billion per year.[112] Statistics from Eurostat evidence the high levels of recorded crime within the EU, with circa 30 million crimes reported to the police each year[113] and an estimated 75 million direct victims of crime each year.[114] For example, in 2011, the year before the publication of the Victims Directive, there were over 5,000 intentional homicides, over a million assaults, 8 million offences of theft and over 55,000 rapes recorded within the EU.[115] The scale of reported crimes and the number of victims highlights the importance of measures to protect and support victims of crime within the EU.

While many of these crimes are committed in one member state against a citizen of that member state, the commission has also recognised that '[m]ore and more people are travelling, living or studying abroad and are therefore potential victims of crimes committed in a country other than their own. The EU has a mandate to ensure that citizens and foreigners moving within its borders are protected.'[116] The importance of this is highlighted by the estimated

1.26 billion journeys by Europeans within the EU in 2008.[117] There are also large numbers of Europeans who reside outside their home country, either permanently (up to 11 million) or for a shorter period; '10% of Europeans have lived and worked abroad during a period of their lives and 13% have gone abroad for education or training'.[118] These statistics highlight the necessity for and value of protections for victims of crime, with a minimum standard of victim's rights applicable irrespective of nationality or the member state in which the crime occurred.

The EU Directive on Victims' Rights became operative in participating member states on 16 November 2015. For the purposes of the Directive, a victim is defined as 'a natural person who has suffered harm, including physical, mental or emotional harm or economic loss which was directly caused by a criminal offence' (Article 1(a)(i)). The definition of victim also includes 'family members'[119] of a person whose death was directly caused by a criminal offence and who have suffered harm as a result of that person's death' (Article 1(a)(ii)). The Directive states that its purpose is 'to ensure that victims of crime receive appropriate information, support and protection and are able to participate in criminal proceedings' (Article 1). Thus, for ease of discussion, the provisions of the Directive on Victims' Rights may be categorised according to three key themes: information and support; protection; and participation.

The provision of information and support is dealt with in Chapter 2 of the Directive. There are two key points in the process where the Directive identifies victims as having specific information entitlements. Article 4 provides victims with a right to receive certain information from first contact with a competent authority without unnecessary delay. It lists the information which should be provided, including details of: available support services; procedures for making a complaint; and the availability of legal advice and compensation. The second key point for information provision arises once a victim has made a formal complaint. Article 6 provides that victims have a right to receive information about their case and must be informed that this information is available to them upon request. This information includes the provision of reasons where a case does not proceed to trial or details of the trial if the prosecution is to proceed, as well as details of the final judgment and other relevant updates on the progress of proceedings. To allow for full realisation of the rights to information entailed in Articles 4 and 6, victims also have a right to understand and be understood (Article 3) and a right to interpretation and translation (Article 7). In relation to support, the EU Directive on Victims' Rights envisages an important role for victim support services. Article 8 provides that victims have a right to access free and confidential support services 'before, during and for an appropriate time after criminal proceedings' and that states have a correlating duty to provide for such services. States must facilitate referral of victims to these services (Article 8(2)) and access must not be dependent upon making a formal complaint

(Article 8(5)). The minimum services which must be available from victim support services are listed in Article 9 and include: information on rights; information about and referral to specialist support services where applicable; and emotional or psychological support.

Chapter 3 establishes the right to participate in criminal proceedings. Article 10 provides that victims have a right to be heard during criminal proceedings and to give evidence, as well as a right to specific safeguards in the context of restorative justice services (Article 12). Victims are also entitled to request a review of a decision not to prosecute (Article 11). Victims who participate in criminal proceedings must be provided with the possibility of reimbursement of expenses incurred as a result of such participation (Article 14) and they have a right to decision on compensation from the offender during the course of criminal proceedings (Article 16). Victims must also have any recoverable property returned to them without unnecessary delay after criminal proceedings are completed (Article 15). Significantly, Article 17 provides specific protection for the participation rights of victims resident in other member states, placing an onus on states to ensure that any difficulties experienced by such victims are minimised.

Finally, Chapter 4 of the Directive provides for the protection of victims and recognition of victims with specific protection needs. Article 18(1) provides that:

> Without prejudice to the rights of the defence, Member States shall ensure that measures are available to protect victims and their family members from secondary and repeat victimisation, from intimidation and from retaliation, including against the risk of emotional or psychological harm, and to protect the dignity of victims during questioning and when testifying.

Specifically, victims have a right to avoid contact with the offender within premises in which criminal proceedings are conducted (Article 19) and a right to protection of privacy throughout criminal proceedings (Article 21). During the investigation, victims have specific protection rights, including an entitlement for interviews to be conducted promptly and for the number of interviews to be kept to a minimum and the possibility of accompaniment by a legal representative (Article 20). To identify victims who may have special protection needs, Article 22 requires states to conduct individual assessments of victims. Child victims will be presumed to have specific protection needs (Article 22(4)). Where a victim is identified as having specific protection needs the measures which must be made available to them during the investigation and court proceedings are listed in Article 23. These include the availability of specialist interview suites and specialist interviewers during the investigation and measures to protect the victim while s/he is giving evidence during criminal proceedings. Further, specific additional protections for child victims such as audio-visual recording of interviews are provided for in Article 24.

While the EU Directive on Victims' Rights is an extremely important measure for victims of crime within the EU, it is just one of a suite of measures which aim to assist and protect victims of crime. In addition to the EU Directive on Victims' Rights, several measures aimed at specific categories of victims have also been introduced by the EU. The Directive on Trafficking in Human Beings, adopted in 2011, aims to combat trafficking in human beings and to protect its victims.[120] The Directive establishes minimum standards in relation to criminal offences and sanctions and introduces provisions to strengthen the prevention of human trafficking and the protection of victims (Article 1). The Directive requires member states to ensure that 'the recruitment, transportation, transfer, harbouring or reception of persons' is punishable (Article 2(1)). Interestingly, trafficking does not require a cross-border element and may be internal, that is, within the borders of one member state.[121] Also in 2011, the Directive on Child Sexual Exploitation, aimed at combating the sexual abuse and sexual exploitation of children and child pornography was adopted.[122] The Directive establishes minimum standards in relation to 'criminal offences and sanctions in the area of sexual abuse and sexual exploitation of children, child pornography and solicitation of children for sexual purposes' (Article 1). The Directive also includes provisions aimed at the prevention of crimes of this nature and the protection of victims.

Two measures have also been adopted which enable victims to continue to benefit from protection measures issued in one member state while travelling in or moving to another member state. The first, the Directive on the European Protection Order (EPO), allows victims with a protection order in criminal matters issued in one member state to request an EPO which applies in other member states.[123] The second, the Regulation on mutual recognition of protection measures in civil matters, enables victims with a civil law protection order to invoke it in another state.[124] Finally, Directive 2004/80/EC on compensation to crime victims ensures that victims can access state compensation when they are victims of violent intentional crime and that compensation is accessible, irrespective of the state in which the crime occurs.

New bills and legislation

The Irish legislature has also indicated an increased willingness to intervene in order to better support and accommodate victims of crime. A Victims' Rights Bill, for example, was initiated in 2008, the purpose of which was to make provision for the treatment of and rights of victims of criminal offences. Although the Bill was never enacted, more recent initiatives carry greater hope. The first commitment in the Justice and Law Reform section of the Programme for Government, 2011–16 indicated a requirement for legislation to strengthen the rights of victims of crime and their families, including greater use of victim impact statements and statutory rights to information. Two new Bills have been introduced on the foot of this commitment. The General Scheme of the Criminal Justice (Victims of Crime) Bill 2015 was introduced in July 2015 as part of the process of implementing the Directive on Victims' Rights. It was passed on 5 November 2017. It incorporates the definition of a 'Victim' from the Directive – 'a natural person who has suffered harm, including physical, mental or emotional harm or economic loss, which was directly caused by an offence'. It also provides for the inclusion of family members of a person who has died as a direct result of a crime in the definition of a victim. The Act is founded upon three key pillars: information; protection; and participation.

One of the significant developments in this legislation is the increased level of *information* which will be provided to victims on first contact, in relation to investigations and criminal proceedings, and decisions regarding prosecutions. Other significant developments in the Act include the requirement that the Gardaí or the DPP are to provide victims with reasons for decisions not to prosecute a crime (section 8) and the introduction of a process for formally reviewing a decision not to prosecute (section 10). The Act also provides for the *protection* of victims by, among other things, creating a mechanism for the submission of complaints (section 12); prescribing the manner in which interviews and medical examinations are conducted (section 14); requiring assessments to determine protection needs; the employment of protection measures at investigation stage (advice regarding personal safety or the protection of property; safety or barring orders; or applications to remand in custody or to have conditions attached to bail) and court stage (the avoidance of contact between victims and offenders during the course of criminal proceedings); and the employment of special measures for a much broader range of offences than currently available at investigation stage (the conduct of interviews by a person of the same sex; the use of specially trained interviewers; the employment of premises designed for the purpose of conducting interviews) and court stage (television links, intermediaries, screens, restrictions on questioning about a victim's personal life). This is a significant extension of the availability of the special measures which are available in the Criminal Evidence Act 1992, which were previously available for only a limited number of offences. A further extension of the availability of live television-link evidence is also included in the Domestic Violence Bill 2017, which will extend the availability of this facility to victims of domestic abuse in civil proceedings for orders under domestic violence legislation such as barring and safety orders and hearings relating to breaches of these orders. As regards *participation*, a notable feature of the Bill is the introduction of victim impact statements for all victims who have suffered harm directly caused by an offence. Previously, such a provision applied to only a limited number of offences.

The Criminal Law (Sexual Offences) Act 2017 increases protection for victims of sexual offences in a number of significant ways. Perhaps most notably, the Act introduces a procedure for regulating the disclosure of counselling records in sexual offence trials. Previously, under Irish law there was no procedure for regulating disclosure of counselling records which were held by third parties such as counsellors or social workers (Leahy, 2012). The Act fills this lacuna, creating a formal application process for the introduction of this evidence which is similar to the process which regulates the disclosure of sexual experience evidence. If the defence seeks disclosure of counselling records, a written application to court must be made. A hearing will then take place to determine whether disclosure should be ordered. The complainant (who is entitled to legal representation) and the record-holder are entitled to be heard at this hearing and the judge must provide reasons for his/her decision regarding disclosure. The section provides useful guidelines to structure judicial discretion in deciding whether to order disclosure. These guidelines, along with the possibility of imposing conditions upon disclosure orders, are designed to ensure that disclosure of records goes no further than is necessary, maximising protection of victims' privacy rights. The Act also amends the special measures for testifying provided for in the Criminal Evidence Act 1992, and introduces the possibility for those under the age of 18 to give evidence from behind a screen to prevent the witness from seeing the defendant. Defendants are also prohibited from personally cross-examining witnesses who are under 14 years of age (Bryan O'Sullivan, 2015). A final important development in the Act is the introduction of harassment orders, which may be imposed upon convicted sex offenders when passing sentence or at any time before their release from prison. Such orders may prohibit the respondent from communicating with the victim and order the respondent to stay within a specified distance of the victim's home, workplace or any other place frequented by the victim.

Civil actions

It has long been recognised by the courts that a victim of a crime may also have available to him or her a civil remedy in the form of an action for damages.[125] This can include non-fatal conduct such as trespass to the person – including assault, battery and false imprisonment – as well as actions which may be brought for the benefit of the relatives of a victim (Quill, 2014: 500–4).[126] This has many possible benefits, not least a greater control of proceedings, as well as the avoidance of the principled protections of the criminal process such as proof beyond reasonable doubt, the presumption of innocence and the right not to give evidence at trial. It has been held that such a remedy is part of the mechanisms made available by the state for the vindication of the human and personal rights of its citizens.[127] In *M.N. v S.M.*,[128] for example, the court considered the appropriate level of damages to order in civil proceedings for a continuum of sexual abuse over five years which culminated in the rape of a teenager. In assessing the level of general damages for sexual assault, it was held that the award of damages must be proportionate and fair both to the plaintiff and to the defendant. The court also held that in assessing the injuries suffered by the plaintiff, it was relevant to consider the actions of the defendant and, in particular, whether he had made an early admission of guilt, whether he had entered an early plea to the criminal proceedings and whether any apology had been given, all of which may have helped to alleviate the suffering of the plaintiff in a particular case. Aggravated damages may also be appropriate.[129]

The law is also constantly evolving in this field. The Statute of Limitations Act 1957 was amended in 2000, for example, to take account of acts of sexual abuse which may result in tort actions, and in particular the capacity of some victims of this abuse to bring actions within the relevant time period. The courts also have made it clear that they will allow 'considerable latitude' to sexual abuse complainants who fail to initiate a civil complaint until a long time after the alleged incidents occurred.[130] The jurisprudence on civil wrongs is also evolving. In a recent case of *Walsh v Byrne*,[131] the plaintiff took an action for personal injuries, loss, damage, inconvenience and expense including aggravated damages for sexual assault and battery and trespass to the person. He also sought a declaration that the entire relationship created by the defendant with the plaintiff constituted oppression, and argued that the court should develop the law by recognising the practice of grooming for the purposes of sexual abuse as either a new tort or the development of existing tort law. White J. accepted this reasoning and recognised the 'continuum of sexual abuse' as a new tort: '[I]t is appropriate to extend the law of tort, to cover what is now a well recognised and established pattern of wrongdoing, where a child is befriended, where trust is established and where that friendship and trust is used to perpetrate sexual abuse.'[132]

The Irish High Court has also recently rejected the common law rule in *Hollington v Hewthorn* which provided that evidence of a conviction was inadmissible in subsequent civil proceedings. In refusing to adopt this persuasive authority, the court ruled that a conviction should be seen as *prima facie* evidence of guilt in a civil case, Kearns P. stating that 'to rule out the conviction as completely inadmissible would ... be contrary to logic and common sense and offend any reasonable person's sense of justice and fairness'.[133] The same court has also extended actionable conspiracy to include battery. In *Madden v Doohan*[134] it was noted:

> There seems no reason whatsoever to exclude battery from the class of wrongful actions which may be the subject matter of conspiracy and which may result in loss and damage. Indeed, it would be quite a travesty of justice if a person who conspired to have another person injured or murdered could not be rendered liable in the civil courts to an action in damages brought by the widow of the victim by virtue of the fact that they were able to solicit a third party to carry out a brutal assault which they themselves were not prepared to execute.[135]

The issue of whether prosecution authorities should enjoy an immunity from suit has also come under closer scrutiny (Walsh, 2013: 1–28). Traditionally it has been held that the Garda Síochána and the prosecuting authorities of the state did not owe the plaintiff a duty of care in relation to *bona fide* actions and decisions taken in carrying out their functions in the investigation and prosecution of crime.[136] In one case, for example, the plaintiff had been the complainant in a rape trial. During the trial it was held that the accused had been detained unlawfully, and as a result his admissions had to be excluded from evidence. The prosecution's case had collapsed as a result. The plaintiff sued for damages in respect of Garda negligence on the basis of a failure to vindicate her constitutional right to bodily integrity and to ensure that justice was achieved. The defendants sought and were granted a preliminary ruling that the Gardaí cannot, in the absence of *mala fides*, be held liable in damages for the performance of their investigative and prosecutorial functions.[137] In reversing this decision, and another one,[138] however, the Supreme Court has recently held that the two cases should now be heard at trial. This was justified on the basis that domestic tort jurisprudence is capable of being tested against the European Convention on Human Rights,[139] particularly having regard to whether or not a rule establishing absolute immunity for public authorities is proportionate.

Conclusion

A state/accused logic of action cast a long shadow over criminal process relations in the nineteenth and twentieth centuries. It defined the accused as the primary (exclusive) rights-bearer, with institutional practice heavily co-ordinated in accordance with this feature. The operational self-enclosure and monopolistic purity provided by this logic is now more open to challenge as the criminal process becomes more attuned to new narratives and value orientations. This reorientation includes victims of crime who are again being recognised as a 'community of identity' (Rose, 2008: 135–6). This reshapes the construction and presentation of intersubjective criminal conflict, not least because pluralism of this kind generates competing interests, priorities and validity claims in the decision-making process. Momentum of this kind makes it more difficult to rely exclusively on tradition and previously settled conventions of practice. The criminal process is thus slowly moving from a monolithic *culture* of rights to *cultures* of rights that reflect 'multiple identities' (Rose, 2008: 178) which are deserving of concern and respect. Law is helping to steer this reintegration, confirming participation and protection claims for victims, while also seeking to secure the fair administration of justice.

Notes

1 [2015] IEHC 824.
2 [2011] 2 ILRM 461.

3 In the same case Fennelly J. noted at paragraph 26: 'I referred, at the outset of this judgment, to the well-known difficulties in ensuring a fair and balanced trial in cases of prolonged and repeated sexual abuse. The State, representing the people, has an interest and a duty to see to it that people are prosecuted in response to legitimate complaints from victims. The victims themselves, as is increasingly recognised, have an interest in seeing that justice is done. The accused person is entitled under the Constitution to a fair trial.'
4 For a previous example of victims interests being subsumed with the community/public interest, see, for example, *EOR v DPP* ([1996] 2 ILRM 128) where Keane J. had stated: '[w]hat is beyond doubt is that where that community right conflicts with due process, it is the latter right that must prevail'. See also *Rattigan v DPP* [2008] 4 IR 639.
5 See *Nulty v Director of Public Prosecutions* [2015] IEHC 758. See also *Irwin v DPP* [2010] IEHC 232, where Kearns P. expressed the view that applications for leave to seek judicial review involving prohibition of a criminal trial on the grounds of failure to preserve evidence represented a 'cottage industry' and, when engaged in as a matter of routine, were 'a grave abuse of the legal process' in the light of their effect on the rights and interests of victims.
6 See *People (DPP) v Kieran Lynch* [2015] IECCA 6 paras 32–3.
7 See Clarke J. in *DPP v JC* [2015] IESC 31 where he noted at para. 4.8: 'On the one hand is the principle that society, and indeed the victims of crime, are entitled to have an assessment carried out at a criminal trial of the culpability of an accused based on the proper consideration by the decider of fact (be it judge or jury) of all evidence, where that evidence is material to the question of guilt or innocence, is potentially probative of guilt, and is not potentially more prejudicial than probative in the sense in which those terms have come to be used in the jurisprudence. That principle is not, of course, an absolute requirement. However, there is, in my view, a high constitutional value to be attached to ensuring that all potentially relevant evidence, which meets the criteria which I have just sought to define, is considered at a criminal trial.' See also *People (DPP) v Cash* [2008] 1 ILRM 443 per Charleton J.
8 See *P.O'C. v D.P.P.* [2000] 3 IR 87, at 105; *II v GG* (Unreported, High Court, 5 July 2012).
9 See *McFarlane v DPP* (Unreported Supreme Court, 5 March 2008). In the *People (DPP) v Nash*, [2015] IESC 32 Clarke J. noted: 'The entitlement of a victim of crime to at least have the evidence which suggests that a particular accused may be guilty analysed at a trial and a proper verdict delivered should not be underestimated.'
10 *P.C. v DPP* [1999] 21R. 25 at p. 77, and *The People (DPP) v J.T.* (1988) 3 Frewen 141.
11 Dworkin (1985: 147) neatly captures this conservative-innovative dynamic: 'propositions of law are not simply descriptive of legal history in a straight forward way; nor are they evaluative in some way divorced from history. Propositions of law are interpretive of legal history, which combines elements of both description and evaluation, but is different from both.'
12 In respect of victims of crime in Ireland, the case of *The People (DPP) v J.T.* (1988) 3 Frewen 141 provides a very good example of how the courts have applied 'fresh moral insight' to a common law provision on spousal incompetence. The case is discussed more fully later in the chapter.
13 The Criminal Evidence Act 1992 originally set this age at 'under 17', but this was amended by section 257(3) of the Children Act 2001.
14 See also *O'Sullivan v Hamill* [1999] 2 IR 9.
15 See section 13(1)(b) of the Criminal Evidence Act 1992; see also *People (DPP) v EC* [2016] IECA 150).

16 [1998] 1 IR 321.
17 [1995] 1 IR 268.
18 For an example of a case where a court refused to grant such an application, see *D.O'D v DPP* [2010] 2 IR 605.
19 [2011] IECCA 32.
20 Since 2001, it also applies to extradition proceedings and in particular to persons whose extradition is being sought. See also section 67 of the Criminal Justice (Mutual Assistance) Act 2008, which provides that a witness can give live television-link evidence from another designated state.
21 Section 5, Criminal Procedure Act 2010.
22 See *K.D. v Director of Public Prosecutions* [2016] IEHC 21.
23 Ibid., at para. 32.
24 The rules set out in section 4F(3) of the Criminal Procedure Act 1967 apply to the taking of evidence under section 255 of the Children Act 2001. These rules provide as follows: (a) when the evidence is being taken, both the accused and a judge of the District Court shall be present; (b) before it is taken, the judge shall inform the accused of the circumstances in which it may be admitted in evidence at the accused's trial; (c) the witness may be cross-examined and re-examined; (d) where the evidence is taken by way of sworn deposition, the deposition and any cross-examination and re-examination of the deponent shall be recorded, read to the deponent and signed by the deponent and the judge.
25 See *DPP v Hanley* [2011] 1 IR 247. See also *DPP v O'Brien* [2011] I IR 273.
26 See *DPP v Collopy* [2016] IECA 149.
27 See *People (DPP) v Murphy* [2013] IECCA 1.
28 See section 18, Criminal Evidence Act 1992.
29 See *DPP v O'Donoghue* [2007] 2 IR 336.
30 Provision is also made for any other witness, with leave of the court, to give victim impact evidence via a television link
31 See section 5B Criminal Justice Act 1993, as inserted the Criminal Procedure Act 2010.
32 See also *People (DPP) v C(M)* (Unreported, Central Criminal Court, 16 June 1995). See also section 23 of the Children Act 2001, which provides that 'any views expressed by any victim in relation to the child's criminal behaviour shall be given due consideration' in relation to the admission of a child offender onto the Garda Diversion programme.
33 See section 28 of the General Scheme of the Bail Bill 2015.
34 The determination as to whether a child understands the nature and consequences of an oath is one for the trial judge. See *AG v O'Sullivan* [1930] IR 553.
35 [1991] IR 253.
36 If a child was capable of giving an intelligible account, but did not understand the importance of telling the truth under oath, it was still possible for him or her to give unsworn testimony under section 30 of the 1908 Children's Act, as amended by section 28(2) of Criminal Justice Act of 1914. Such testimony, however, needed to be corroborated.
37 See *R v Brasier* (179) 1 Leach 199.
38 See *R v Hayes* [1977] 2 All ER 288.
39 *R v Hill* (1851) 2 Den 254.
40 (Unreported, Court of Criminal Appeal, 14 December 1998).
41 (Unreported, Circuit Court, 1983).
42 (Unreported, Circuit Court, 1983).

43 [1999] 3 IR 9.
44 (Unreported, Court of Criminal Appeal, 28 July 28 1995).
45 See *R v Lapworth* [1931] 1 KB 117. There were also some other specific statutory exceptions.
46 (1988) 3 Frewen 141.
47 Significantly, spousal privilege does not cover civil partners or those in long-standing partnerships. This was challenged in the case of *Van der Heijden v The Netherlands* [2012] ECHRR 588, where the applicant was the unmarried life partner of a man accused of shooting and killing someone in a café; she was believed to have been with him at the time. In the Netherlands a spousal privilege applied to spouses or registered partners preventing them from testifying against their partners. Because she was neither, she was compelled to testify. It was held that there was no breach of Article 8 of the ECHR, as she had not registered as a partner.
48 See section 7 Criminal Law (Rape) (Amendment) Act 1990.
49 (1946) 80 ILTR 45.
50 The unsworn evidence of a child could always be corroborated by sworn evidence.
51 See, for example, the Australian case of *Bromley v R* (1986) 161 CLR 315.
52 (Unreported, Court of Criminal Appeal, 28 July 1995).
53 It should be noted, however, that the Law Reform Commission in Ireland suggested in 1990 that there should be no corroboration requirement in respect of persons with an intellectual disability (LRC 33 -1990: 24).
54 [1987] ILRM 225.
55 See *Eviston v DPP* [2002[3 IR 260. See also *Hanrahan v District Judge Mary Fahy and DPP* [2016] IEHC 266.
56 See, for example, *People (DPP) v DR* [1998] 2 IR 106. See also Charleton and Byrne (2010: 1–83). In a case involving a sexual offence, a voluntary complaint made at the first reasonable opportunity after the commission of the alleged offence is admissible to demonstrate consistency and credibility on the part of the complainant.
57 Section 3(4)(b) of the Domestic Violence Act 1996, for example, permits an applicant for a barring order to provide opinion evidence that he or she has a legal or beneficial interest in the place of residence that is not less than that of the respondent.
58 Section 9 of the Criminal Law (Rape) (Amendment) Act 1990; see also Campbell et al. (2010: 556).
59 Section 3 of the Criminal Law (Rape) Act 1981, as amended by section 13 of the Criminal Law (Rape) (Amendment) Act 1990, now provides that, except with leave of the court, no questions shall be asked in cross-examination about the sexual experience of a complainant. Previously in a rape case where the defence was one of consent, the trial judge was obliged 'to allow unpleasant charges to be made against the complainant in connection with her past; he should not indicate to the jury that he disapproves of this being done'. See *People (DPP) v McGuinness* [1978] IR 189. More recently, see *People (DPP) v GK* [2007] 2 IR 92.
60 Section 34, Sex Offenders Act 2001; see also Counihan (2013: 115–23).
61 See, for example, section 7 of the Criminal Law (Rape) Act 1981, as amended; section 11 of the Criminal Law (Human Trafficking) Act 2008; and section 252 of the Children Act 2001. See also *LK (a minor suing by her mother and next friend MK) v Independent Star Limited, The Dundalk Democrat Limited and Independent Broadcasting Corporation Limited (trading as LMFM)* [2011] 2 ILRM 272.
62 See section 181 of the Criminal Justice Act 2006.

63 Section 33, Criminal Procedure Act 2010.
64 See section 120 of the Succession Act 1965. See also section 120(4) of the same Act, which provides that anyone guilty of an offence against the deceased, or against the spouse, civil partner or child of the deceased punishable by a sentence of two years or more, shall be prevented from taking a share in the estate as a legal right. But see also *Nevin and Lavelle v Nevin* [2013] IEHC 80.
65 Part 3, Criminal Procedure Act 2010.
66 Section 2, Criminal Justice Act 1993, as amended.
67 *DPP v Gerald McNeill* [2011] 2 ILRM 461.
68 This includes a prosecution for rape, rape under section 4 of the Criminal Law (Rape) (Amendment) Act 1990, aggravated sexual assault, sexual offences against children or incest.
69 Section 26(3B) of the Civil Legal Aid Act 1995.
70 Section 4A of the Criminal Law (Rape) Act 1981 (as amended). See also section 28(5A) of the Civil Legal Aid Act 1995.
71 Section 10, Non-Fatal Offences Against the Person Act 1997; see also *O'Raithbheartaigh v Judge McNamara and the Director of Public Prosecutions* [2014] IEHC 406.
72 Section 9, Non-Fatal Offences Against the Person Act 1997, section 170 and Schedule, Part 5 of the Civil Partnership and Certain Rights and Obligations of Cohabitants Act 2010.
73 Section 41, Criminal Justice Act 1999, as amended. See also *McNulty v Ireland, the AG, DPP and the Irish Human Rights Commission* [2015] 2 ILRM 269.
74 Criminal Law (Human Trafficking) Act 2008. But see also *FAFCE v Ireland* [2015] 61 EHRR SE2.
75 Sections 3–6, Child Trafficking and Pornography Act 1998.
76 Section 5, Non Fatal Offences Against the Person Act 1997; see also *DPP v Dundon* [2008] IECCA 14.
77 Section 13 of the Post Office (Amendment) Act 1951, as amended.
78 Section 13, Non Fatal Offences Against the Person Act 1997.
79 Sections 16–17, Non Fatal Offences Against the Person Act 1997.
80 These offences will be included in the proposed Non-Fatal Offences (Amendment) Bill 2017.
81 See section 3 of the Criminal Justice (Withholding Information on Offences Against Children and Vulnerable Persons) Act 2012.
82 Section 176, Criminal Justice Act 2006.
83 Section 26, Criminal Justice Act 2007.
84 Section 28, Children First Act 2015.
85 Section 5, Criminal Law Rape (Amendment) Act 1990
86 *People (DPP) v Barnes* [2006] IECCA 165; Criminal Law (Defence and the Dwelling) Act 2011.
87 Section 12, Child Care Act 1991
88 Section 12, Mental Health Act 2001.
89 Sections 10 and 14 of the Children First Act 2015 (not yet commenced).
90 See National Vetting Bureau (Children and Vulnerable Adults) Act 2012; see also Criminal Justice (Spent Convictions and Certain Disclosures) Act 2016.
91 Redress for Women Resident in Certain Institutions Act 2015.
92 See Protections for Persons Reporting Child Abuse Act 1998.

93 See section 103 of the Health Act 2007. More generally, see Protected Disclosures Act 2014.
94 *Osman v The United Kingdom* [1998] EHRLR 228, *X and Y v The Netherlands* [1985] 8 EHRR 2350, *MC v Bulgaria* [2003] ECHR 3927/98), *A v UK* [1999] 27 EHRR 611, *Söderman v Sweden* (2013) EHRR 128; and *KU v Finland* [2008] 48 EHRR 1237.
95 [1996] 22 EHRR 330.
96 *Hajduová v Slovakia* (2011) 53 EHRR 8.
97 *Opuz v Turkey* (2010) 50 EHRR 28.
98 *Perevedentsevy v Russia* (2016) 62 EHRR 16.
99 *Kalucza v Hungary* (57693/10).
100 *A v Croatia* (2015) 60 EHRR 26.
101 *Perevedentsevy v Russia* (2016) 62 EHRR 16.
102 *Rowe and Davis v United Kingdom* (2000) 30 EHRR 1.
103 *Y v Slovenia* (41107/10) 28 August, 2015 at para. 106.
104 *Al-Khawajah v UK* (2011) ECHR 2127; Heffernan (2013: 132–60).
105 *Maiorano v Italy* (case no. 28634/06).
106 [2007] IEHC 108.
107 (1986) 8 EHRR 235.
108 [2007] IEHC at para. 50.
109 (2014) 59 EHRR 15.
110 The Stockholm Programme – An Open And Secure Europe Serving And Protecting Citizens 2010/C 115/01, available at http://eur-lex.europa.eu/legal-content/EN/TXT/?uri=uriserv:OJ.C_.2010.115.01.0001.01.ENG; COM (2011) 274; European Commission, DG Justice (2013) Guidance Document Related To The Transposition And Implementation of Directive 2012/29/EU of the European Parliament and of the Council of 25 October 2012 establishing minimum standards on the rights, support and protection of victims of crime, and replacing Council Framework Decision 2001/220/JHA, p. 3.
111 Replacing the 2001 Council Framework Decision on the standing of victims in criminal proceedings.
112 http://europa.eu/rapid/press-release_MEMO-11-310_en.htm, accessed 16 February 2017.
113 Excluding minor offences. See http://ec.europa.eu/justice/criminal/victims/index_en.htm, accessed 16 February 2017.
114 http://eur-lex.europa.eu/legal-content/EN/TXT/PDF/?uri=CELEX:52011DC0274&from=EN, accessed 16 February 2017.
115 For full details seethe detailed tables available at http://ec.europa.eu/eurostat/statistics-explained/index.php/Crime_and_criminal_justice_statistics#Source_data_for_tables_and_figures_.28MS_Excel.29, accessed 16 February 2017.
116 http://ec.europa.eu/justice/criminal/victims/index_en.htm, accessed 16 February 2017.
117 COM(2010) 352, based on Eurostat, Tourism Statistics 2008.
118 http://eur-lex.europa.eu/legal-content/EN/TXT/PDF/?uri=CELEX:52011DC0274&from=EN, accessed 16 February 2017. See also Eurostat, Statistics in Focus 94/2009; Eurobarometer 337/2010.
119 'Family members' means the spouse, the person who is living with the victim in a committed intimate relationship, in a joint household and on a stable and continuous basis, the relatives in direct line, the siblings and the dependants of the victim: Article 1(b).

120 Directive 2011/36/EU on preventing and combating trafficking in human beings and protecting its victims, and replacing Council Framework Decision 2002/629/JHA.
121 See https://ec.europa.eu/anti-trafficking/citizens-corner/trafficking-explained_en., accessed 16 February 2017.
122 Directive 2011/92/EU on combating the sexual abuse and sexual exploitation of children and child pornography, and replacing Council Framework Decision 2004/68/JHA.
123 Directive 2011/99/EU on the European protection order.
124 Regulation (EU) No. 606/2013 on mutual recognition of protection measures in civil matters.
125 *Whelan v Lawn* [2014] IESC 75.
126 See, for example, sections 48 and 49 of Civil Liability Act 1961.
127 *Grant v Roche Products (Ireland) Limited*, [2008] 4 IR 679.
128 [2005] 4 IR 461 at 472.
129 See *O'Donnell v O'Donnell* [2005] IEHC 216; see also *L.O'K. v L.H* [2006] IEHC 393.
130 See *Moloney v Kelleher* [2014] IHC 358; *Doherty v Quigley* [2015] IESC 54; *II v GG* (unreported, High Court, 5th July, 2012; *Hayes v McDonnell* [2011] IEHC 530, *Mr C v His Honour Judge Sean O Donnabhain and the DPP* [2016] IEHC 74.
131 [2015] IEHC 414.
132 Ibid., at para. 22.
133 *Nevin and Lavelle v Nevin* [2013] IEHC 80.
134 [2012] IEHC 422.
135 Ibid., para. 18.
136 See *W v Ireland (No.2)* [1997] 2 IR 141 and *BL v Ireland* [2010] IEHC 430.
137 *Lockwood v Ireland* [2010] IEHC 430.
138 *L.M. v The Commissioner for An Garda Síochána, The Minister for Justice, Equality and Law Reform, The Director of Public Prosecutions, Ireland and The Attorney General* [2012] 1 ILRM 132.
139 *Osman v The United Kingdom* (2000) 29 EHRR 245.

4

Service provision for victims of crime in Ireland

The previous chapter detailed the legal rights which victims of crime have been afforded in Ireland. This chapter focuses on service rights which complement these legal rights. Service rights 'refer to services which do not affect procedure, such as information provided about case progress' (Hoyle, 2012: 407). These rights are representative of the 'welfare model' of victims' rights protection (Rogan, 2006a). Since the provision of services to victims does not interfere with criminal procedure or potentially affect defendants' due process rights, service rights are less controversial than legal ones. As Rogan notes, 'alleviating the effects of victimisation is uncontentious' (Rogan, 2006a: 143).

This chapter will map the services which are available to victims at each stage in the criminal justice process, from reporting through to offender release. Many of the organisations discussed here also offer counselling services and/or emotional support to victims outside of the criminal justice process, but the focus in this chapter will be on services relating directly to the victim's passage through the formal process. The chapter will also explore the gaps between the rhetoric and the realities of service provision for victims of crime in Ireland with reference to available research on their experiences.

Guidelines on service provision for victims of crime

International instruments emphasise the importance of the effective provision of services to crime victims. The UN Declaration of Basic Principles of Justice for Victims of Crime and Abuse of Power (UN Doc A/RES/40/34 (1985)) (hereafter the UN Declaration) provides that '[v]ictims should receive the necessary material, medical, psychological and social assistance through governmental, voluntary, community-based and indigenous means' (Principle 14). Moreover, the EU Directive on Victims' Rights (2012/29/EU) is predominantly concerned with the provision of service rights, with its specific purpose stated as being 'to ensure that victims of crime receive appropriate information, support and protection and are able to participate in criminal proceedings' (Article 1).

In Ireland, victims' service rights are outlined and protected within the Victims Charter and Guide to the Criminal Justice System (hereafter Victims Charter) which was originally enacted in 1999 and revised in 2010. The Charter was created by the Commission for the Support of Victims of Crime in consultation with the various criminal justice system stakeholders and contains commitments from each of these stakeholders regarding the level of service which victims can expect from them. However, while the Charter contains undertakings with regard to service provision, it does not create legally enforceable rights Thus, as Rogan suggests, '[t]erming it a charter is perhaps giving it a little too much credit, as it really just sets out existing protections for victims in consolidated format' (Rogan, 2006b: 152–3). Similarly, McGovern notes that the Charter 'acknowledges its own inherent limitations as a tool for instantiating the rights of victims by placing considerable emphasis on how to make complaints about criminal justice agencies and on where to obtain further information' (McGovern, 2002: 398). Concerns may also be raised about the approach adopted in the Charter, as it mirrors similar measures in the UK in the 1980s and 1990s where victims began to be cast as 'consumers'. However, as Goodey notes with reference to the 1996 English Victims Charter, 'victims [were] consumers of services with very little recourse to justice should these services fail to match what they indicate victims can expect to receive' (Goodey, 2005: 131). Despite its limitations, the Charter provides an important benchmark for service provision. It will be referred to throughout this chapter when the services available at each stage in the criminal justice process are described. Further, with the implementation of the Directive on Victims' Rights and the consequent commencement of the Criminal Justice (Victims of Crime) Act 2017, victims now have legally enforceable service rights which will offer greater recourse to justice if their entitlement to adequate service provision is not met.

The right to information: cornerstone service right

The cornerstone of effective service provision for victims is the provision of information, making the right to information the most important service right to which victims are entitled. As the EU Agency for Fundamental Rights notes: '[l]ack of information not only represents a serious obstacle to the enjoyment of victims' rights, but research on victim satisfaction with support services has also repeatedly identified the lack of information as a prime source of dissatisfaction with criminal proceedings, and one which discourages them from actively participating' (2014a: 49).

Services and supports for victims are effective only if victims know that they exist. It will be seen in the following discussion that effective information provision about the criminal justice process (e.g. progress of investigation, timings of hearings, release of offenders etc.) is vital to empower victims and minimise the potential for secondary victimisation as a result of feeling isolated within the process. Based on consultations with Irish support service providers for its report in 2008, the Irish Council for Civil Liberties (ICCL) concluded that 'the availability of timely and clear information can have a huge impact on the experience of a victim' (ICCL, 2008: 14). Information provision 'is a vital element in the creation of a fairer and more humane system' (Rogan, 2006b: 155).

The importance of the right to information is stressed in international instruments. The UN Declaration provides that '[v]ictims should be informed of the availability of health and social services and other relevant assistance and be readily afforded access to them (Principle 15). Further, Article 4 of the EU Directive on Victims' Rights creates the right to receive information from the first contact with a competent authority. There is thus a clear obligation imposed upon the agencies of the criminal justice system to make sure that, from first contact with the system (i.e. report to the Gardaí), the victim is kept fully informed about both the progress of the case and all available support services. Information provision 'must be an active and continuing process' (ICCL, 2008: 20). It is vital that it is effectively achieved throughout the criminal justice process from report through to the release of an offender. The importance of information provision, along with shortcomings in the delivery of information to victims at various stages of the process, will be a recurring theme in this chapter.

Information and support for victims who choose not to report: the role and availability of support organisations

When considering service provision for victims within the criminal justice process, it must be remembered that a significant proportion of victims do not engage formally with the system by reporting to the Gardaí (for full discussion see Chapter 6). Where victims do not report, 'a clear challenge exists in relation to the provision of information' (Grozdanova and de Londras, 2014: 35). In particular, 'victims who do not report crimes may miss a key opportunity to receive information about victim support organisations' (Kilcommins et al., 2010: 172).

For victims who do not report, the various support organisations are an important source of information, advice and services. There are a wide variety of support organisations in Ireland that offer specialist support to victims of all types of crime. The most prominent support organisations are perhaps those that support victims of sexual violence (e.g. Rape Crisis Centres, or OneinFour, which supports adult survivors of child sexual abuse) or domestic abuse (e.g. Women's Aid, ADAPT or AMEN, which supports male victims of domestic abuse). There are a wide range of other organisations which support the families of victims of unlawful killing (e.g. AdVIC or Support After Homicide), tourist victims (Irish Tourist Assistance Service) or victims of road traffic incidents (PARC Road Safety Group). Individuals who do not report to the Gardaí are very likely to seek help from such organisations, often by contacting their helpline or visiting their website. Helplines are particularly closely associated with victims of domestic abuse or sexual violence, both of which are characterised by especially high levels of under-reporting. The importance of helplines in this area is evidenced in the available statistics from rape crisis and domestic abuse support services. In 2015, Dublin Rape Crisis Centre (DRCC) received 11,789 helpline contacts (DRCC, 2016: 4). Women's Aid experienced similar levels of demand in 2015, responding to 9,308 calls on their national Freephone helpline (Women's Aid, 2016: 12). The websites of these organisations also receive significant levels of traffic. In 2015, DRCC's website recorded 83,478 visits and Women's Aid reported 167,229 visits to its website. Although all of these visits would not have been by victims, the figures demonstrate high levels of reliance on supports outside of the formal criminal justice system. This support is vital for those who do not make a formal complaint but still wish to access services such as counselling.

Outside of specialist organisations like those listed above, the Crime Victims Helpline (CVH) represents an important source of support for victims who do not report. As will be seen below, the Gardaí inform all victims about the CVH, but the service is equally important for those who do not make a formal complaint or who are still deciding whether to do so. The CVH was established in 2005 and is a national freephone helpline staffed by trained volunteers which is funded by the Commission for the Support of Victims of Crime. It also offers a text service and a website (www.crimevictimshelpline.ie) which the organisation itself describes as 'one of the most comprehensive information sites for victims of crime in Ireland' (CVH, 2015: 3). It is labelled as 'a one-stop shop for victims seeking emotional support; information about the criminal justice system; and assistance in coping with the effects of crime' (Ibid.), and CVH volunteers advise callers on how to report to the Gardaí and/or on specialist support services which are available in their area. Volunteers can liaise with Gardaí or other services on behalf of a victim if s/he requests this (Ibid: 4).

The CVH is a crucial service within the criminal justice system, as evidenced by its inclusion within the Victims Charter, which details the level of service which victims can expect from the helpline (Victims of Crime Office, 2010: 12). The CVH commitments in the Charter include a guarantee of confidentiality as well as the promise to provide various types of advice, including: general information about the criminal justice system; the process involved in reporting to the Gardaí; details of relevant specialist support services; and how to apply for compensation. The importance of the helpline is evident in the increase in callers since its introduction in 2005. In its first year, the CVH received 168 calls. In 2015 it received over 3,200 contacts by phone, email and text message (CVH, 2016: 2). Three-quarters of these contacts were with victims and the remainder were with 'friends or family members; other service providers (such as GPs or counsellors); and members of An Garda Síochána' (Ibid.: 6). The most common offences of which callers to the CVH had been victims of were assault (26%) and burglary/robbery/theft (20%) (Ibid.: 8). The primary purposes for contact were for emotional support (40%) and information regarding the criminal justice system (37%) (Ibid.: 9).

It is clear from these statistics that the CVH has a significant reach. Research with victims conducted by Kilcommins et al. has demonstrated that the CVH is effective in its service provision. Just over a third of the participants surveyed in this research had used the CVH (Kilcommins et al., 2010: 72). Well over half (65.8%) of respondents reported using the CVH for general information. A similar number (64%) said they had accessed the CVH for emotional support. Nearly half of respondents had accessed information about other support organisations (42.3%) and just over a third had accessed information about state agencies (33.3%) (Ibid.: 75–6). Drawing on the respondents' accounts of their experience with the CVH, Kilcommins et al. concluded that the CVH 'provides a very useful and effective service which acts as an entry point allowing victims to access not only information but also ongoing emotional support and reassurance' (Ibid.: 76). Significantly, the report also showed a very high rate of satisfaction with the CVH. Of the 104 valid responses to this part of the survey, fifty-three respondents (51%) stated that they were very satisfied with the CVH. Another thirty-nine (37.5%) indicated that they were satisfied (Ibid.: 78).

Given the importance of the CVH as a source of information and support for victims (particularly those who have not made or may not make a formal complaint), awareness of this service within the community generally is very important. As will be seen below, the Gardaí inform all victims about the CVH when they make a complaint, but visibility within the community generally is vital if those who do not engage with the formal criminal justice process are to access it. Unfortunately, Kilcommins et al. found a lack of awareness about the CVH among both the general public and professionals and representatives of community groups (Kilcommins et al., 2010: 81) and recommended a 'systematic information-giving programme targeted at key professionals and community organisations who are likely to be in contact with victims' (Ibid.: 173).

The CVH has recently invested much energy and resources in raising awareness about their services. Such awareness-raising was a key component of the CVH *Strategic Plan 2011–2014*. The CVH now has an increased presence on social media and is connected with a broader audience on Twitter and on Facebook (CVH, 2015: 3). In 2015 it also launched a short film about its work which was shown in cinemas across Ireland (CVH, 2016: 2). Initiatives like these have increased societal awareness about the important services offered by the CVH.

Report to the Gardaí and investigation

Gardaí play a crucial role in the support of victims of crime, not least because a Garda is often the first person to whom a victim recounts the incident (ICCL, 2008: 50). Article 4 of the EU Directive on Victims' Rights places a clear onus on police to provide adequate services to victims, setting out a comprehensive list of information which victims must receive 'from the first contact with a competent authority'. The Gardaí are the organisation within the criminal justice system who fulfil this role. Article 4 stipulates that victims must be given information about: available support (medical, specialist, psychological, accommodation); the process involved in making a formal complaint; available protection measures; availability of legal aid and/or how to access legal advice; availability of compensation; interpretation and translation services; relevant protections for individuals who have been victimised outside of their resident member state; complaints/redress procedures; contact details for communications about developments in the case; available restorative justice services; and the possibility of reimbursement of expenses.

Further, Article 5 provides that victims are entitled to a 'written acknowledgment of their formal complaint … stating the basic elements of the criminal offence concerned'. This must be in a language which the victim can understand. Victims must also be facilitated to make their complaint in a language they understand by 'receiving the necessary linguistic assistance'. Finally, Article 6 provides that victims are entitled to receive information about the progress of their case, a decision not to prosecute and/or impending trials. Thus, there are high expectations about the level of service provision (and in particular, information provision) which the Gardaí should be delivering to victims. At national level, as with all criminal justice system stakeholders, the basic entitlements which victims can expect from the Gardaí are listed in the Victims Charter. Given the breadth of their obligations, for ease of discussion and critique, the services provided by the Gardaí will be considered here under three headings: (1) report and recording practices; (2) information provision; and (3) protection of vulnerable groups.

Report and recording practices

When a victim contacts the Gardaí about a crime or traumatic incident, the Victims Charter states that the Gardaí will 'respond quickly to the call and investigate the complaint'. The Report of the Garda Inspectorate on Crime Investigation found that, despite this commitment, victims have experienced some issues with this stage of the process, including the physical environment of Garda stations and crime recording. These issues need to be addressed if victims are to receive an effective service at this stage of the process.

Information provision

The Victims Charter places significant recurring responsibilities on the Gardaí to provide information to victims. When a victim makes a complaint, s/he must be informed of the name, telephone number and station of the investigating Garda and the PULSE (Police Using Leading Systems Effectively) incident number. The Gardaí must also '[e]xplain what will happen and keep the victim informed of the criminal investigation' and '[t]ell the victim in writing about the [CVH] and the other services available for victims' (Victims of Crime Office, 2010: 16).

The obligation to provide information continues throughout the investigation and trial of the offence. The Gardaí also have specific responsibilities to provide victims with the following information when a suspect is due to appear in court:

- whether the suspect is being held in prison or is on bail (and any conditions which attach to bail);
- the time, date and location of the court hearing;
- details of the prosecution process, including information about support which is available from voluntary organisations in relation to attendance at court (e.g. accompaniment services);
- whether a victim impact statement is possible; and
- the final result of the trial (Victims of Crime Office, 2010: 16).

Previously, the Gardaí would automatically pass details of victims to Victim Support (a voluntary organisation which provided support to victims of crime in Ireland until 2005). Concerns arose as to whether this practice was compatible with data protection rules. Having reviewed the matter, the Data Protection Commissioner advised that the Gardaí could no longer engage in this practice. If a referral to a victim support organisation was to be made, this could only be done with the victim's informed consent (Office of the Data Protection Commissioner, 2001). The Data Protection Commissioner cautioned that 'even when acting in furtherance of "good causes" – organisations must be sensitive to people's privacy rights, to ensure that inadvertent breaches of data protection law are averted' (Ibid.). Thus, the Gardaí now advise victims about relevant organisations but do not inform these organisations about victims.

The Gardaí formally communicate information to victims via standardised letters that are generated by the PULSE system and are signed by or on behalf of the District Officer (Garda Inspectorate, 2014: 4). The first letter empathises with the victim and provides the PULSE reference number, the investigating Garda's name and the Garda station contact number, as well as the contact details for the CVH. A leaflet with the contact details of other support organisations is also enclosed (Ibid.). The second letter will be sent once an offender has been identified and the case has progressed (Ibid: 5). Despite these arrangements and the commitments made in the Victims Charter, several studies have identified shortcomings in the information provided by the Gardaí to victims during investigations (Garda Inspectorate, 2014: 5; An Garda Síochána, 2015: 11; Kilcommins et al., 2010: 45).The results of these surveys are disappointing and highlight significant shortcomings in the service being delivered to victims by the Gardaí. As noted in the introduction to the chapter, the right to information is one of the cornerstone rights for victims as it makes them aware of available supports and protections and helps to minimise feelings of loss of control or isolation which victims can experience within the criminal justice process (for full discussion see Chapter 6).

Protection of vulnerable groups

A number of key services are offered by the Gardaí to ensure that all victims, regardless of any special sensitivities they might have, are treated equitably at the reporting and investigation stages of the criminal justice process. For victims of sexual offences, a Garda of the same gender will be provided to investigate the offence and, as far as possible, a doctor of the same gender will also be provided for examination purposes (Victims of Crime Office, 2010: 17). Details of relevant support organisations in the locality will also be provided (Ibid.). There are also special services for families of victims of unlawful killings, most notably, the family's local Garda Superintendent will keep contact directly with it and any support organisation with which the family is engaging (Victims of Crime Office, 2010: 17). This contact will be maintained via a Garda Family Liaison Officer (FLO,) who is a specially trained member of An Garda Síochána. There are 474 trained FLOs throughout Ireland (Garda Inspectorate, 2014: 30). Although FLOs are primarily appointed in cases of unlawful killings, they can be appointed in any other case where the District Officer deems it appropriate (McMahon, 2015). Victims of domestic abuse will be advised about local support agencies. They will also be notified that the Gardaí have a pro-arrest policy in domestic abuse cases (Victims of Crime Office, 2010: 17). For victims who do not speak English, free translation services are provided by the Gardaí (Ibid.: 18). Finally, there is special provision for members of the LGBT (lesbian, gay, bisexual and transgender) community, who may be referred to an LBGT Liaison Officer, and for victims of racist incidents, who may have the support of Ethnic Liaison Officers (ELOs). Access Officers are also available for victims with disabilities. These officers provide additional assistance and guidance for these victims to allow them to overcome any challenges they might face in accessing Garda services.

The Gardaí also have specialist interviewers who are trained to interview children under 14 years of age and persons with an intellectual disability who are making complaints in relation to sexual crime, or offences involving violence or threats of violence (An Garda Síochána, 2013: 71). These specialist interviewers can also interview victims of sexual crime or serious crime or witnesses to those crimes, where they are directed to do so (Ibid.). Generally, specialist interviewers will interview children and persons with intellectual disability in plain clothes 'unless the circumstances dictate otherwise' (Ibid.: 72). There are also 'dedicated interview suites' at 'strategic locations throughout the country designed to provide appropriate facilities for interviewing complainants in accordance with the provisions of ... the Criminal Evidence Act 1992' (i.e. recording of interviews) (Ibid.). The details of these provisions have been discussed in Chapter 4. The interview suites are located away from Garda stations. They may also be used for interviewing complainants of other serious crimes when this is appropriate (Ibid.: 73).

Kilcommins et al. found that FLOs have a positive influence on the experience of the families of victims of unlawful killing. Although the sample of victims who had experienced the support of an FLO was small, the researchers found that the majority were satisfied with the service provided and noted the 'very positive contribution which [FLOs] can make to victim experiences' (Kilcommins et al., 2010: 57). However, the Garda Inspectorate was somewhat less positive about the role of LGBT officers and ELOs, particularly the fact that both of these roles are now linked (Garda Inspectorate, 2014: 46). Issues have also been raised about the response of the Gardaí to domestic abuse incidents. Although it is stated that the Gardaí have a 'pro-arrest' policy, it would seem that arrests are typically made only for breach of a domestic violence order, and not for crimes such as assault (Garda Inspectorate, 2014: 20).

Strengthening Garda service delivery to victims: Garda Victims' Service Offices and the Criminal Justice (Victims of Crime) Bill 2016

Garda Victim Service Offices were launched by Garda Commissioner Nóirín O'Sullivan in Waterford Garda Station on 9 December 2015. The creation of twenty-eight Victims of Crime Offices within the Gardaí aims to ensure that victims are kept informed about the progress of their cases. These offices were originally piloted in Dublin and Waterford and, since December 2015, there is one within every Garda Division. The offices are staffed by specially trained Gardaí who operate to a Standard Operating Procedure. The offices are open between 9am and 5pm, Monday to Friday. Victims of crime can choose between receiving contact by phone, letter or email. The central role of these offices is to keep victims informed of all significant developments associated with their case and to provide contact details for relevant support/counselling services. In crimes such as burglary, assault or criminal damage, victims receive a follow-up call from the Victim Service Office to ensure that they have all the information they require, including contact details of the investigating Gardaí. Victims can also raise any concerns they have in the wake of the crime, or issues with the investigation. They will be provided with crime prevention advice and details for external services available from other state and/or non-governmental agencies. Victims of domestic abuse, sexual crime or other crimes where there is trauma will continue to be given advice and support in person from investigating or specialist Gardaí. Significantly, in light of criticism from the Garda Inspectorate about monitoring of victim treatment, the Gardaí have undertaken to assess victim satisfaction with their services via their quarterly Public Attitude Survey and engagement with victims and their representative groups. The improvement of victim satisfaction will also be furthered by changes to the PULSE system which will allow for the capture of more information about victims' needs (McMahon, 2015). There will also be 'enhanced functionality in relation to the printing of letters to victims of crime including two additional letters' (Ibid.). Given the recent introduction of these offices, it is too soon to tell whether they will be successful in meeting some of the problems highlighted in the 2014 Garda Inspectorate report and other studies discussed above. However, since their introduction, the CVH has already reported a 'notable decrease in calls to the helpline where the caller in unable to make contact with the investigating Garda' (CVH, 2016: 1). Thus, it seems that this initiative holds significant promise for improving the service which the Gardaí deliver to victims.

Garda service delivery to victims of crime will also be strengthened by the commencement of the Criminal Justice (Victims of Crime) Act 2017, which places many of the existing Garda commitments on a statutory footing, creating legally enforceable rights for victims. Section 7 creates a list of information which all victims are entitled to upon first contact with the Gardaí. This includes information about available support services, reporting procedures and the availability of legal aid, compensation or expenses. Further, section 8 creates an obligation for Gardaí to inform victims that they are entitled to request certain other information about investigations and criminal proceedings, such as information about developments in the investigation or a decision not to prosecute. The Act also places special protections for vulnerable victims on a statutory footing. Section 12 entitles victims to be accompanied by a person of his/her choice, including a legal representative, when making a complaint. Section 15 also places an obligation on Gardaí to assess victims to determine whether they have any special protection needs which may require special measures to be employed during the investigation. Examples of special measures which might be made available include the use of specially trained interviewers, conducting interviews in adapted premises, continuity of interviewers and the availability of interviewers of the same gender as the victim where the offence involves sexual or gender-based violence or violence in a close relationship.

Sexual Assault Treatment Units (SATUs)

Given the special circumstances of sexual violence, particularly the importance of gathering forensic evidence quickly and effectively, SATUs offer a very important service for victims. There are six SATUs in Ireland (Cork, Donegal, Dublin, Galway, Mullingar and Waterford), as well as Sexual Assault Services Midwest in Limerick. The units are 'geographically distributed around the country … to maximise equitable ease of access' (Kennedy et al., 2016: 3) Victims may approach a SATU directly or be referred by a medical practitioner (e.g. GP or hospital emergency department), or Gardaí may refer victims to SATUs for the collection of forensic evidence which will be used to investigate the offence. Forensic samples may be collected up to seven days after a rape or sexual assault. If the victim has reported to the Gardaí, a Garda will be present to collect the forensic samples. For victims who present to the SATU outside of the seven-day period, an examination and after-care will also be provided and the examiners will document any injuries the victim may have. All SATU services, including follow-up appointments, are provided free of charge. Upon arrival at a SATU, victims meet with a support worker from a rape crisis centre who will support them throughout the forensic examination process and provide them with information about support services which are available from the rape crisis centre. There were 685 attendances at the six SATUs in 2015 (Eogan, 2016: 6). The majority of victims attended the SATU within 72 hours of the incident (Ibid.).

A significant recent development for victims attending at SATUs is that forensic samples can now be collected and stored even if the victim has not or is not going to immediately report to the Gardaí. Previously, samples could not be used in a criminal investigation unless there was a Garda presence during the collection process, as it was felt that this was necessary to preserve the chain of evidence. Where the victim consents, new protocols now allow for collection without Garda involvement and storage for up to one year to allow the victim some time to decide whether to proceed with a formal complaint (SATU, 2014: 102). Examiners at the SATU will write and store a medico-legal report and this will be provided to the Gardaí along with the samples if the victim decides to proceed with a formal complaint. After one year of storage the samples will be destroyed unless the victim requests in writing that they be stored for another year (Ibid.). This service commenced in July 2016 (Rogers, 2016).

Victims who are under the age of 18 will require the consent of a parent or legal guardian before an examination may be carried out. Children who are below the age of 14 will not be examined in SATUs but will be referred to the Child and Adolescent Sexual Assault Treatment Service (CASATS) in Galway or examined by another agency within the Health Service Executive. For example, examinations may take place in St Louise's Unit in Crumlin Children's Hospital or St Claire's Unit in Temple Street Children's Hospital. Examinations may also be carried out by a suitably qualified medical practitioner where this is appropriate. CASATS provides a 24-hour service for child victims of sexual abuse under the age of 14. In June 2014, Children At Risk In Ireland (CARI) (a support organisation for child victims of sexual abuse) began providing accompaniment services to CASATS. This service is available on a 24/7 basis, 365 days a year (CARI, 2015: 17).

Victims from outside of Ireland

The primary support for visitors to Ireland who become victims of crime is the Irish Tourist Assistance Service (ITAS), a voluntary organisation which offers a free and confidential support service. The ITAS was founded in April 1994 and supports victims of all types of crime. Services offered by ITAS include: helping to address medical needs; provision of telephone/fax/email facilities; interpretation services; liaison with embassies, Gardaí and other agencies on behalf of the victims; help with arrangement of emergency travel documents; cancellation of credit cards; organising money transfers; re-issue/re-schedule of stolen travel tickets; arrangement of accommodation/meals in emergency situations; and transport.

There are good links between the ITAS and the Gardaí, who refer tourist victims to them for support. The strength of the working relationship between the ITAS and the Gardaí is evidenced in the fact that the ITAS opened a satellite centre in Pearse Street Garda Station on 16 June 2016. The ITAS provided assistance in 445 incidents of crime or other traumatic events in 2015, assisting 823 tourists (ITAS, 2016: 12). Eighty-six per cent of these individuals were referred to ITAS by the Gardaí. Eighty-three per cent of these referrals were from Garda stations in Dublin (Ibid.). In 6% of cases, tourist victims contacted the service directly and referrals also came from embassies (5%), the tourist industry (2%) and other sources (1%) (Ibid.: 13).

Crimes committed against tourists are relatively common. In 2015, seven tourists a day reported a crime in Ireland (ITAS, 2016: 4). Thus, the services provided by the ITAS are an important part of the criminal justice system infrastructure for individuals who fall victim to crime while visiting Ireland. However, despite seemingly good links between the ITAS and the Gardaí who refer tourist

Service provision for victims of crime

victims to them for support, only one in eleven tourists who reported crime contacted the ITAS (Ibid.). Thus, only approximately 10% of tourist victims are receiving assistance. There may be a number of reasons for this, including not requiring special assistance. However, Lisa Kennedy (chief executive officer of ITAS) suggests that other reasons may also contribute to these victims not availing themselves of assistance, including: (1) not being informed of the service; (2) language barriers, resulting in victims not understanding what the ITAS offers; and (3) information about the ITAS being offered in a manner which discourages victims from approaching the service (Kennedy, 2015). Kennedy suggests that appropriate referral processes and training for Gardaí should be put in place to ensure that tourist victims receive appropriate support and assistance. Given the numbers of tourist victims in Ireland each year, this is an important aspect of service provision for victims which should not be overlooked.

Rights in relation to prosecution decisions

The process surrounding prosecution decisions can often be very distressing for victims, who may be disappointed with the charge decision which is made and will feel disillusioned if a decision not to prosecute is taken. To help them to understand and accept a decision not to prosecute, victims are entitled to request reasons for such a decision. If they are not satisfied that these reasons are valid, a review can be requested. The right to review of a decision not to prosecute is provided for in Article 11 of the EU Directive on Victims' Rights.

For less serious offences such as minor assaults or public order offences, the Gardaí will make the decision on whether to prosecute and will prosecute the offence in the name of the Office of the DPP. Victims can request a summary of reasons for the decision of the Gardaí not to prosecute. Forms for this request are available on the Garda website. The application must be made within twenty-eight days of the victim's finding out that no prosecution will take place and must be sent to the relevant Superintendent. If the victim is not satisfied with these reasons, s/he can request a review of the decision. This request must be made within twenty-eight days of provision with the summary of reasons. The review will be carried out by the relevant Chief Superintendent in the area.

The Victims Charter provides that the Office of the DPP will take the views of a victim into account when deciding whether to prosecute (Victims of Crime Office, 2010: 30). Information about a decision not to prosecute may be provided for fatal cases which occurred on or after 22 October 2008 or for any case which occurred on or after 16 November 2015 (Victims of Crime Office, 2015: 4). The extension of the scheme to all offences in 2015 is due to the Victims of Crime

Office's new obligations under the EU Directive on Victims of Crime and is a very welcome move from a victims' rights perspective. Victims, or the families of victims in fatal cases, who wish to obtain a summary or reasons for a decision not to prosecute must complete a 'request for reasons' form which is available on the Office of the DPP's website or from Garda stations (Ibid.: 5). This request must be sent within twenty-eight days of the date when the victim was informed of the decision not to prosecute, but this time period might be extended 'if there is good reason and if it is in the interests of justice' (Ibid.: 5). A summary of reasons should be provided in writing within twenty-eight days. If this period is to be extended, the victim will be informed in writing that it may take longer to release the information and will be provided with an indication of when the information may be available (Ibid.: 6). The DPP cannot provide a summary of reasons where a suspect was dealt with under the Garda Síochána Adult Caution Scheme or the Juvenile Diversion Programme or where the information would: interfere with an ongoing criminal investigation; prejudice a future court case; or jeopardise the personal safety of any person or the security of the state (Ibid.: 4–5).

In the period from October 2008 (i.e. the introduction of the policy on giving reasons for decisions not to prosecute in fatal cases) to November 2015, ninety-seven requests for reasons were made (Office of the DPP, 2016a: 25). Sixty-four per cent of these requests related to fatal road traffic incidents. Ninety-two of these requests were granted. Unsurprisingly, when the facility to ask for reasons not to prosecute was extended to all crimes in November 2015, the number of requests increased considerably. Between November 2015 and June 2016, 333 requests for reasons were made, with reasons being given in 216 cases (Ibid.). Examples of instances where requests are refused include requests relating to decisions made prior to 16 November 2015, or where giving a reason may prejudice a future court case (Ibid.).

It is possible to ask for a review of a decision made by the DPP. Such requests must be made within twenty-eight days of the date on the letter informing the victim of the reasons not to prosecute or, where reasons were not sought, within fifty-six days of the date when the victim was informed of the decision not to prosecute (Office of the DPP, 2015: 7). These time limits may be extended if there is a good reason and an extension is in the interests of justice. The review is performed by a lawyer who was not involved in making the original decision and should be completed within six weeks of receipt of the request but may take longer in complex cases. There are two possible outcomes in a review: reversal of the original decision (in which case the Gardaí will be instructed to start court proceedings) and confirmation of the original decision. When the latter decision is issued, there is no further right of review but a victim who is unhappy with how his/her request for reasons or review was dealt with can make a complaint (Ibid.: 8). In the period from November 2015 to June 2016, 135 requests for review were received by the Office of the DPP (2016a: 25). The original decision was upheld in 106 cases. Eleven requests were deemed to be invalid for various reasons (e.g. because the decision not to prosecute was taken by the Gardaí) and eighteen requests were still pending when the Annual Report was published.

The Office of the DPP set up a Communications and Victims Liaison Unit in July 2015 (Office of the DPP, 2016a: 24). The aim of this unit is to ensure that the Office meets its obligations under the EU Directive on Victims Rights. The Unit deals with all requests for reasons not to prosecute and reviews requests received from victims and provides information to victims who contact the Office. The Unit has produced two information booklets for victims: *How We Make Decisions* and *How to Request Reasons and Reviews* (Ibid.). Both of these booklets are available on the website of the Office. These initiatives should have a positive effect on victim satisfaction levels with the DPP and ensure that victims will have consistent access to information which they are entitled to, as well as meeting some of the criticisms which victims have previously expressed about the Office of the DPP (ICCL, 2008: 17; Kilcommins et al., 2010: 124). The right to seek reasons for a decision not to prosecute and the right to review decisions in relation to prosecutions are now provided for in the Criminal Justice (Victims of Crime) Act 2017 (sections 8(2)(d) and 10, respectively). There are no substantive changes to the procedure itself but the creation of legally enforceable rights in this area further strengthens protection for victims.

Trial support

Attending court as a witness can be traumatic for victims. As victims attend as witnesses for the state and not as parties in their own right there is often a sense of powerlessness, and indeed some victims (especially victims of serious crimes such as sexual or violent offences or the families of victims of unlawful killings) can experience the trial process as a form of secondary victimisation. In Ireland a number of initiatives and services provided by both criminal justice stakeholders (i.e. the Courts Service and the Office of the DPP) and voluntary support organisations seek to ensure that attendance at court is not unduly distressing.

Pre-trial support for victims

'Courts are rarely victim-friendly places' (Mawby, 2007: 220) and '[i]ncomprehension as to the workings of the judicial system pose[s] significant hurdles to the uninitiated' (Mulkerrins, 2003: 125). Information about the process is vital to offset victims' feelings of isolation and confusion. To deal with victims' concerns and queries about the court process and arrange advance visits to courthouses prior to the trial, the Courts Service has 'customer liaison officers' (Victims of Crime Office, 2010: 24). In a study by Kilcommins et al. many of the victims surveyed expressed satisfaction with the service provided by court officials (Kilcommins et al., 2010: 117). Victim support organisations also perform an important role in supporting victims at this stage of the process and providing them with relevant information. The study by Kilcommins et al. recorded 'a very positive response' regarding information provided by support organisations about court procedures (Ibid.: 118).

The Office of the DPP also has significant responsibilities for information provision, as well as an obligation to meet with victims pre-trial if this is requested. The Victims Charter states that when victims are attending court as witnesses the relevant representatives of the DPP must:

- treat the victim with respect, taking account of his/her personal situation, rights and dignity;
- liaise with the Gardaí to ensure that the victim is kept up to date (especially if the offence is of a violent or sexual nature);
- arrange for the victim to speak with the prosecution barrister or solicitor before the court case if the victim wishes to do so. The purpose of this meeting is to explain what will happen in court (Victims of Crime Office, 2010: 30).

The pre-trial meeting with the prosecution legal team is a key support for victims. Although the conversation which occurs is necessarily limited because the lawyers cannot be seen to 'coach' the witness, these meetings provide victims with important information so that they can feel that they are not forgotten within the process. If evidence is to be given by video-link, the victim is brought to the video-link room and shown where s/he will sit and how the evidence will be taken (Grozdanova and de Londras, 2014: 11). The Rape Crisis Network of Ireland has praised the introduction of meetings between representatives from the Office of the DPP and victims, noting that this process (which includes a tour of the courts) 'though very simple ... has a profound effect on victims and has been very helpful in alleviating fear of unknown surroundings and procedures' (ICCL, 2008: 18). Research conducted by Grozdanova and de Londras found that meetings between representatives of the Office of the DPP and victims are 'extensively held' (Grozdanova and de Londras, 2014: 11).

Another important resource for victims at the pre-trial stage is the material which is provided on the websites of the various criminal justice agencies. The Courts Service provides access to both a DVD and a booklet entitled *Going to*

Court for Young Witnesses. Two booklets, *Going to Court as a Witness* and *The Role of the DPP* are available on the website of the Office of the DPP. Further, for victims who have the option of providing a victim impact statement, the Gardaí, the Office of the DPP and the Victims of Crime Office have collaborated to develop guidelines entitled 'Making a Victim Impact Statement' to help victims to draw up their statements.

Services available for victims during the trial

During the trial, victims are entitled to special arrangements to protect them from coming into contact with the accused, and court accompaniment. The customer liaison officers within the Courts Service can arrange access to victim rooms and reserve family seating in murder and manslaughter cases (Victims of Crime Office, 2010: 24). A dedicated suite of four rooms and reception area for victims are available within the Criminal Courts of Justice in Dublin and waiting rooms are available in 'almost all refurbished courthouses and also in a number of other courthouses' (Ibid.). The Victims Charter also contains a commitment that 'rooms will be set aside for victims in all future refurbishment projects' (Ibid.). These assurances are mandated by Article 19 of the EU Directive on Victims' Rights. Interpretation services are also available by order of the court for witnesses who do not speak English to aid them in giving evidence or making a victim impact statement (Victims of Crime Office, 2010: 25). A legal entitlement to translation and interpretation services for victims throughout the criminal justice process is included in section 21 of the Criminal Justice (Victims of Crime) Bill 2016.

Although efforts are made by the Courts Service to provide special waiting rooms to protect victims during the trial, the architecture of many Irish court buildings means that this is not always possible, causing concern for victims (Bacik et al., 2007; ICCL, 2008; Kilcommins et al., 2010: 127; Mulkerrins, 2003: 127; for full discussion see Chapter 6). Court accompaniment is an essential service for victims, as it provides them with support and a source of information throughout the trial, which can be a very confusing and traumatic process. One of the main providers of court accompaniment is Victim Support at Court (VSAC), an independent voluntary organisation which is dedicated solely to supporting victims in court. VSAC also organises pre-trial court visits for victims and their families to familiarise them with the court setting before the trial. Other specialist support agencies also offer court accompaniment services. A key service provider in this context is Children at Risk in Ireland (CARI), which offers specialist Child Accompaniment Support Services (CASS) (court accompaniment and pre-trial court familiarisation) for children. This service was first introduced in 2005 and was originally provided only to child victims of sexual abuse who were testifying in court. Since 2009 the service is available to all children who are attending court as witnesses in any criminal trial. In 2014 CARI supported thirty-one children going to court to give witness testimony in criminal trials (CARI, 2015: 15). Other voluntary agencies that provide specialist accompaniment services for victims include Rape Crisis Centres, OneinFour and domestic abuse support services such as Women's Aid and ADAPT. In relation to the latter, however, it is important to note that support workers can attend only criminal proceedings. They are not permitted to support their clients in civil proceedings pertaining to applications for orders under the Domestic Violence Act 1996 (as amended), as these proceedings are held in camera. This gap in protection for domestic abuse victims whose protection is dependent upon the civil law system as well as the criminal justice process will be ameliorated by the provisions of the Domestic Violence Bill 2017, which strengthens protections available to victims of domestic abuse during civil proceedings. Section 22 allows an applicant for an order under the domestic violence legislation to be accompanied in court by a person of his/her choice (including a support worker). Significantly, section 24 of the Bill also imposes an obligation on the Courts Service to provide applicants with information on, and contact details for, domestic violence support services.

Coroner's service

Coroners inquire into sudden, unnatural or violent deaths with a view to establishing a cause of death and issuing a death certificate. This may involve a post-mortem and/or an inquest. An inquest is a public inquiry but, unlike criminal court proceedings, the purpose is not to establish blame for the death. An inquest will usually take place between four and ten months after a death. However, it cannot be concluded before any criminal proceedings relating to the incident are completed. If there is going to be a criminal trial, a preliminary inquest will open within the four to ten month period after the death but it will be adjourned until the criminal trial is concluded.

One of the key services guaranteed by the Coroner's Service to victims in the Victims Charter is the provision of information. Victims are promised information at each stage of the process. Where a post-mortem is carried out, the Coroner's Service will tell families where to get information about the process (Victims of Crime Office, 2010: 50). Families are also entitled to request the findings of the examination on payment of a set fee (Ibid.). Where an inquest is to take place, the Gardaí should inform the family as soon as possible of the date, time and place of the inquest (Ibid.). Coroners must also demonstrate sensitivity towards victims' families, for example, by providing them with the option to leave the courtroom when potentially distressing information is being provided (e.g. evidence from the pathologist) (Ibid.). After the inquest, families can request copies of documents such as post-mortem reports from the Coroner's Office on payment of a set fee (Ibid.).

Reimbursement of expenses and compensation

Victims will frequently be disadvantaged financially because of their victimisation. At the very least, they will incur travel and/or accommodation expenses if their case goes to court, particularly if the trial is held far away from their own home. However, this is often the least of the costs an individual will face as a result of being a victim of crime. Victims are likely to face medical and/or counselling fees as well as loss of income because of absence from work or the expense of having to replace belongings which have been lost as a result of the crime. Victims should have access to recompense for the harms which have been visited upon them, or at the very least access to reimbursement of expenses for attending court for the trial of the offence. It was seen in the last chapter that offenders may be ordered to pay compensation to victims. However, this does not always occur and many offenders may not have the means to provide adequate compensation. Consequently, the state must take some responsibility for both reimbursement of expenses incurred when attending court and the payment of compensation. Minimising the pecuniary effects of victimisation is a very important service for victims.

Reimbursement of expenses

Article 14 of the EU Directive on Victims' Rights states that victims should be able to apply for reimbursement of expenses incurred as a result of their active participation in criminal proceedings. The Victims Charter provides that the Gardaí must inform victims about the possibility of reimbursement of court expenses (Victims of Crime Office, 2010: 16). Where a victim's case goes to court, s/he may apply to the Gardaí for payment of the expenses incurred in attending court as a witness to give evidence. Expenses which may be reimbursed include travel costs, meals and, where appropriate, accommodation. The expenses will be paid by the Garda Superintendent in the area where the case is being prosecuted. Victims can liaise with the investigating Garda about applying for reimbursement of expenses. It may also be possible for victims to have these expenses paid in advance if this is necessary to facilitate their attendance at court (An Garda Síochána Victim Information Letter). Research suggests that the Gardaí are not consistently advising victims of their entitlements in this regard, which is out of step with their commitments in the Victims Charter (Kilcommins et al., 2010: 164). This practice will need to change in future as the Victims of Crime Act 2017 requires the Gardaí to inform victims upon first contact of 'any entitlement to expenses arising from the participation of a victim in any proceedings relating to an offence' (section 7(1)(o)).

State-funded compensation

The EU Directive on Victims' Rights does not discuss state-funded compensation schemes for victims, concentrating instead on the right to obtain a decision on compensation from the offender (Article 16). However, there are other relevant international and EU provisions which create obligations regarding state-funded compensation. Principle 12 of the UN Declaration provides that:

> When compensation is not fully available from the offender or other sources, States should endeavour to provide financial compensation to:
>
> (a) Victims who have sustained significant bodily injury or impairment of physical or mental health as a result of serious crimes;
> (b) The family, in particular dependants of persons who have died or become physically or mentally incapacitated as a result of such victimization.

The Declaration also provides that '[t]he establishment, strengthening and expansion of national funds for compensation to victims should be encouraged' (Principle 13). A European Convention on the Compensation of Victims of Violent Crimes was introduced in 1983. This Convention obliges states to establish compensation schemes for the benefit of victims of serious crimes or their surviving families. Ireland has, however, never signed this Convention. Finally, a Council Directive on Compensation to Crime Victims was introduced in 2004 (2004/80/EC). This Directive requires EU member states to co-operate with each other to facilitate access to compensation where an individual falls victim to a crime in a member state where s/he does not reside.

In Ireland, state-funded compensation for crime victims is available via the non-statutory Scheme of Compensation for Personal Injuries Criminally Inflicted (the Scheme), which was introduced in 1974 after the Dublin and Monaghan bombings which occurred on 17 May 1974, resulting in the deaths of thirty-three people. Although the scheme was introduced in 1974, it was backdated to 1 October 1972, meaning that victims could make claims for crimes committed from that date onwards. Under the scheme, damages are payable for 'out-of-pocket expenses, loss of income (including future losses), loss of opportunity, and damages for mental distress in fatal cases' (Murray, 2008: 17). Due to an amendment to the Scheme in 1986, damages are no longer payable for pain and suffering. The Criminal Injuries Compensation Tribunal (CICT) administers the scheme. The CICT is composed of seven members (a chairperson and six ordinary members), all of whom are qualified solicitors and barristers who work on a part-time basis and are paid fees for the work they perform for the

CICT. Members of the CICT are appointed by the Minister for Justice, Equality and Law Reform.

The scheme applies only to victims of violent crime. Applications for compensation may be made via application forms which are available on the website of the Department of Justice. Article 3 of the Scheme provides that the following individuals are eligible to apply for compensation:

(a) the person who sustained the injury (the victim);
(b) any person responsible for the maintenance of the victim who has suffered pecuniary loss or incurred any expenses as a result of the victim's injury;
(c) where the victim has died as a result of the injury, any dependent of the victim or, if he has no dependent, any person who incurred expenses as a result of his death;
(d) where the victim has died otherwise than as a result of the injury, any dependent of the victim.

It is also possible for individuals to claim compensation under the scheme where they have sustained injuries as a result of: coming to the assistance of a member of An Garda Síochána; attempting to prevent a crime or to prevent the escape of someone who has committed a crime; or trying to save a human life (Article 4). Applications for compensation must be made within three months of the occurrence of the crime which gave rise to the injury but the CICT can extend this time limit where the circumstances of the case 'justify exceptional treatment' (Article 21). Murray notes that the CICT can 'exercise considerable discretion' in relation to these restrictions and '[i]ncidents that occurred many years outside the three-month time limit have been treated as being exceptional where an applicant can show good grounds for such treatment' (Murray, 2008: 17). In general, Murray suggests that the CICT will allow a period of twelve months for bringing an application 'and will, for good cause shown, extend the time further' (Ibid.). There is no time limit for applications relating to fatal injuries. Article 23 provides that '[t]o qualify for compensation it will be necessary to indicate to the Tribunal that the offence giving rise to the injury has been the subject of criminal proceedings or that it was reported to the Gardaí without delay'. However, the CICT will have discretion to dispense with this requirement 'where they are satisfied that all reasonable efforts were made by or on behalf of the claimant to notify the Garda Síochána of the offence and to co-operate with them' (Ibid.).

There are a number of restrictions regarding eligibility for compensation. Compensation will not be payable 'where the offender and the victim were living together as members of the same household' when the injuries occurred (Article 10). Compensation is also not payable where the CICT 'is satisfied that the victim was responsible, either because of provocation or otherwise, for the offence giving rise to the injuries', and the CICT may reduce the amount of an award where it is of the opinion that the victim has been partially responsible for the offence (Article 13). There is no compensation available for injuries incurred as a result of road traffic offences unless the CICT believes that there has been a deliberate attempt to run down the victim (Article 12). Compensation is also not payable 'where the Tribunal is satisfied that the conduct of the victim, his character or his way of life make it inappropriate that he should be granted an award' (Article 14). The CICT may also reduce an award where 'it is appropriate to do so having regard to the conduct, character or way of life of the victim' (Ibid.). Proceedings of the CICT are informal (Article 20). Applications are first considered by the staff of the CICT, who make sure that all the relevant information is present and that the application is suitable for consideration (Article 24). Once the staff have completed their enquiries into the incident, the application is then forwarded to a member of the CICT who will make a decision on it.

The CICT makes a number of commitments to victims in the Victims Charter, including: the provision of information about and support in completing an application form for compensation; polite and professional treatment; provision of written decisions; prompt payment of compensation; and provision of information about rights of appeal (Victims of Crime Office, 2010: 54). It also promises to provide support to victims who are seeking compensation from another EU member state. However, there is evidence that the CICT is not delivering on its commitments to victims as comprehensively as it could, and there are limits to the service which it provides. Most notably, the scheme is a 'cash-limited grant scheme' which means that the CICT has no capacity or authority to pay out more funds in any one year than have been voted by the Dáil. If the CICT funding becomes exhausted before the end of a financial year it has to wait until the next financial year, when it has been granted more money, before making any further payments to applicants. This naturally results in delays in some instances and may mean that the CICT is quite restricted in the amounts of compensation which it can pay out. As the CICT does not publish annual reports, it is not possible to properly assess its workings or how it is affected by the 'cash-limited' nature of its operation. Figures released to the *Sunday Independent* in 2014 showed that the CICT budget in 2013 was €11.297m, amounting to 396 payments (Griffin, 2014). The *Sunday Independent* also found some evidence of delay, interviewing one woman who had been waiting three years for €31,000 compensation after her son was murdered in 2011. However, without further details on the average waiting times for compensation, it is not possible to comment authoritatively on the extent to which delay is an issue for victims who are granted compensation by the CICT.

The provision of state-funded compensation for victims is by no means a straightforward element of service provision. The current system requires some improvement if it is to offer an appropriate level of service to victims. Its cash-limited, non-statutory nature means that the service provided by the CICT is necessarily restricted. Extension of the scheme would be highly resource intensive but it is something which must be considered if the state is to provide optimum support and protection to victims.

Restorative justice

Article 12 of the EU Directive on Victims' Rights provides that victims have a right to safeguards in the context of restorative justice services. In Ireland, restorative justice services are managed by the Probation Service and tend to be used most often in relation to young offenders. However, there are some restorative justice initiatives for adult offenders also. The *Restorative Justice Strategy: Repairing the Harm: A Victim Sensitive Response to Offending* emphasises that the Probation Service has a 'victim-sensitive' response to restorative justice. The Probation Service makes clear that one of the core principles underpinning restorative justice practice is provision of information and support to victims 'to enable them to make an informed decision as to whether they participate in the restorative process, which includes determination of the most appropriate form of offender reparation' (Probation Service, 2013: 7).

For young offenders (under the age of 18), restorative justice takes the form of family conferencing. A family conference may be ordered by the Court under the Children Act 2001 (as amended) and is run by Young Persons Probation. A family conference is a meeting between the young offender, members of his/her family, the victim and others who may be involved with the young offender (e.g. a social worker). The aim of the conference is to discuss the offender's actions and to devise an action plan which will seek to prevent re-offending. The Probation Service has a guide for victims who are involved in family conferences which explains the process. Victims are entitled to bring a support person along with them. If victims do not wish to be present, they may nominate someone to attend on their behalf or express their views via letter or through the Probation Officer (Probation Service Information Leaflet). Victims are also entitled to be informed of the outcome of the Action Plan which is agreed at the conference.

For adult offenders, a cautioning scheme, operated by An Garda Síochána, came into force in Ireland in February 2006. An adult caution may be administered instead of a prosecution where there is evidence that an offence has been committed and the individual admits the offence and gives informed consent to being cautioned (An Garda Síochána, 2006: 3). The offence and offender must be suitable for an adult caution and it must be in the public interest for one to be administered (An Garda Síochána, 2006: 1). The scheme applies to more minor offences such as public order, minor assaults or minor acts of criminal damage. The principal purpose of the scheme is to divert from prosecution adults who are unlikely to re-offend (Ibid.: 1). If 'reasonably possible', the views of any victims must be obtained before an offender is considered for an adult caution. Garda guidance on the scheme provides that '[t]he effect on the victim of the offence in question, and, any reason advanced by him/her as to why a caution should not be applied must be carefully considered before a decision is taken on whether to prosecute or to caution' (Ibid.: 3). However, the victim's views are not necessarily determinative and a caution may be appropriate even if the victim is opposed to it.

Another form of restorative justice which may be used where the offender is an adult is Victim Offender Mediation (VOM), which provides an opportunity for mediation between the victim and offender. A mediator will prepare with each participant prior to the meeting and then facilitate discussion during the meeting. The Court might request VOM post-sentence, but the participation of the service user is voluntary. A pilot programme to provide a VOM for victims of sexual crime, approved by the Minister for Justice and Equality, commenced in September 2015. The Probation Service's National Victim Services Team co-ordinates and oversees the delivery of the pilot through a core group of probation staff who have participated in specialised mediation skills and dedicated training on sexual trauma (Probation Service, 2016: 22).

Restorative justice offers victims an opportunity for more direct involvement in the criminal justice process than does the traditional criminal process of trial and punishment. For some victims, there may be significant cathartic benefits in discussing the harms visited upon them with the offender and they may feel more confident that victimisation will not re-occur. Positive outcomes for victims who engage in restorative justice are evidenced in research carried out by Le Chéile (a non-statutory youth restorative justice service in Limerick). As part of an analysis of the services provided by Le Chéile, interviews were conducted with six individuals who had acted in the capacity of direct victim or victim representative in a restorative intervention (Quigley et al., 2014: 43). 'All those interviewed stated that Restorative Justice is a more inclusive, respectful and meaningful approach' (Ibid.). The report also found that those victims who engaged with restorative justice experience two final outcomes, which were each considered independent, namely, an increase in their perception of safety or a decrease in fear of crime, and an ability to attain closure on the event (Ibid.: 89).

Imprisonment and release of offenders: victims' information entitlements

The interests of victims and their families in the criminal justice process do not cease when the trial concludes. While some victims may not want to know about an offender's engagement with the Probation Services or imprisonment and release, such information is very important for others, particularly where a very serious crime is involved and/or when the offender may be returning to live in the same locality as the victim and/or his/her family after release. Article 6(5) of the EU Directive on Victims' Rights provides that victims must be 'offered the opportunity to be notified, without unnecessary delay, when the person remanded in custody, prosecuted or sentenced for criminal offences concerning them is released from or has escaped detention'. The Victims of Crime Act 2017 imposes an obligation on the Irish Prison Service (IPS) to provide information about an offender upon the request of a victim (section 8(2)(m)).

Both the Probation Service and the IPS have demonstrated their cognisance of and commitment to victims' rights. In the *Joint Probation Service and Irish Prison Service Strategic Priorities* 2015–17, upholding the rights, supports and protection of victims' is listed as one of eight strategic priorities. In the Victims Charter, the Probation Service guarantees a number of services to victims, including preparation of a victim impact report when requested by the courts; support for victims if a family conference is taking place for a young offender; and provision of information about various orders which an offender may have received instead of a prison sentence (i.e. probation, community service or supervision by the Probation Service) (Victims of Crime Office, 2010: 34). The IPS similarly commits to providing victims and their families with updates about an offender's time in prison if this is requested. The IPS will provide information about a prisoner's release (either temporary release or release upon sentence completion), as well as other 'relevant developments regarding the prisoner's sentence … such as transfers between prisons or parole board hearings (for prisoners sentenced to eight years or more)' (Victims of Crime Office, 2010: 38). The Parole Board also 'seriously considers' representations from victims in relation to parole decisions for offenders (Parole Board, 2016: 5).

To fulfil its commitments to victims, the Probation Service has a Victim Services Team which responds to victim queries. The *Probation Service Annual Report 2015* noted that the Victim Services Team responded to a range of queries from victims in 2015, including 'requests for clarification regarding the nature of our work with offenders, the meaning and responsibilities attached to particular Court Orders (Probation) or information in relation to support services' (Probation Service, 2016: 22). The IPS launched its Victims Liaison Service (VLS) in 2000 (Burke, 2016). In May 2016, VLS had 294 live cases of prisoners in custody or released on licence in the community under supervision. Forty-nine per cent of those cases involved a prisoner who was serving a life sentence. However, the VLS is available to victims or victims' families regardless of the crime committed (Ibid.). It is important to note that the IPS offers services to victims on an 'opt-in' basis. If victims request information, the VLS will enter into direct contact with them to inform them of any significant development in the management of the perpetrator's sentence as well as any impending release (IPS website). Where people opt in, AdVIC reports that the system works very well (Grozdanova and de Londras, 2014: 12). The Court can also order such notification at the time of sentencing (Ibid.). However, victims and their families may not always be aware that they are entitled to information from the IPS or how to access it (Kilcommins et al., 2010: 228). It has been recommended that the right to information for victims be extended to the work of the Mental Health (Criminal Law) Review Board, which reviews the detention of offenders who have been found not guilty by reason of insanity or who were found to be unfit to stand trial (Ibid.).

Conclusion

This chapter has detailed the services available to victims from complaint (or even a decision not to report) right through to an offender's imprisonment and eventual release. It is evident from the discussion here that the various criminal justice system stakeholders and voluntary organisations have, in recent times, significantly increased their commitment to provide effective support for victims at all stages of the process. What is also apparent, though, is that while service rights are uncontentious at the level of principle and do not encroach upon the formal criminal justice process, there is room for improvement, especially in light of new obligations under the EU Directive on Victims' Rights. There are already efforts to further improve services for victims, with notable developments such as the introduction of Garda Victim Service Offices and the extension of the provision of reasons for decisions by the Office of the DPP. Other changes, such as improvement of the infrastructure of the courts and reform of state-sponsored compensation will involve significant capital investment and will inevitably take more time. Overall, however, Irish criminal justice stakeholders have demonstrated a firm commitment to effective service provision for victims, and recent initiatives would seem to indicate that the momentum to further improve upon these services will continue in the future.

5

Ongoing challenges for victims of crime and the criminal justice sector

The coming years provide an exciting opportunity to improve the experience of victims of crime in Ireland and to give practical effect to the rights of victims in this jurisdiction. The focus of the EU Directive on Victims' Rights is on the availability of high-quality services delivered in a respectful, sensitive, professional and non-discriminatory manner, and it recognises victims of crime as bearers of rights rather than mere 'consumers of criminal justice' (Zedner, 2004: 146). We must take this opportunity to build upon the many positive developments and practices in recent years, while remaining cognisant of the many challenges facing the sector.

Given the variety and extent of the rights afforded victims under the EU Directive on Victims' Rights, ensuring effective access to protections and services will pose a significant challenge. This chapter documents a variety of issues which continue to concern victims of crime in Ireland and those working on their behalf. The absence of comprehensive, accurate and reliable data on the experience of victims of crime while engaging with the criminal justice system and support services is raised as a concern, particularly given the potential value of such information in decisions on public policy, infrastructure and funding. The challenges facing the state in tackling the problem of under-reporting and attrition in this country are also examined, including the vital importance of acknowledging the existence of victims who do not engage with or disengage from the criminal justice system, and understanding the scale of under-reporting and attrition and the multiplicity of reasons for this. The burden placed on victims and the potential for disillusionment and further trauma through engagement with the system are documented, focusing on the potential to minimise risk through comprehensive training programmes designed to enable front-line workers to provide a sensitive and compassionate service to victims. Innovative policy options adopted in other jurisdictions, including the creation of an Ombudsman for Victims of Crime and measures to unify service provision within the sector, including Witness Care Units, are also explored. It is hoped that the significant developments in the creation of a more just and supportive environment for victims of crime to date can be built upon to transform the experience of crime victims in Ireland.

Transposition of the EU Directive on Victims' Rights

While the EU Directive on Victims' Rights represents a great opportunity for criminal justice systems across Europe to strengthen the rights of victims and their families and to improve their experiences following a crime, positive steps must be taken to transpose the Directive and enshrine these rights in national law.[1] The Irish legislature and courts have taken steps over many years which seek to enhance the status of victims (see Chapter 4 for more detail). However, we await the comprehensive reform necessary to reflect our new obligations under the EU Directive. The Irish government proposes to enshrine many of the rights of victims in this jurisdiction in one key piece of legislation, the Criminal Justice (Victims of Crime) Act. The drafting of a bill along the lines of the General Scheme of the Criminal Justice (Victims of Crime) Bill was approved by government on 14 July 2015 and the Criminal Justice (Victims of Crime) Bill 2016 was published on 29 December 2016.[2] The Act was passed by the Oireachtas in November 2017, significantly later than the required date of transposition of 16 November 2015, with the result that victims of crime did not benefit from the positive measures contained therein for more than two years. It remains to be seen when the Act will come into effect and when victims will be able to assert their rights under the Act in reality. This represents a failure on the part of the state to protect victims and their families and a failure of Ireland's obligations under EU law. However, Ireland was not alone in failing to transpose the directive into national law in a timely manner. At the end of January 2016 the European Commission opened infringement proceedings against sixteen member states for non-communication of the measures taken to fulfil their obligations under the Directive.[3] While some countries had simply failed to communicate details of the steps which they have undertaken, several countries had failed to transpose the Directive outright.[4] Ireland was the final state to notify the Commission of national implementing measures.[5] Ireland's failure to implement the Directive in a timely manner, despite broad political support and the 'lucrative political appeal of the crime victim' (Doak, 2015: 139), is regrettable. It leaves the state open to significant fines and, more importantly, signifies a lack of urgency and concern for victims of crime in Ireland today.

Further concerns persist as to whether the state's planned implementation measures will in fact fully comply with Ireland's obligations under the Directive. As discussed in Chapter 4, several bills have been published, including the Domestic Violence Bill 2017 and the Criminal Law (Sexual Offences) Act 2017, which supplement existing legislation and fulfil some of the obligations under the Directive. However, the primary piece of legislation in this regard is the Criminal Justice (Victims of Crime) Act 2017, the long title of which identifies it as 'an act to give effect to provisions of Directive 2012/29/EU ... establishing minimum standards on the rights, support and protection of victims of crime'. This Act therefore purports to fulfil Ireland's obligations under the Directive, yet it focuses exclusively on the right to information (Part 2) and the protection of victims during investigations and criminal proceedings (Part 3), limiting its reach to victims who engage with An Garda Síochána or the Garda Síochána Ombudsman Commission.

Under the Directive, victims have the right to receive information from the point of first contact with a competent authority (Article 4). However, under the Act, victims have a right to information when they contact or are first contacted by the Garda Síochána or the Garda Síochána Ombudsman Commission in relation to an alleged offence, making their right to information contingent on contact with one of these two organisations.[6] This points to a wider concern with the focus on the Garda Síochána and the Garda Síochána Ombudsman Commission in the Act as the sole authorities receiving and investigating complaints, that is, the competent authorities. This is noteworthy, given range of agencies investigating and prosecuting criminal offences in this jurisdiction and has the potential to exclude victims of certain types of crimes, such as regulatory or environmental crimes, from protection. While it may be more difficult to prove direct harm to an individual person as a result of a crime of this nature, it is not inconceivable, particularly given that both the Directive and the Act define a victim widely, as 'a natural person who has suffered harm, including physical, mental or emotional harm or economic loss' caused directly by an offence.[7]

The narrow focus of the Act is also reflected in the failure to include in legislation wider rights afforded to victims under the Directive such as the right to access victim support services, which under Article 8(5) of the Directive is not dependent on a formal complaint being made to a competent authority. While Section 7(9) of the Act provides that a member of An Garda Síochána or an officer of the Ombudsman Commission may arrange for the victim to be referred to a victim support service with their consent, the obligation is limited to these organisations. This is not reflective of Article 8 of the Directive, under which the obligation to facilitate referrals of victims to victim support services applies to both competent authorities and 'other relevant entities', which include 'public agencies or entities, such as hospitals, schools, embassies, consulates, welfare or employment services, who are in contact with victims and identify the need for the victim to seek the specialised services of a VSO [victim support organisation]'.[8]

It is unfortunate that wider rights given under the Directive are not accommodated within the Act, for example, the right to access support services mentioned above or the broad rights to information, advice, support, referral, emotional and psychological support, where available, under Article 9 of the Directive. While accompanying policies may be announced, it is important to remember that a scheme of this nature may not fulfil Ireland's obligations under the Directive. While states have freedom as to the manner of implementation of the Directive, this

> does not however release it from the obligation to give effect to the provisions of the Directive by means of national provisions of a binding nature ... Mere administrative practices, which by their very nature may be altered at the whim of administration, may not be considered as constituting the proper fulfilment of the obligation deriving from the Directive.[9]

Individuals must be in a position to clearly recognise their rights and obligations under EU law.[10] It is therefore clear that while the Criminal Justice (Victims of Crime) Act 2017 is an important piece of legislation in the advancement of victims' rights in this jurisdiction, it has significant shortcomings which will need to be addressed if Ireland is to fulfil its obligations under each article of the Directive.

Resources

It is vital that the victims of crime and their families have access to justice, adequate information and services in practice, not just in theory, a fact emphasised by the European Court of Human Rights in *Al-Skeini and Others v The United Kingdom* in 2011; 'the object and purpose of the Convention as an instrument for the protection of individual human beings requires that its provisions be interpreted and applied so as to make its safeguards practical and effective'.[11] The difficulties for victims and support services in Ireland, both statutory and non-statutory, resulting from inadequate resourcing have long been recognised (Bacik et al., 2007; Cooper, 2008; Duffy, 2008; Grozdanova and de Londras, 2014; Mulkerrins, 2003). Many services within the sector have been hit by reductions in funding since the onset of recession in Ireland in 2006/2007 and it is important the state should protect funding to existing services. However, continuing to fund existing services will not be sufficient; it will also be necessary to identify new streams of funding to fulfil new obligations arising from the Directive. In order to ensure that the rights of victims enshrined in the Directive move from theory to reality, the state must allocate significant resources in both the short and long term (FRA, 2014a: 12; O'Malley-Dunlop, 2015). This will include investment in personnel to provide services, for example, court accompaniment and individualised assessment of needs. The requirement under Article 8 of the EU Directive on Victims' Rights that free support services must be provided 'before, during and for an appropriate time after criminal proceedings', irrespective of whether a victim has made a formal complaint to the Gardaí, is likely to significantly increase the demands on such services, and there will be associated funding demands. Funding for training of police officers, court staff, judges and prosecutors is also vital if the experience of victims of crime when they engage with the criminal justice system is to be improved. Capital investment will also be required in the coming years to provide further equipment for video-links and recording and separate waiting areas.

Worryingly, in the Regulatory Impact Analysis of the General Scheme of the Victims of Crime Bill, which aims to transpose the Directive,[12] the state indicates that it was not possible 'to estimate the likely cost of implementation of the procedures in the proposed Bill but it is likely that it can be met from within existing resources'.[13] It is very difficult to imagine the implementation of the Act on a cost-neutral basis. Despite this rhetoric, some increase in funding to the sector has been announced. A 21% increase in funding to the Victims of Crime Office was announced in October 2015 to support victim support services and to supplement the establishment of Garda Victim Liaison Offices throughout the country.[14] This brings the total budget to almost €1.5 million in 2016. The Tánaiste and Minister for Justice stated that:

> This increased funding will assist community and voluntary organisations in meeting the additional demands for support services, such as the provision of information on the rights of victims and court accompaniment, arising from both the implementation of the provisions of the EU Victims' Directive and the landmark new Victims' Rights Bill which I am introducing.[15]

An increase in funding to COSC (the National Office for the Prevention of Domestic, Sexual and Gender-based Violence, from €1.9 million to €2.4 million was also announced.[16] While on a percentage basis these amounts may seem significant, in total the investment is less than €800,000. The Victims' Rights Alliance raised concerns about the adequacy of this funding to provide the additional supports required and to vindicate the rights of victims under the Directive.[17] As COSC funds circa forty organisations and the Victims of Crime Office supports fifty victim support organisations, approximately €12,500 extra will be available per organisation funded by COSC, and €6,000 extra per organisation funded by the Victims of Crime Office.[18] A further €250,000 in funding for the Victims of Crime Office was announced for 2017.[19] Given the significant under-resourcing of the sector to date, it is questionable whether these rather small increases in funding will be sufficient to meet increased demands under the Directive and to ensure adequate and effective access to services.[20] As noted by Williams, the danger with the creation of new rights without adequate support or funding from central government is that victims are led to expect a certain standard of service which stakeholders are not in a position to deliver (Williams, 1999: 391). More problematically, frustration is directed at individual services and criminal justice agencies and attention is distracted 'from the possibility that there might be structural problems underlying crime and criminal victimisation' (Ibid.: 394). If victims are to be given rights and develop expectations, it is incumbent upon central government to adequately resource the agencies and services which are required to deliver upon these expectations.

Reliance on volunteers

One consequence of the limited funding available to support services is the relative importance of volunteers, and concerns have been raised about a potential over-reliance on volunteers within the sector and the sustainability of services staffed solely by volunteers.[21] Many victim support services in the country are provided solely by volunteers, for example AdVIC, SAH (Support after Homicide), IRVA (Irish Road Victims Association).[22] Research conducted by the Victims of Crime Office found that 9% of the total spending of funded organisations related to costs associated with volunteers (Victims of Crime Office, 2015: 10). While volunteers play an important role in the provision of support services to victims, are cost effective, motivated and have an ability to engage with victims, there are disadvantages associated with over-reliance on volunteers within the sector (FRA, 2014a: 14). Given a lack of training, qualifications and experience, there is a danger that volunteers may provide a more limited and less professional service for victims. The financial implications of volunteering may lead to high staff turnover and high-quality staff not being available to work (FRA, 2014a: 14). In light of these factors, the European Union Agency for Fundamental Rights (FRA)has stressed the importance of an appropriate balance between the number of volunteers and the number of professional staff:

> [i]n particular, organisations relying on volunteers should make sure that permanent staff offer effective guidance to volunteers and supervise the quality of their work. Tasks performed by professionals or volunteers of victim support organisations must be in line with quality standards and appropriate to the professional background of the person providing the support or advice. (FRA, 2014a: 14)

Given the increase in demand for services amid economic constraints, it will be important to ensure an appropriate balance between professional and volunteer staff within the sector in Ireland and that those volunteers who are in place are properly trained, supervised and quality assured.

Distribution

Another concern facing victims in Ireland is disparity in the distribution of resources for service provision throughout the country. Supports to victims are currently ad hoc and piecemeal, with the nature and quality of the supports available dependent on geographic location and the individual or organisation providing services to the victim (Hanly et al., 2009: 13; Spain, Gibbons and Kilcommins, 2014: 27). For example, it has been suggested in the Rape and Justice in Ireland Report that 'it is quite possible that the very low rate of rape reports in the far west of Ireland may be due, in part, to a complete lack of SATU services in this area at the time of the study' (Hanly et al., 2009: 12). This impacts on the victim in a number of ways, reducing the quality of service provided to victims (if any), increasing the potential for trauma and increasing rates of under-reporting and attrition. It is necessary to rectify the disparity in the distribution of resources for service provision throughout the country to ensure equal access to a high standard of care for victims. A nationally co-ordinated approach to the funding, 'planning, delivery and ongoing evaluation of support services for victims' (Hanly et al., 2009: 14) will be important in this regard.

Research

Quality assurance

Recital 63 of the EU Directive on Victims' Rights states that 'it is essential that reliable support services are available to victims and that competent authorities are prepared to respond to victims' reports in a respectful, sensitive, professional and non-discriminatory manner'. As part of this process, the state and service providers must ensure not just the existence, but the adequacy of such services. Accordingly, if the experience of victims is to improve in a real and meaningful way, quality assurance processes must be put in place to evaluate the standard of service being provided to victims and to record their experiences of those services. The absence of a formal process to monitor the quality of services provided to victims of crime by An Garda Síochána was noted in the *Report of the Garda Inspectorate on Crime Investigation* (Garda Inspectorate, 2014: 20) and the Inspectorate recommended the implementation of a system of quality assurance on victim contact, including a quality call-back system 'which monitors the quality of the service provided to victims of crime to ensure that the good work of Gardaí is acknowledged as well as dealing with those who consistently provide a poor service' (Garda Inspectorate, 2014: Part 7: 15). In a report on Victims of Crime in the EU, the European Union Agency for Fundamental Rights (FRA) suggested that:

> clear and consistent quality control mechanisms should be established ... [it is the] responsibility of EU Member States ... to monitor support services' performance, ensuring that they conform to designated standards while also respecting the independence of civil society. (FRA, 2014a: 14)

The adoption of a system of quality control for victim support services, including key performance indicators and benchmarks, would enable transparent assessment of services over time and across jurisdictions and ensure access to rights in practice. This is particularly important given Ireland's obligations under Article 28, which requires member states to provide the European Commission with available data on how victims have accessed the rights established in the EU Directive on Victims' Rights. The first communication is required in November 2017 and data must be shared every three years thereafter. This data should be collected in a systematic manner and include assessment in light of key performance indicators and data collected directly from the victim (FRA, 2014a: 16, 92). In furtherance of these aims, the FRA has suggested the adoption of a system of peer review or accreditation of victim support services (FRA, 2014a: 100).[23]

Accuracy of data

The requirement to share data with the European Commission on how victims have accessed their rights under the Directive (Article 28; Recital 64) makes clear that this should at a minimum include 'the number and type of the reported crimes and, as far as such data are known and are available, the number and age and gender of the victims'. Given well-documented difficulties with official crime statistics in Ireland, steps must be taken to ensure that they are investigated to ascertain their accuracy and completeness. For example, the *Report of the Garda Síochána Inspectorate: Crime Investigation* published in 2014 raised serious concerns with the recording of crimes on the Garda PULSE system, which is the source from which official crime statistics are calculated. The Inspectorate found that the average conversion rate from the call for service to the creation of a PULSE incident number (i.e. the unique computer-generated number which is allocated to an incident on the Garda computer system) was 63%, which was categorised as low (Garda Inspectorate, 2014.: 26). The Inspectorate 'learned of an unacceptable practice where individual gardaí were deciding not to record a crime' (Ibid.: 29). Examples of situations where this might occur included assault cases where the Gardaí might give the victim some time to consider whether they will report or not (particularly where alcohol is involved). There was also evidence that some Gardaí did not record incidents involving tourist victims, as it was felt that these victims would not follow up on the report. Domestic violence cases were particularly problematic, as some Gardaí did not record the offence where the victim was not willing to proceed with a formal complaint (Ibid.: 29).

The concerns raised about the recording of crime in Ireland prompted a review of PULSE data by the CSO (CSO, 2015; CSO, 2016). Two such reviews have been undertaken to date, and while the impact of inaccurate data on recorded crime in 2015 was significantly less than for 2011, ongoing difficulties with the data being provided for the purposes of calculating official crime statistics were highlighted. It was found that circa 17% of crime reported to An Garda Síochána in 2015 was not recorded on the PULSE system (CSO, 2016: 4). Further analysis demonstrated that 3% of incidents included in a non-crime category on PULSE (Attention and Complaints) should have been classified as a crime (CSO, 2016: 4). Additionally, it was found that there was no justification provided in the narrative in PULSE for downgrading the seriousness of a crime in 33% of all cases downgraded in 2015 (CSO, 2016: 5). Similarly, '21% of invalidated crimes lacked sufficient explanation as to why they were classified as such' (CSO, 2016: 5). It was found that removing crimes incorrectly given the status of detected, but without a charge or summons sheet attached, would reduce the number of crimes detected by 10% (CSO, 2016: 5). It is important that the CSO continues to work with An Garda Síochána to improve the reliability of the data and to review the quality of data provided at regular intervals, as planned.

Depth of understanding of the experience of victims

It is important that we have a holistic understanding of the experience of victims, including those who do not report to official authorities, and an over-reliance on official crime statistics should therefore be avoided. Victims' surveys are an extremely important tool from which to assess the true state of crime within Ireland, and as an alternative crime measurement technique (Hall, 2010: 16). Victims' surveys give victims an opportunity to tell their story in a more complete manner, providing detail which may not be gathered in the course of an investigation or report to formal authorities such as the Gardaí, and allowing space to record not just the occurrence of a crime but its impact on the victim (Davies et al, 2004; Davies et al., 2007). They also provide detail on the experience of victims which is not otherwise available because they have not reported their experiences to formal authorities (see below for full discussion on under-reporting of crime). For example, the Rape Crisis Network of Ireland (RCNI) stresses that the experience of the 64% of its clients who did not report to any formal authority would be lost in the absence of victims' surveys and that this 'is an essential part of the story. It is the only place where these survivors have their experiences documented publicly to support and influence national policy' (RCNI, 2014: 23). The collection of such data ensures that policy is not based exclusively on the experience of the cohort of victims who report to a formal authority and 'allows us to ask if there are patterns ... that make it more or less probable that the crime will be formally reported' (RCNI, 2014: 23). The Crime and Victimisation surveys conducted by the CSO are an important source of information in this regard in Ireland and should be facilitated and funded in the coming years.

While state-wide generic research conducted by bodies such as the CSO is vital, it is also important that NGOs, particularly those receiving state funding, continue to undertake research which elucidates the experience of victims of crime using their service and to hear the voice of service users while quality assuring their services. It has been suggested that 'all NGOs operating in the criminal justice area produce and publish high quality statistics relating to their operations ... NGOs should be required, at a minimum, to co-operate with all legitimate research projects to the maximum extent consistent with their resources and requirements.' (Hanly et al., 2009: 14). Data might also be collected from the broader criminal justice sector, including prosecuting authorities and the courts, and from health care and social welfare professionals (FRA, 2014a: 92). An example of good practice in this regard is a large-scale research project (n=7,723) into victims' and witnesses' experiences of the criminal justice system commissioned by the Crown Prosecution Service (CPS) in England and Wales (Crown Prosecution Service, 2015).

The adoption of strong quality-control standards and the collection of high-quality and comprehensive data will be very important in the coming years in ensuring that victims' needs are being met. Thorough interrogation of official statistics provided by criminal justice agencies is important, as are victim surveys which provide a useful counterpoint to official statistics.

Under-reporting of crime

The failure of victims to report crime is a significant, ongoing problem in Ireland. The consequences of non-reporting are varied and noteworthy and impact on both the individual victim and society. First, as already documented, a failure to report to the Gardaí will result in the crime being excluded from official crime statistics. The crime will not be investigated and the offender will not be held to account. Second, and importantly, victims may not have access to information on their rights and the support services they may need (FRA, 2014b: 61; Hanly et al., 2009).

While rates of reporting vary across crime categories, across jurisdictions and over time, studies consistently show that many victims of crime fail to report their experiences to formal authorities. In the EU a number of large-scale studies conducted by the FRA on the victimisation of minority and immigrant groups (FRA, 2009), LGBT persons (FRA, 2013a), Jewish persons (FRA, 2013b) and female victims of violence (FRA, 2014b), consistently identify under-reporting of crime as an issue of concern (FRA, 2014a: 11). For example, more than half of victims of anti-Semitic crime (harassment, vandalism, physical violence or threats) in the preceding five years did not report the crime (FRA, 2013b: 48). Just 22 % of LGBT persons reported the most serious incidents of violence (FRA, 2013a: 24). The FRA *Report on Violence Against Women* in the EU found that the most serious incidents of partner violence came to the attention of authorities in just 20% of cases; where the violence was inflicted by a non-partner only 19% of cases were reported (FRA, 2014b: 61).

Studies undertaken in Ireland since the late 1980s point to under-reporting as a significant issue. For example, a study in Dublin in the early 1990s noted that 19% of those surveyed did not report the crime (O'Connell and Whelan; 1994: 85). In a follow-up study a few years later, the figure was reported at 20% (Kirwan and O'Connell, 2001: 10). The Quarterly National Household Survey also provides interesting information on the rate of under-reporting. In a survey published in 2016 26,000 households were asked about experiences of crime in the previous 12 months among those over 18 years of age. It was found that 42% of violent thefts (36% in 2010, 39% in 2006, 41% in 2003), 42% of assaults (45% in 2010, 47% in 2006, 49% in 2003), and 50% of acts of vandalism (45% in 2010, 57% in 2006 and 61% in 2003) were not reported (CSO, 2003; CSO, 2006; CSO, 2011; CSO, 2016). Twenty-seven per cent of burglaries were not reported, an increase of 2% on the non-reporting figures recorded in the 2010 Quarterly National Household Survey (CSO, 2011; CSO, 2016). Interestingly, reporting trends as recorded in the Quarterly National Household Survey have fluctuated quite considerably. In six of eight categories of crime reporting, rates decreased between 1998 and 2003 (CSO, 2006: 3). In 2006 there were modestly increased rates of reporting in five of the eight categories (CSO, 2006: 3), and the downward trend was replicated in 2010 and 2015 (CSO, 2011; CSO, 2016). High levels of under-reporting were also identified in the most recent *An Garda Síochána Public Attitudes Survey*, with 26% of those who disclosed victimisation not reporting the incident (An Garda Síochána, 2015: 9).

The SAVI Report into sexual abuse and violence in Ireland, which involved a study of 3,120 participants in 2002, noted that disclosure rates to the Gardaí were very low (McGee et al., 2002: 128–32). Only 1% of men and 8% of women had reported their experiences of adult sexual assault to the Gardaí (6% overall) (McGee et al., 2002: 128). Only 8% of adults had reported previous experiences of child sexual abuse to the Gardaí (McGee et al., 2002: 128). While positive trends are evident among victims of this category of crime, reporting levels remain strikingly low. Statistics published by the RCNI demonstrate that an increasing number of users of its service are reporting the crime committed against them to police, with 18% reporting in 2007 and 27% reporting in 2009 (Hanly et al., 2009: 11). The number of victims of sexual violence reporting to police in 2014 had risen to 33% (RCNI, 2014: 23). Interestingly, 3% reported exclusively to another formal authority including the Redress Board, Health Services Executive, church or education authorities and representatives processing asylum applications (RCNI, 2014: 23).

In Ireland too there are high levels of under-reporting of violence against women. Women reported the most serious incident of partner violence perpetrated against them in just 28% of cases, while violence inflicted by a non-partner was reported in just 24% of cases (FRA, 2014b: 61). While this was above the EU averages of 20% and 19%, respectively, noted above; such high levels of under-reporting are of great concern and must be tackled if all victims of crime are to be supported.

It is important to note that these statistics represent the population as a whole and fail to capture the different levels of reporting across different sectors of the community. The issue of under-reporting among particularly vulnerable groups will be discussed later in this chapter. However, the findings of a study of 2,752 students on their experience of crime are instructive, particularly as this group is not traditionally considered to be vulnerable. The study explored experiences of harassment, stalking, violence and sexual assault and indicated great variation in reporting rates across different categories of crime, with 10% of students reporting physical violence to the Gardaí, 6% reporting obsessive behaviour and just 3% reporting unwanted sexual experiences (USI, 2013: 7).

Reasons for not reporting

It is very important that measures are taken to encourage victims to report crimes to the relevant authorities, and in this context effort must be made to understand and to tackle the varied and complex reasons for non-reporting. Some victims, for example, do not wish to involve policing authorities as they do not think that the incident is a crime. Others do not deem the incident sufficiently serious to report it and/or prefer to handle it themselves (CSO, 2006: 3; CSO, 2016: 4, 6; Garda Síochána Public Attitudes Survey, 2015: 9; FRA, 2014a: 64; McGee et al., 2002: 129; USI, 2013: 6, 26). In an Irish context, victims have reported lack of time as a consideration in failing to report a crime (CSO, 2011: 11; CSO, 2016: 4, 6). Other victims have reported that a fear of reprisals inhibits them from reporting to police (FRA, 2014a: 64; CSO, 2006: 3; CSO, 2016: 4, 6; USI, 2013: 7). Victims may not know where or how to report (USI, 2013: 6, 26) or may report to another authority (CSO, 2011: 6; FRA, 2014a: 64).

The relationship between police authorities and victims may also be a factor influencing reporting rates. For example, victims may fear that they would not be believed, should they report, or fear feeling uncomfortable talking to Gardaí (USI, 2013). In an EU study on anti-Semitism, 20% indicated that they did not trust the police (FRA, 2013b: 48). Other victims have cited a lack of confidence in the ability of policing authorities to do anything as a reason for failing to report (CSO, 2016: 4, 6; FRA, 2012; 14; Garda Síochána Public Attitudes Survey, 2015: 9; McGee et al., 2002: 131). Worryingly, some victims also report 'the perception that they could not deal with the difficult demands of pursuing a case' as the most common reason for not reporting to Gardaí (Hanly et al., 2009: 12).

Victims may not report these incidents because they were ashamed or embarrassed or feared being blamed (FRA, 2014a: 64; McGee et al., 2002: 131). The desire to keep the incident private is often cited as a reason for failing to report certain types of crime. For example, 21% of victims of sexual violence at the hands of a partner did not report the most serious incident because of a desire to keep the incident private, as compared with 11% of victims of physical violence (FRA, 2014a: 64; USI, 2013: 7). In some limited circumstances victims may not wish the offender to be arrested. For victims of intimate partner violence, very particular concerns apply and victims have reported concerns about losing custody of children or the ending of a relationship as reasons for not reporting to police (FRA, 2014a: 64).

Given the complex and varied nature of reasons why victims fail to report a crime, it will not be possible, or necessarily desirable, to reach 100% reporting rates in the near future. However, a multi-pronged approach to improving reporting rates must be taken in Ireland. This may involve addressing the feelings of shame and embarrassment associated with being a victim of crime in some circumstances, increasing the confidence of victims in the ability of investigating authorities to respond to the crime and ensuring that all crimes are taken seriously and victims are dealt with compassionately by police (FRA, 2014a).

Attrition rates

In addition to significant numbers of crimes going unreported, the rate of attrition in criminal cases has long been documented as a serious concern in the Irish criminal justice sector (Bartlett and Mears, 2011; Hamilton, 2011; Hanly et al., 2009; Leahy, 2014; Leane et al., 2001; O'Mahony et al., 2009). The reasons for attrition are complex and multi-faceted. Victims may withdraw their statements: following a poor reaction from police (Hanly et al., 2009: 7; Hohl and Stanko, 2015: 337); at the encouragement of family, friends and Gardaí (Hanly et al., 2009: 7); through fear of retaliation (IPA, 2011); or as a result of the trial process (Hanly et al., 2009: 9; Lovett and Kelly, 2009). Decisions by the DPP not to prosecute, often on evidentiary grounds, also contribute to attrition rates (Hanly et al., 2009: 8; Lovett and Kelly, 2009: 77). In a study of rape cases published in 2009, it was found that under one third of prosecutable cases were prosecuted in Ireland, resulting in a conviction or guilty plea in respect of at least one charge in almost 60% of cases (Hanly et al., 2009: 8). Difficulties with the trial process itself, including multiple adjournments and delay, personal cross-examination of the victim by the defendant, the release of counselling notes and the potential for intimidation of victims and witnesses have also led to confusion, an erosion of confidence and attrition (Bryan O'Sullivan, 2015; Counihan, 2013; Fisher, 2011; IPA, 2011: 17; Leahy, 2008; Leahy, 2014; Lovett and Kelly, 2009).

Given the complexities, it is difficult to rectify all of these issues within a short time frame. Longer-term options put forward include trial preparation programmes (Leane et al., 2001), prohibition of cross-examination by the defendant (Bryan O'Sullivan, 2015), victim information packs (Leane et al., 2001) and public awareness campaigns (Leane et al., 2001). Mechanisms to maximise victim safety, including the use of specialised domestic violence courts and/or fast-track systems, have also been suggested (Women's Aid, 2010). Such courts are staffed by specially trained staff and are designed to increase victims' confidence and feelings of safety and to decrease rates of attrition (Bowen et al., 2014; Cook et al., 2004). Reviews of the operation of twenty-three such domestic violence courts in England and Wales show moderately increased rates of conviction (66%, as compared with CPS Area average of 64%) (Home Office et al., 2008). It is hoped that the initiatives currently underway, such as training for individuals with whom victims come into contact (discussed below) and the 'What would you do?' campaign on domestic violence announced by the Tánaiste and Minister for Justice in November 2016,[24] will increase awareness of the problem among family and friends and reduce attrition rates. However, given the limited effectiveness of ad hoc attempts to reduce attrition in other jurisdictions (Brown, 2011; Cook, 2011), it is suggested that a much more comprehensive, evidence-based approach is required to tackle the multiple causes of attrition in Ireland.

Traumatisation of victims

Victims of crime, particularly victims of serious crime, are often traumatised by their experience (Doak, 2015; Herman, 2003; Kilpatrick and Acierno, 2003), experiencing feelings of helplessness, a disrupted sense of control, terror and catastrophe (Herman, 1992). The impact of trauma is broad, deep and life shaping (Fallot, 2011). It has an effect on mental and physical health (Newmann and Sallman, 2004) and affects 'the way people approach the human service setting, heightening fear and suspiciousness' (Fallot, 2011: 98). The potential for further traumatisation of victims engaging with the criminal justice system and support services is well documented (Coen, 2006; Fallot, 2011; Kelleher et al., 1999; Zedner, 2004). The requirement in Article 1 of the EU Directive on Victims' Rights, that victims be treated with respect and in a 'sensitive, tailored, professional and non-discriminatory manner, in all contacts … in the context of criminal proceedings', hits at the heart of the well-documented problem.

Many victims are frustrated by the general insensitivity of the court process, and the lack of sensitivity among criminal justice agencies and actors remains a central concern (Joyce and Keenan, 2013; Mulkerrins, 2003; Parkinson, 2010; Zedner, 2004). Research conducted by COSC in 2014 highlighted concerns about a lack of empathy and understanding of the impact of crime on victims when they access front-line services. Adapt House Limerick note that '[i]t is the experience of women survivors that frontline staff often do not have the understanding of domestic abuse nor the sensitivity to the traumatic impact of abuse on the victim' (Spain et al., 2014: 14). As police are the first point of contact for many victims, it is vitally important that victims have a positive experience when in contact with them (Zedner, 2004: 144). Victim support groups have reported that '[w]omen accessing our member services consistently report that they are not taken seriously when they come into contact with the legal system. They are often not believed, their cases are often trivialised …' (Spain et al., 2014: 14). This is reflected in the Guerin Report, which highlighted a lack of empathy in dealings between An Garda Síochana and victims and recommended that An Garda Síochana review all guidance given to Gardaí on dealing with victims, including ensuring that the process was not intimidating (Garda Inspectorate, 2014; 335–6). In an earlier study by Kilcommins et al., circa 70% of respondents indicated satisfaction with Garda sensitivity during the statement-taking process; however, the authors emphasised the importance of Gardaí remaining 'constantly vigilant about their potential to cause secondary victimisation during the statement-taking process through invasive questioning, victim-blaming attitudes (especially in relation to hate crimes, sexual offences and domestic violence), and general insensitivity to the needs of victims' (Kilcommins et al., 2010: 176).

Improvements in the front-line experience of victims has been noted from 2014 onwards, where pockets of good practice now exist, due in part to increased awareness among service providers including the Gardaí, staff of the court service, probation officers and health professionals (Spain et al., 2014: 14). A number of initiatives by An Garda Síochána, such as the development of a Garda Strategic Transformation Office to co-ordinate and implement recommendations for change, including in relation to improving customer care (Garda Inspectorate, 2015), and the establishment of Garda Victim Service Offices, should go some way towards ameliorating the concerns raised by vicitms. Pre-trial meetings between victims of violence or sexual offences and the prosecution legal team are another example of an initiative which can reduce stress for victims (Grozdanova and de Londras, 2014: 11; ICCL, 2008: 18). However, it is clear that this is not something which can be achieved overnight and it will be necessary to strive for continued improvement in the service provided by An Garda Síochána and others to victims. In this respect, it is important to note that victims interact with a variety of different organisations and support services, including health care services, police, social services, victim support groups, legal professionals and faith-based organisations (FRA, 2014a). The standard of service and sensitivity varies greatly across the sector and awareness and training on minimising revictimisation of victims must be directed across the board (Hanly, Healy and Scrivner, 2009, Strand 1: 162; FRA, 2014a).

Efforts must focus on ensuring that victims do not suffer further traumatisation when they engage with the criminal justice system and support services, and different models of intervention to protect victims should be reviewed. One method may be to apply a 'trauma lens' in the provision of services and to recognise the emotional impact of crime on victims. The traditional approach to trauma and the resulting emotional experience has been to ignore, minimise or medicalise the experience. When trauma has been acknowledged, focus has been placed on PTSD (post-traumatic stress disorder) and the victim's need for 'treatment', implying passivity and deficiency. Victims who do not fit the criteria receive little or no recognition of the emotional impact and trauma associated with their experience. Fallot and Harris (2008a; 2008b) have developed a model of trauma-informed care based on the core values of safety, including physical and emotional safely, trustworthiness, choice, collaboration and empowerment:

> Basic shifts in both understanding and practice are fundamental ... Rather than asking, implicitly or explicitly, 'What is wrong with you?' or 'What is your problem?' we ask 'What have you been through?' and 'How have you tried to cope with it?' This basic change in orientation affects the organization's view ... Collaborative decision making and planning pervade trauma-informed cultures; not only are consumers' opinions frequently sought and incorporated into individual service planning and organizational strategies, but also staff perspectives become central to administrators' thinking ... (Fallot, 2011: 100)

The focus on empowering victims reflects evidence that victims who feel control over their decisions are likely to have a reduced level of PTSD symptoms, as compared to those who lack control over decision making (Hanly et al., 2009: 13, Strand 1 191).

One special (although controversial) category of victims is worthy of consideration in this context: prisoners. It is recognised that those engage with the criminal justice system as perpetrators are more likely than the general population to have experienced victimisation and trauma (Broskey and Lally, 2004). For example, high levels of victimisation and trauma were found in a 2013 study on women ex-prisoners in Ireland, with 75% of the women involved in the study having experienced violence or abuse (McHugh, 2013). Research also suggests that prisoners are subject to frequent and routine victimisation within the prison setting (O'Donnell and Edgar, 1996). This fact must be considered by criminal justice agencies and the risk of and potential for retraumatisation of victims who engage with the criminal justice system must be highlighted and should be averted where possible.

Concerns have also been raised about the impact of delay, the crowded nature of the proceedings and the shortcomings of physical facilities, and the potential for these to result in further traumatisation of victims (Bacik et al., 2007; Garda Inspectorate, 2014; Garda Inspectorate, 2015; Kilcommins et al., 2010; O'Higgins,

2016). The *Report of the Garda Inspectorate on Crime Investigation* found that the physical environment of the public offices in Garda stations 'varied greatly from station to station' (Garda Inspectorate, 2014: 20), with lack privacy being a particular problem; '[s]ome stations did not have a suitable room available for a person who wished to discuss a matter in a private setting' (Ibid.). Although efforts are made by the Courts Service to provide special waiting rooms to protect victims during the trial, the architecture of many Irish court buildings means that this is not always possible. The experience of victims in a study by Kilcommins et al. (2010) suggests that the architecture and design of court facilities is not 'fit for purpose'. Only 27% of respondents (38) reported having access to a separate waiting facility (Ibid.: 127). As Mulkerrins notes, '[e]vidence of low-grade intimidation abounds where complainants have to share waiting/cloakroom facilities with the defendant and his family while awaiting hearings' (Mulkerrins, 2003: 127). The adequacy of reserved seating or space provided for victims and their family/friends in the courtroom must also be examined (Kilcommins et al., 2010: 127). Thus, to protect victims appropriately, investment in appropriate facilities for victims in all courtrooms is necessary.

A variety of protections contained within the EU Directive on Victims' Rights are designed to reduce the risk of further victimisation for victims throughout the trial process, including the right to be accompanied in court by support persons (Article 20) and the right of vulnerable victims to protections when testifying (Article 23) – rights which are available to some extent in Ireland, as discussed in Chapter 4. The structure of courtrooms and the processing of the lists of cases should be reviewed in order to utilise resources to maximum effect. In the case of in camera hearings, which could potentially take place in smaller venues, consideration should be given to using smaller, less intimidating settings. This would also have the effect of freeing up larger venues and would ensure a more effective overall use of courtrooms, and hence reduce delays. Better audibility and seating arrangements for all should be provided, and all courtrooms should in future be designed or upgraded with this in mind. The option of a separate waiting room for victims should be provided in all cases, but its utilisation should remain a matter for the victim's choice. Support organisations should use the Court Service's bi-annual meetings of regional user panels to highlight the concerns of victims and work towards practical ways of improving the situation. Good-practice solutions arising from this process in one region should be copied in other regions.

Training

While it is necessary to introduce a variety of measures to reduce the potential for further traumatisation of victims, including the provision of appropriate facilities, a reduction in delays and the inclusion of the victim as much as possible in the criminal justice process, arguably, the primary means by which the potential for further traumatisation of victims can be reduced is through the education of stakeholders with whom the victim comes into contact. Training is also vital to ensure that the suite of rights afforded to victims of crime under the EU Directive will be realised. Training must be a priority to ensure that victims of crime receive accurate, comprehensive information on their rights and that their rights are realised through the provision of the best possible service. The necessity for training staff who engage with victims of crime in Ireland has long been recognised (Kilcommins et al., 2013). The UN Declaration provides that '[p]olice, justice, health, social service and other personnel concerned should receive training to sensitize them to the needs of victims, and guidelines to ensure proper and prompt aid' (Principle 16). However, the urgency to provide comprehensive training has increased, given Ireland's obligations under the EU Directive, including the need to provide appropriate information, support and protection (Article 1) and 'emotional and, where available, psychological support' (Article 9), for example. Article 25 specifically requests both general and specific training for police officers, court staff, judges, prosecutors, lawyers, victim support and restorative justice organisations. The Directive recognises the range of roles and varying degrees of contact between victims and practitioners and that the type of training required varies depending on the duties and nature and level of contact. Ultimately, the 'training shall aim to enable the practitioner to recognise victims and to treat them in a respectful, professional and non-discriminatory manner' (Article 25).

There may be a tendency to focus on basic service rights in training, such as the right to information (under Article 4 and 6) or the right to written acknowledgement of a formal complaint (under Article 5), as lawyers, police officers and other criminal justice workers are likely to be more comfortable with such rights and their ability to deliver on them. However, the focus on the victim's experience in a broader sense in the Directive will require training front-line professionals on how best to engage with victims sensitively and with compassion. Many of those working within the criminal justice system may possess an ability to communicate respectfully and with sensitivity; however, it is clear that many front-line workers will require help in the acquisition of such skills (Kilcommins et al., 2010: 177). The FRA has highlighted that 'to be effective, training needs to cover both the need for a sensitive approach to victims, especially regarding particularly vulnerable groups such as child victims, and specialised knowledge, again with an emphasis on certain groups of victims' (FRA, 2014a: 51). Training should therefore aim to do more than inform service providers of their obligations; rather, it should provide them with the support they need to provide victims with the sensitive approach mandated under the Directive.

It is therefore recommended that all agencies and organisations with responsibility for providing services to victims of crime should implement a training needs assessment and provide training in a systematic and comprehensive fashion. As a key front-line service provider, An Garda Síochána is a vital stakeholder, yet, as noted above, significant shortcomings have been identified in relation to the level of service provided to victims (Garda Inspectorate, 2014: 7.11; Kilcommins et al., 2010: 55). While training has been provided to Gardaí on an ad hoc basis in the past, this has been neither systematic nor comprehensive. The Garda Inspectorate recommended that clear guidance and, where necessary, training be provided to all Gardaí and supervisors on their roles and responsibilities toward victims of crime, including victims of domestic violence (Garda Inspectorate, 2014: 7.10). This is particularly important, given the concerns which have been raised in the past about the response of the Gardaí to domestic abuse incidents. Although it is stated that the Gardaí have a 'pro-arrest' policy, the Garda Inspectorate noted that arrests are typically made only for breach of a domestic violence order and not for crimes such as assault (Ibid.: 20). Victims who do not have such orders in place cannot rely on this 'pro-arrest' policy and may not receive adequate protection. Moreover, '[d]uring field visits, the Inspectorate found a complete absence of supervision in [domestic violence] cases and an absence of management data on how divisions were performing' (Ibid.: 20).

In addition, it was recommended that specialist officers should be trained to deal with certain categories of particularly vulnerable victims (Ibid.: 7.11) and that victims and support organisations should be utilised as part of a Garda training and awareness programme (Ibid.: Part 6). Positive steps have been taken by An Garda Síochána in this regard, including the inclusion of education on the rights and needs of victims in the foundation training programme. There are also many specially trained officers now in place throughout the country, including Family Liaison Officers, Ethnic Liaison Officers, LGBT Liaison officers and specialist interviewers.[25] Garda Victim Service Offices have also been established throughout the country (see Chapter 4 for full discussion). Despite pockets of good practice, a systematic, compulsory and comprehensive training programme for all Gardaí on the broad range of victims has not yet been implemented. Every member of the force who encounters victims in their everyday working life must be responsive to the needs and rights of victims.

Training cannot focus only on An Garda Síochána, as victims interact with a variety of different organisations and support services, including health care services, police, social services, victim support groups, legal professionals and faith-based organisations (FRA, 2014a). As observed earlier, volunteers make up a significant proportion of those who come into contact with victims of crime, and training of this special cohort and their supervisors must be completed to ensure that victims' rights are realised. There is evidence of other actors within the criminal justice sector engaging in training on an ad hoc basis. For example, a training and information session for front-line staff of the Courts Service who interact with victims was developed in 2015 for delivery in 2016 in conjunction with Victim Support at Court (Courts Service, 2016, p 16). All front-line staff in the Office of the DPP who meet with victims, including state solicitors, receive training on their obligations to victims (Loftus, 2015). As judicial training is not as developed in Ireland as in other jurisdictions, funding for such training is limited. At present, the Judicial Studies Committee in Ireland is limited to providing one-day conferences for judges of the District Court, the Circuit Court and the combined High and Supreme Courts, respectively, as well as an annual one-day 'National Judges Conference' (Association of Judges of Ireland website). Although issues related to victims are discussed in these fora via invited presentations, this is no substitute for targeted judicial training on victims' needs, and judicial education in this area is in need of improvement.

Encouragingly, a number of Irish partners, led by the Irish Council for Civil Liberties, have been successful in obtaining funding from the European Commission to support the training of European lawyers, prosecutors and the judiciary on the rights and needs of victims as provided for by Article 25 (3) of the EU Directive on Victims' Rights. The project draws on project partners in five jurisdictions, including the Bar Council of Ireland, the Law Society of Ireland, the Department of Justice (Hungary), Human Rights Monitoring Institute (HRMI) (Lithuania), APAV (Portugal) and the Peace Institute (Slovenia). A variety of victim support groups, including Victim Support Europe, will also lend their expertise, ensuring that the voice of the victim is at the forefront. This project aims to 'greatly increase victims' access to justice in criminal proceedings by focusing on the training of stakeholders who have a key role to play in implementing the Directive'.[26] A needs assessment will be conducted in each jurisdiction, with input from victims and other stakeholders leading to the development of a training programme and material, for delivery in Ireland first before modification and delivery in the other partner jurisdictions.

Given the great potential for health care professionals to identify and channel cases of violence and to ensure that victims are better served, steps should be taken to maximise their potential (FRA, 2014a). A European-wide study on violence against women showed that doctors and health care providers are most likely to be the first point of contact for victims of domestic violence (FRA, 2014b: 13). Eighty-seven per cent of the 42,000 women surveyed said that they would 'welcome further questions from doctors if they showed signs of abuse' (FRA, 2014b: 13). Health care professionals will also often have a role in dealing with victims of physical and sexual violence and 'initiatives to train and inform healthcare professionals could be considered promising practices' (FRA, 2014b: 13).

Independent oversight

The inclusionary logic being embraced by the criminal justice system has the scope to deliver positive change for victims. Independent oversight of those with responsibility for victims would do much to ensure that change is effected and that victims receive and continue to receive the best possible service. There are a number of government offices in Ireland at present which fulfil some of this role for victims of certain types of crime, including COSC and the Anti-Human Trafficking Unit. More generally, the Victims of Crime Office was established as an executive office in 2008 and promotes a co-ordinated policy response and supports service providers, both state agencies and non-governmental organisations, throughout Ireland. It also has a role in promoting awareness on the needs of victims and advising the Minister for Justice and Equality on relevant issues on victims of crime, including international developments. The Commission for the Support of Victims of Crime is an independent body which operates under the aegis of the Department of Justice and Equality and provides financial assistance to voluntary sector organisations to provide support to victims of crime and works to promote co-operation and co-ordination in service provision and improve the consistency of service provided to victims. The Commission and the Victims of Crime Office have a role 'to assist' in the development of 'strategies and policies to support victims of crime with a view to improving cohesion and consistency of service and information available to victims of crime'. The Commission's stated role includes 'develop[ing] strong links with Government Departments and agencies of the criminal justice system, in the interest of victims of crime'.[27] While these agencies fulfil important roles, they have no role in identifying systemic issues and advocating with government.

It is suggested that the creation of an independent office such as that of the Office of the Federal Ombudsman for Victims of Crime (OFOVC) in Canada should be considered in Ireland. The OFOVC is independent and was set up in 2007 to assist victims on both an individual and collective basis. In addition to promoting access to services, informing victims of services and beneficial laws and referring them to appropriate services, the Ombudsman identifies systemic issues facing victims, promotes the needs and concerns of victims and makes recommendations to government for changes to laws, policies or programmes, to better support victims of crime. The OFOVC sent sixty separate submissions and recommendations to government between 2007 and 2015 on matters such as mental health and justice, sex offender registration, firearms, online crime, protection for seniors, employment protection and leave for victims, offender accountability for debts to victims and the release of offenders.[28]

Another important role fulfilled by the OFOVC relates to complaints from victims. Any victim who is of the view that their rights have been infringed or denied by a federal department, agency or body has the right to file a complaint to the OFOVC. The complaints department handled 1,233 issues in 2014–2015. However, the Office's powers are somewhat limited, as it does not have investigative powers to review complaints. In a public consultation on priorities for the creation of a Canadian Victims Bill of Rights a suggestion to grant the OFOVC investigative powers was ultimately rejected.[29] In the US, the Office of the Victims'

Rights Ombudsman has been established under the auspices of the Department of Justice 'to receive and investigate complaints filed by crime victims against its employees', which may result in disciplinary proceedings against employees.[30]

At present, it not always clear to whom service providers in Ireland, both state and non-governmental, are answerable, if indeed they are answerable to any independent body. For example, possible misconduct by members of An Garda Síochána is investigated by the Garda Síochána Ombudsman Commission,[31] while complaints against the Office of the DPP are dealt with internally.[32] The creation of an independent officer with powers to investigate complaints and to monitor the needs of victims and advocate on their behalf would be a positive development for victims in Ireland and should be considered.

The perfect victim

Another challenge facing the criminal justice system is the continued adherence to an outdated notion of the stereotypical, perfect victim. The ideal victim as described by Nils Christie is one who bears no responsibility for the harm suffered and who is therefore deserving of compassion and justice, while those victims who do not fit the ideal are entitled to neither pity nor protection (Christie, 1986: 17, 19; Minow, 1993: 1413). Culturally and institutionally entrenched stereotypes of the 'ideal victim' (McAlinden, 2014: 185) create an expectation of a victim who is vulnerable (Walklate, 2011) and innocent (McEvoy and McConnachie, 2012: 531–2). Victims of domestic abuse, for example, 'are passive, loyal housewives, acting as loving companions to their abusers. These women must have flawless characters and continually appeal to the police and courts for help, regardless of the futility of their efforts' (Dowd, 1992: 581). Victims of gender violence should be 'helpless, virginal, and completely without fault' (Kelly, 2000: 580), while victims of ' "real child abuse" – [are] young, pure, passive and blameless' (McAlinden, 2014: 185). Such victims are at the top of a hierarchy of victims (Carrabine et al., 2004) that is reflected in official and media discourses:

> At one extreme, those who acquire the status of 'ideal victim' may attract massive media attention, generate collective mourning on a near global scale, and drive significant change to social and criminal justice policy and practice (Greer, 2004; Valier, 2004). At the other extreme, those crime victims who never acquire legitimate victim status or, still worse, are perceived as 'undeserving victims' may receive little, if any, media attention, and pass virtually unnoticed in the wider social world. (Greer, 2007: 22)

The attribution of ideal victim status and the place of the victim within the hierarchy and related levels of media interest are influenced by demographic characteristics such as race, class, gender, as well as notions of 'respectability'

(Greer, 2007: 23–4). In this way entrenched conceptions of those legitimate or ideal victims and those deserving of public support and media attention 'do much to reify dominant white, male, middle-class, heterosexual discourses on crime and control. They reinforce rather than challenge existing structures of power. In so doing, they help to maintain the social, political and economic conditions under which much victimisation takes place' (Davies et al., 2007: 15–16).

However, there is a fundamental dissonance between the constructed and actual identities of victims and offenders (McAlinden, 2014: 182). Acceptance of the binary logic of the 'the worthy sufferers and the unworthy remainder' (McAlinden, 2014: 182; Tilly, 2008: 94), whereby the victim is conceived of as wholly blameless and the defendant necessarily becomes wholly blameworthy, results in the complexity and nuance of the victim/perpetrator relationships being lost. As Srikantiah notes 'victims are not perfectly innocent and perpetrators are not perfectly evil' (Srikantiah, 2007: 196; McAlinden, 2014; McEvoy and McConnachie 2012; Heber, 2014).

In addition to an understanding of the ideal victim, a perception of the ideal crime also exists (Hohl and Stanko, 2015: 328). Leahy has identified myths and stereotypes in relation to the crime of rape in Ireland including, 'the idea that the only "real" rape is the aggravated stranger rape or sexist ideals of "deserving" rape complainants (*i.e.* complainants who have not in any way "asked for" the attack)' (Leahy, 2008). Crimes which do not fit our traditional understanding of a crime are less likely to result in prosecution and conviction. For example, the RAJI study identified that rape perpetrated by a stranger is most likely to be prosecuted, despite being relatively uncommon (Hanly et al., 2009: 6). As Hanly notes, 'reading RAJI one can only conclude that culture, beliefs and attitudes have a significant and negative impact on the pursuit of justice … these attitudes and beliefs were perpetuated and reinforced at every point in the criminal justice system' (Hanly et al., 2009: 6).

Vulnerable groups

Bound by a system which favours the ideal victim as described above, the criminal justice system also poses significant additional challenges for 'atypical' victims, including victims with a physical or intellectual disability, or victims who are socially, economically, culturally or politically marginalised. While many of these victims are high on the hierarchy of ideal victims, due to their inherent vulnerability and blamelessness, they face particular challenges and have particular needs. Kilcommins and Moffiett observe that, to the extent that it accommodates victims of crime, [the criminal justice system] remains epistemically rooted in mainstream accounts of victims' needs and concerns (Kilcommins and Moffitt, 2015: 53).

It is clear from both national and international research that certain groups are at an increased risk of victimisation on the basis of a variety of factors, including gender, race, religion, gender identity, sexual orientation, age, marital status, family status, membership of the Traveller community, or disability. For example, individuals with disabilities are at an increased risk of sexual violence as compared to the general population (Bartlett and Mears, 2011), and disability is the second-highest risk factor for rape, preceded only by gender (Hanly et al., 2009: 10). Homeless persons are also particularly vulnerable to crime (Kilcommins, 2004: 103). While violence may contribute to homelessness, victimisation is often 'a consequence rather than a cause of their homelessness' (Mayock and Sheridan, 2012: 10).[33] Almost one in three Irish women (31% or 470,157) have experienced some form of psychological violence by a partner and 15% of Irish women (227,495) have experienced physical or sexual violence by a partner (FRA, 2014b). Members of the LGBT community in Ireland and ethnic minorities, including members of the Traveller community, are also at risk of crime on the basis of their membership of these communities (Schweppe et al., 2014: 19). Given the ripple effect of crime targeting against an individual on the basis of their membership of a community or group, whereby the reverberations of a crime committed against one member of an identity group are felt throughout the community, it is particularly important to tackle crimes of this nature (Haynes et al., 2015).

Victims who are socially, economically, culturally or politically marginalised may be reluctant to report in an unfriendly climate, as they do 'not expect recognition or sympathy' (FRA, 2014a: 26; Kilcommins, 2004: 103; Kilcommins et al., 2010; Schweppe et al., 2014; Spain et al., 2014). As discussed above, this lack of trust leads to significant under-reporting in these communities. Victims of crime from certain identity groups may also find that their crimes are not prosecuted. For example, prosecution is less likely when a complainant has mental health difficulties, irrespective of the severity of the psychiatric illness (Hanly et al., 2009: 10). While this may relate in part to concerns about the complainant's reliability as a witness, it is 'essential that every individual in the state have equal access to the protection of the law. Where some groups, in particular those with psychiatric illnesses are seen to be excluded from the justice system due to personal attributes or disabilities a violation of human rights may have occurred' (Hanly et al., 2009: 10).

Victims of crime who have a disability pose difficulties for the legal system 'in relation to information gathering and fact finding for an adversarial justice system which for the most part refuses to engage with the ontological dimensions of disability' (Kilcommins et al., 2013; Kilcommins and Moffett, 2015). These victims must fit 'within an adversarial paradigm of justice that emphasises orality, lawyer-led questioning, observation of the demeanour of a witness, the curtailment of free-flowing witness narrative, confrontation and robust cross-examination' (Kilcommins and Moffiett, 2015: 53). Specific improvements in the accommodation of victims, including those with disabilities, have been made in Ireland, reflective of a more inclusionary ethos (Kilcommins et al., 2013; for full discussion see Chapter 4). However, much remains to be done to overcome the very particular challenges faced by members of vulnerable groups when they interact with the criminal justice system, including the increased risk of victimisation. Safeguards to protect and support these victims are envisaged in the EU Directive and will now be discussed.

Supports for vulnerable victims

The protections to be provided to vulnerable victims and the requirement for specific needs assessments under the EU Directive have been outlined in Chapter 4. Under Article 9 member states are obligated 'to encourage victim support services to pay particular attention to the specific needs of victims who have suffered considerable harm due to the severity of the crime' (Article 9 (2)) and to provide targeted support to victims with specific needs, including victims of gender-based or sexual violence and victims in a close relationship with the perpetrator (Article 9(3)). Unfortunately the new Criminal Justice (Victims of Crime) Act 2017 does not incorporate this provision. Victims will now be assessed to identify specific protection needs and the extent to which they would benefit from special protection measures in the course of criminal proceedings (Section 15, Criminal Justice (Victims of Crime) Act 2017). Such assessments will consider the personal traits of the victim and the nature and circumstances of the crime and should prove to be a valuable tool in the protection of individuals who are vulnerable due to their status or the nature of the crime, particularly as

> particular attention shall be paid to victims who have suffered considerable harm due to the severity of the crime; victims who have suffered a crime committed with a bias or discriminatory motive which could, in particular, be related to their personal characteristics; victims whose relationship to and dependence on the offender make them particularly vulnerable. In this regard, victims of terrorism, organised crime, human trafficking, gender-based violence, violence in a close relationship, sexual violence, exploitation or hate crime, and victims with disabilities shall be duly considered. (Article 22 (3))

Child victims shall be presumed to have specific protection needs (Section 15(7)). Importantly, the wishes of the victim, including their desire not to receive special protection measures during criminal proceedings, must be respected. The onus on the state goes beyond the provision of the assessment: the state must also provide specialist services to address those needs. The nature of the support provided will also be important, and it may be provided by a specialist unit within a generic organisation or a specialised support organisation (FRA, 2014a). The FRA has highlighted the need for

> support services, including trauma support and counselling, that provide targeted support for victims with specific needs. These include child victims, victims of sexual violence and other gender-based violence, victims with a disability, victims who are irregular migrants and victims of violence in close relationships. In accordance with the Victims' Directive, these services must, as a minimum, develop and provide suitable interim accommodation for victims in need of a safe place due to an imminent risk of repeat victimisation, of intimidation and of retaliation. (FRA, 2014a: 15–16)

While the EU Directive does not aim to address all the issues facing vulnerable victims, if the rights set out are effected in full they will go some way towards improving the experience of victims of crime and ameliorating some of the challenges they face when they engage with the criminal justice system.

Unified service provision

The services offered to victims in Ireland are provided by a wide variety of organisations and individuals and involve both statutory and non-statutory organisations, providing general and specialist support across the country. Victims of crime can struggle to engage with the variety of relevant agencies, and navigating a fragmented response system in a vulnerable state creates further stress for victims. It is therefore important that victims can access information on available services, and better mapping of options and supports is required (Spain, Gibbons and Kilcommins, 2014: 15). Research has highlighted the difficulty victims experience in identifying and accessing the range of services which exist, often due to a lack of co-operation between the statutory and non-statutory agencies working in the field: '[o]verall the lack of a joined up approach is a major difficulty. To effect change individual women still rely on individual responses – e.g. by the Gardaí, by a Judge, by a housing officer, by a social worker. Supporting infrastructure and leadership needs to be developed as to how agencies all interact to help make victims safer (Women's Aid)' (Ibid.: 22).

A strategy to encourage closer working relationships among key stakeholders in the field is vital to ensuring victim safety and to reducing the risk of retraumatisation. There have been some successes in this regard since 2000, including the Memoranda of Understanding settled between Office of the DPP and service providers, including an agreement with the DRCC and with the Health Services Executive relating to the disclosure of material held by therapists/social workers/counsellors. Other examples of successes in this regard include the appointment of a Detective Inspector Domestic Violence and Sexual Assault Investigation Unit as national liaison between An Garda Síochána and the NGO sector and the development of 'Guidelines for Making a Victim Impact Statement' by the Office of the DPP in collaboration with a working group comprising staff from the Victims of Crime Office of the Department of Justice and Equality and An Garda Síochána. Joint training sessions involving the Probation Service, An Garda Síochána, RCNI, Ruhama and Adapt, among others, are also examples of positive steps in this area (Spain et al., 2014: 22–3). The FRA has highlighted the importance of co-ordinated and effective referrals between support organisations, particularly for those victims with special protection needs, and has suggested that they 'should be organised in a manner that allows victims, as much as possible, to benefit from a relation of trust' (FRA, 2014a: 14).

Given the importance of a unified service to victims, the co-location of services in a one-stop-shop setting might be considered (COSC, 2010: 13; Hoyle, 1999). The creation of witness care units for victims and witnesses, such as those developed in England and Wales, might also be considered. Witness care units manage cases from the point when the defendant is charged to the conclusion of the case and provide a single point of contact for victims and witnesses where they can access information on the progress of their cases. The units provide a full needs assessment for victims and witnesses who are required to attend court and a dedicated officer supports individuals through the process and co-ordinates support and services during the trial process and offers post-case support.[34] Witness Care Units are in place across England and Wales and are jointly staffed by the police and the CPS.

Conclusion

The EU Directive on Victims' Rights marks a significant shift in victims' rights in Europe. It has the potential to promote and support victims, requiring stakeholders to re-examine the nature of their engagements with them. The state is now under a legal obligation to give effect to the rights afforded victims of crime in the Directive and to prevent them from becoming victims of the criminal process (Zedner, 2004: 143). Political and media circles have embraced the renewed appeal of the victim in recent years, with politicians accepting the public relations benefits attached to advocating for victims, implying a concern for victims and the community while being tough on criminals (Zedner, 2004: 144). The broad political appeal of the victim, coupled with a societal preoccupation with victims, has placed victims at the centre of debates on crime control and punishment (Ibid.). These debates are now highly politicised, with punishment of offenders the 'most satisfying method of honouring the righteous victim' (McEvoy and McConnachie, 2012: 530). Not only are offenders being punished in the name of victims but, as Ashworth has noted, victims have become 'potent rhetorical devices or symbolic tools to lever up punitiveness' (Ashworth, 2000: 186; Zedner, 2004: 144; Hoyle and Zedner, 2007). It will be important in the coming years to recognise that realising the rights of victims should not be at the expense of the rights of offenders, nor should law and policy reform focus on increasing the severity of punishment of the perpetually wicked offender in order to vincidate the rights of the eternally virtuous and worthy victim (Heber, 2014).

The benefits accruing to victims of a more inclusionary logic in recent years have been multifarious, ranging from an increased profile in criminal justice discourse to the juridifciation of victims' rights in the courts and on Ireland's statute books. Notwithstanding the many positive developments and practices, including the increased recognition of victims in the criminal process, it remains the case that many of the needs of victims continue to be unmet. While victims have become a focus of political concern, significant investment in service provision, research, training and education is required. Efforts must also be made to address the systemic problems which impact on victims of crime, particularly those affecting rates of reporting and attrition. The state must act to move from the rhetoric of legal and service rights to a reality where victims of crime are respected, accommodated and provided for. As Theodore Roosevelt once said: '[r]hetoric is a poor substitute for action, and we have trusted only to rhetoric. If we are really to be a great nation, we must not merely talk; we must act big.'

Notes

1 Following the date of transposition, directives may have vertical direct effect if unconditional and sufficiently precise, *Grad v Finanzamt Traunstein* (Case 9/70) [1970] ECR 825; *Van Duyn v Home Office* (1974) C-41/74).
2 http://www.justice.ie/en/JELR/Pages/Criminal_Justice_Victims_of_Crime_Bill_2016, accessed 8 February 2017.
3 Austria, Belgium, Bulgaria, Croatia, Cyprus, Finland, France, Greece, Ireland, Latvia, Lithuania, Luxemburg, Netherlands, Romania, Slovakia, Slovenia. For more detail see http://ec.europa.eu/atwork/applying-eu-law/infringements-proceedings/infringement_decisions/index.cfm?lang_code=EN&r_dossier=&decision_date_from=26%2F01%2F2016&decision_date_to=28%2F01%2F2016&DG=JUST&title=&submit=Search.
4 http://victimsupport.eu/news/the-eu-victims-directive-on-eu-day-for-victims-of-crime-2016-infringement-cases-opened-against-16-member-states/, accessed 8 February 2017.
5 http://eur-lex.europa.eu/legal-content/EN/NIM/?uri=CELEX:32012L0029&, accessed 10 November 2017. Denmark has opted out.
6 Further rights to information 'during the course, or at the conclusion, of an investigation of the alleged offence or following any subsequent criminal proceedings' from the Garda Síochána, the Ombudsman Commission, the Director of Public Prosecutions, the Irish Prison Service, the director of a children detention school or the clinical director of a designated centre, as the case may be under section 8.
7 Section 2, Criminal Justice (Victims of Crime) Act 2017. Reflects Article 2(1)(a) of the EU Directive on Victims' Rights.

8 European Commission, DG Justice (2013) Guidance Document Related To The Transposition And Implementation of Directive 2012/29/EU of the European Parliament and of the Council of 25 October 2012 establishing minimum standards on the rights, support and protection of victims of crime, and replacing Council Framework Decision 2001/220/JHA, p. 25.
9 Case 96/81. See also European Commission, DG Justice (2013) Guidance Document Related To The Transposition And Implementation of Directive 2012/29/EU of the European Parliament and of the Council of 25 October 2012 establishing minimum standards on the rights, support and protection of victims of crime, and replacing Council Framework Decision 2001/220/JHA, pp. 4–6.
10 C-361/88.
11 ECtHR, *Al-Skeini and Others v The United Kingdom* [GC], No. 55721/07, 7 July 2011, para. 162. See also El-Masri v The Former Yugoslav Republic of Macedonia [GC], No. 39630/09, 13 December 2012, para. 255.
12 http://www.justice.ie/en/JELR/Pages/Criminal_Justice_(Victims_of_Crime)_Bill, accessed 20 August 2016.
13 http://www.justice.ie/en/JELR/Criminal%20Justice%20Regulatory%20Impact%20Analysis.pdf/Files/Criminal%20Justice%20Regulatory%20Impact%20Analysis.pdf, accessed 20 August 2016.
14 http://www.justice.ie/en/JELR/Pages/PR15000535, accessed 20 September 2016.
15 Press release, 13 October 2015, available at http://www.justice.ie/en/JELR/Pages/PR15000535, accessed 20 August 2016.
16 Ibid.
17 https://victimsrightsalliance.com/2015/10/14/budget2016-21-increase-in-funding-for-victims-of-crime-office-this-amounts-to-an-increase-of-e300000-for-50-victim-support-organisations-e6000-each/, accessed 15 September 2016.
18 Ibid.
19 http://www.justice.ie/en/JELR/Pages/PR16000311 accessed 1 November 2016. €600,000 in funding was also announced for COSC and Victims of Crime to facilitate an awareness-raising campaign on domestic and sexual violence and to fund domestic violence perpetrator programmes required under the Council of Europe Convention on preventing and combating violence against women and domestic violence, http://www.merrionstreet.ie/MerrionStreet/en/News-Room/Releases/Tanaiste_welcomes_extra_funding_for_Garda_recruits_more_civilian_staff_and_sustained_additional_overtime_in_2017.html#sthash.jKJ1Ppxl.dpuf, accessed 24 October 2016.
20 See written response to a question put to the Minister for Justice and Equality by Jim O'Callaghan TD, accessed 17 November 2016.
21 https://victimsrightsalliance.com/2015/10/14/budget2016-21-increase-in-funding-for-victims-of-crime-office-this-amounts-to-an-increase-of-e300000-for-50-victim-support-organisations-e6000-each/, accessed 26 September 2016.
22 Ibid.
23 Minimum criteria could include independence from political activities, confidentiality, funding transparency and separation between victim support and probation services (FRA 2014a: 100).
24 http://www.justice.ie/en/JELR/Pages/PR16000347, accessed 16 November 2016.
25 http://www.garda.ie/Controller.aspx?Page=1662, accessed 16 November 2016.
26 https://victimsrightsalliance.com/, accessed 30 September 2016.
27 http://www.csvc.ie/en/CSVC/Pages/WP09000162, accessed 4 October 2016.

28 http://victimsfirst.gc.ca/vv/rtgrag-y.html; http://victimsupport.eu/activeapp/wp-content/files_mf/1433500280P4_Sue_OSullivan_Lisbon_May2015.pdf, accessed 7 October 2016.
29 http://www.justice.gc.ca/eng/cj-jp/victims-victimes/vrights-droitsv/, accessed 7 October 2016.
30 https://www.justice.gov/usao/resources/crime-victims-rights-ombudsman, accessed 22 October 2016.
31 http://www.gardaombudsman.ie/about/about.html, accessed 22 October 2016.
32 https://www.dppireland.ie/victims_and_witnesses/complaints/, accessed 22 October 2016.
33 It has been suggested that the experience of homeless persons is reflective of that of recognised hate crime groups (National Coalition for the Homeless, 2010; Cowburn, Duggan, and Robinson, 2015).
34 http://www.cps.gov.uk/news/fact_sheets/witness_care_units/, accessed 3 September 2016.

Conclusion

This book has sought to examine the criminal justice system's interactions with victims of crime. It is a relationship which has changed irrevocably over time. A significant discontinuity occurred in the nineteenth century when a new architecture of criminal and penal semiotics slowly emerged. An institutional way of knowing interpersonal conflict crystallised, one which reified system relations over personal experiences. It also emphasised new ideals and values such as proportionality, legalism, procedural rationality, equality and uniformity. New commitments, discourses and practices came to the fore in the criminal justice network. Prosecutorial practices, for example, began to focus on more analytic considerations such as the accused's conduct rather than his or her character. More mechanical determinants (such as rulebook formalism) took priority over contextual experiences. The state came to dominate the crime conflict, positioning itself as the only legitimate means of coercion. Monopolisation of this kind recalibrated the circuits of governance, resulting *inter alia* in the construction of *l'égalité des armes* to rebalance dissymmetries in power relations.

The ontological dimensions of crime – so personal and subjective – were also increasingly institutionalised and systematised. The depersonalisation of these experiences occurred via the filtering mechanism of the 'public interest'. In modernity, the problem of criminal wrongdoing became a rationalised domain of action, a site which actively distrusted and excluded 'non-objective' truth-claims. The state, the law, the accused and the public interest became the principal claims-makers within this institutional and normative arrangement, an arrangement which dominated criminal and penal relations for the next 150 years. This newly established configuration suppressed the emotive and personal elements of crime. It did so by denying ownership claims over the conflict to victims and by removing any pathways which permitted the possibility of self-interest. Facticity, objectivity, rationality and neutrality – coalescing with the filtering fiction of the 'public interest' – facilitated this drive from personal to institutional referents. The victim was thus displaced, rendered neutral by the hegemonic impulses of a State/accused logic of action. Victims became non-subjects, disenfranchised and dispossessed of all legal and claims-rights. They were no longer recognised (or recognisable) in the justice system, their non-status and non-presence legitimate and legitimising features of the modern institutional process.

In Chapter 2 we sought to demonstrate the 'conditions of possibility' (Foucault, 2007 repr: xxiv) of the return of victims of crime by examining the factors that shaped this emergence and informed its assumptions. Thus, rather than seeking linear patterns, and the unity and timelessness of phenomena or practices across broad historical spans, we focused again on 'rupture', 'discontinuity' and the 'incidence of interruptions' in order to produce a proper understanding of this emergence (Ibid., 3–4). It is structured around certain causal factors that provided both impetus and shape. At a very general level, the emergence of victimology as a discipline shone a light on the individual experiences of victims and their needs and concerns. This in turn helped to illuminate the intersectional nature of crime, moving the discourse on from conventional criminological accounts that framed and explained the phenomenon exclusively through offender theories of causation. During the 1970s the women's movement also began to 'consciousness raise' about female victimisation, highlighting previously invisible and unvoiced social problems. Campaigning activists started to establish support networks such as rape crisis centres and women's refuge centres, while simultaneously drawing attention to the limitations and challenges posed by an exclusively State/accused model of criminal justice.

Such initiatives inspired broader concerns about victims in the criminal process. Victim surveys helped to gather data on experiences of crime and fear of crime, providing insights quite different from institutional representations. The systemic abuse that occurred in the archipelago of institutions that existed in post-Independence Ireland – and the harrowing accounts of the 'endemic' of deaths, beatings, assaults, molestations, rapes, neglect and ritual humiliations – firmly placed experiences of victimhood on the public agenda. It was aggravated by the horrors of brutal clerical abuses in parishes in different parts of the country. The flood of delayed sexual offence cases coming before the courts from the mid-1990s onwards cast further light on institutions and clerics, and also on the dark dimensions of abuse perpetrated on children by family members, neighbours, teachers and so on. The horrific and tragic details of this maelstrom of abuse details – and the existential despair that it gave rise to – have forced Irish society to confront widespread experiences of victimhood. Events of the kind were also covered by a media industry that was becoming more specialised and instantaneous. The media was also increasingly adept at individualising the experiences of victimhood through focused analysis and imagery. Aside from consciousness raising, these insights have also contributed to the development of a healthy scepticism of institutions of power, and any uncritical deference to such power. This has been aided, no doubt, by repeated findings of corrupt practices in political and executive circles.

The noble post-war dream of winning the war on crime began to fade in Western countries from the 1970s onwards as the nihilism of 'nothing works' took hold. As crime became accepted as a normal social phenomenon, discourse and practice moved away from an exclusive focus on normalising the wrongdoer. A new emphasis on pragmatism was espoused, one which was agnostic as regards the social or psychological causes of deviancy. Instrumental reasoning of this kind accepts the normality of crime and seeks strategies and practices to prevent or displace it. The victim is much more central and visible under such a framework of understanding. Moreover, and in managing an incident, effective service provision to a victim provides relatively quick, attractive and measurable outputs from criminal justice agencies, at least when compared with more long-term and contingent results such as convictions or successful rehabilitative outcomes.

The legal system has also acted as a steerer of reintegration. This is occurring through the deliberative capacity of domestic and EU legislatures, and through expansive judicial interpretation of constitutional and convention texts. The emerging 'rights revolution' is evident in both criminal and civil spheres, and it serves to open up the operational self-enclosure that exists under a state/accused model of justice. Juridification of this kind is providing victims with a stronger legal status and permits their claims to be severed from more public-interest considerations. It will help to ensure that the intersubjective dimensions of the crime conflict are increasingly recognised.

Chapter 4 considered service provision for victims of crime. Service rights represent, in practice, the most significant source of support and protection for victims as they journey through the criminal justice system. Although there was already a commitment to effective provision of services to victims in Ireland by both state agencies and various non-governmental victim support groups, service rights have been considerably strengthened with the implementation of the EU Directive in November 2015. The practical effect of this Directive is to elevate effective service delivery from a commitment to best practice (evident in the pledges proffered in the Victims Charter) to a fully justiciable suite of rights which victims are entitled to rely on at any stage in the criminal justice process. In light of this, it is to be hoped that service provision for victims will continue to improve in the coming years. Indeed, early signs of state commitment to honouring the intent of the EU Directive are evident in initiatives such as the extension of the 'reasons for decisions' scheme to all offences by the Office of the DPP and the introduction of Victim Services Offices by An Garda Síochána. However, in light of the significant capital investment and resource allocation required to achieve full compliance with the objectives of the Directive, the goal of pitch-perfect service provision for victims of crime will take some time to realise.

While it is positive, the re-emergence of the victim in criminal justice discourse and the juridification of victims' rights witnessed in recent years should not be viewed as a panacea. Chapter 5 charted the challenges which continue to face service users, providers and the wider criminal justice sector in the delivery of services which are responsive to the needs of victims and meet increased demands under the EU Directive on Victims' Rights. Systemic problems, including the fragmented nature of service delivery, under-resourcing, high levels of under-reporting and attrition, a continuing commitment to an 'ideal' victim and crime, and a lack of commitment to research and quality assurance in the sector are highlighted. Despite rhetoric to the contrary, it is questionable whether the state is committed to or will be able to deliver the comprehensive and compassionate service demanded under the Directive, and it appears that the dissonance which has existed between criminal justice policy and practice will continue in the coming years.

While this book has charted the return of the victim to criminal justice discourse in Ireland and has advocated for a greater commitment to the delivery of victims' rights, it is recognised that a balance must be struck in the coming years between ensuring that victims are identified as a strategic policy priority while guarding against the use of victims as a political tool. We must guard against binary thinking, where the rights of the victim and the offender are seen to be 'diametrically opposed' (Garland, 2001: 180) and victims are used as 'potent rhetorical devices or symbolic tools to lever up punitiveness' (Ashworth, 2000: 186; Zedner, 2004: 144). There must be space to accommodate the rights of both the offender and the victim in the criminal justice system in the twenty-first century.

Bibliography

Ahern, B. (1999) 'Sheedy Case Representation', *Dáil Debates*, vol. 504, no. 2, c. 180 *et seq* (5 May 1999).
Aldana-Pindell, R. (2004) 'An emerging universality of justiciable victims rights in the criminal process to curtail impunity for state-sponsored crimes', *Human Rights Quarterly*, 26:3, 605–686.
Allen, C. (1931) *Legal Duties and other Essays in Jurisprudence* (Oxford: Clarendon Press).
Andrews, J. A. (ed.) (1982) *Human Rights in Criminal Procedure: A Comparative Study* (Leiden, The Netherlands: Marinus Nijhoff).
An Garda Síochána (2006) *Adult Cautioning Scheme*. www.garda.ie/Documents/User/adult%20cautioning%20final%20for%20publication.pdf (last viewed 26 January 2017)
An Garda Síochána (2013) *Garda Síochána Policy on the Investigation of Sexual Crimes against Children, Child Welfare*, 2nd edn, www.garda.ie/Documents/User/Policy%20on%20the%20Investigation%20of%20Sexual%20Crime,%20Crimes%20Against%20Children%20and%20Child%20Welfare%202014%2002%2024%20HQ%20Dir%2048%2013.pdf (last viewed 26th January 2017)
An Garda Síochána (2015) *An Garda Síochána Public Attitudes Survey* www.dataprotection.ie/docs/Case-Study-8–01-Victim-Support/128.htm (last viewed: 25 January 2017).
Amir, M. (1971) *Patterns in Forcible Rape* (Chicago: University of Chicago Press).
Ashworth, A. (2000) 'Victim's Rights, Defendants' Rights and Criminal Procedure' in A. Crawford and J. Goodey (eds), *Integrating a Victim Perspective within Criminal Justice* (Aldershot: Ashgate), pp. 185–204.
Bacik, I., C. Maunsell and S. Grogan (1998) *The Legal Process and Victims of Rape* (Dublin: Dublin Rape Crisis Centre).
Bacik, I., L. Heffernan, P. Brazil and M. Woods (2007) *Report on Services and Legislation Providing Support for Victims of Crime* (Dublin: Commission for the Support of Victims of Crime).
Baker, J. H. (1977) 'Criminal Courts and Procedure at Common Law 1550–1800' in J. S. Cockburn (ed.), *Crime in England 1550–1800* (London: Methuen), pp. 15–48.
Balance in the Criminal Law Review Group (2007) *Final Report* (Dublin: Department of Justice).

Bartlett, H. and E. Mears (2011) *Sexual Violence against People with Disabilities: Data Collection and Barriers to Disclosure* (Dublin: Rape Crisis Network Ireland).

Baumer, E. and J. Lauritsen (2010) 'Reporting crime to the police, 1973–2005: a multivariate analysis of long-term trends in the national crime victimisation survey', *Criminology*, 48:1, 131–185.

Beattie, J. (1986) *Crime and the Courts in England, 1660–1800* (Princeton: Princeton University Press).

Beattie, J. (1991) 'Scales of justice: defence counsel and the English trial in the eighteenth and nineteenth centuries', *Law and History Review*, 9:2, 221–67.

Beccaria, C. (1995 repr.) *On Crimes and Punishment* (Cambridge: Cambridge University Press).

Bellamy, R. (1992) *Liberalism and Modern Society: An Historical Argument* (London: Polity Press).

Bentham, J. (1830) *The Rationale of Punishment* (London: University of London Press).

Bentham, J. (1970 repr) *An Introduction to the Principles of Morals and Legislation* (London: Athlone Press).

Berlin, I. (1969) 'Two Concepts of Liberty' in I. Berlin (ed.), *Four Essays on Liberty* (Oxford: Oxford University Press), pp. 118–172.

Bevocqua, M. (2000) *Rape on the Public Agenda: Feminism and the Politics of Sexual Assault* (Boston: Northeastern University Press).

Birmingham, G. (2006) *The Report of the Commission of Investigation: The Case of Dean Lyons* (Dublin: Government Stationery Office).

Black, L. (2016) 'Media, Public Attitudes and Crime' in D. Healy et al. (eds) *The Routledge Handbook of Irish Criminology* (Abingdon: Routledge), pp. 399–415.

Blackburn, R. (1999) *Towards a Constitutional Bill of Rights for the United Kingdom* (London: Pinter).

Blackstone, W. (1765) *Commentaries on the Laws of England*, Vol. IV (Boston: Beacon Press).

Blumstein, A. and J. Wallman (2000) *The Crime Drop in America* (New York: Cambridge University Press).

Bohan, P. and D. Yorke (1987) 'Law enforcement marketing: perceptions of a police force', *Irish Marketing Review*, 2, 72–86.

Bowen, P., A. Qasim and L. Tetenbaum (2014) *Better Courts: A Snapshot of Domestic Violence Courts in 2013* (London: Centre for Justice Innovation).

Bowling, B. and J. Ross (2006) 'A brief history of criminology: on the evolution of an academic discipline', *Criminal Justice Matters*, 65:1, 12–15.

Boyle, K. (1972) 'Police in Ireland before the Union I', *Irish Jurist*, VII, 115–137.

Breen, R. and D. Rottman (1984) *Crime Victimisation in the Republic of Ireland* (ERSI Paper no. 121) (Dublin: Economic Social Research Institute).

Breslin, J. (2004) 'McGovern settles claim with victim support', *Irish Examiner* (20 October 2004).

Brewer, J. (1980) 'Law and disorder in Stuart and Hanoverian England', *History Today*, 30, 18–27

Bridgeman, I. (2003) 'The Constabulary and the Criminal Justice System in Nineteenth Century Ireland' in F. McAuley and I. O'Donnell (eds), *Criminal Justice History:*

Themes and Controversies from Pre-Independence Ireland (Dublin: Four Courts), pp. 113–141.
Brienen, M. and E. Hoegen (2000) *Victims of Crime in Twenty-two European Criminal Justice Systems: The Implementation of Recommendation (85)11 of the Council of Europe on the Position of the Victim in the Framework of Criminal Law and Procedure* (Nijmegan, The Netherlands: Wolf).
Brosky, B. A. and S. J. Lally (2004) 'Prevalence of trauma, PTSD, and dissociation in court-referred adolescents', *Journal of Interpersonal Violence*, 19:7, 801–814.
Brown, J. (2011) 'We mind and we care but have things changed? Assessment of progress in reporting, investigating and prosecution of rape', *Journal of Sexual Aggression*, 17:3, 263–272
Bryan O'Sullivan, S. (2015) 'Protection against cross examination by the accused in sexual offence trials', *Irish Criminal Law Journal*, 25:3, 54–64.
Burke, H. (1999) 'Foundation Stones of Irish Social Policy, 1831–1951' in B. Kiely et al. (eds), *Irish Social Policy in Context* (Dublin: University College Press), pp. 11–32.
Burke, R. (1991) 'Garda Training', *Dáil Debates*, vol. 407, no. 8, c. 2002 (2 May 1991).
Burke, W. J. (2016) 'Irish Prison Victim Liaison Service', presentation delivered at Victim Support Europe Conference, 24–26 May 2016.
Byrne, P. (1997) *Social Movements in Britain: Theory and Practice in British Politics* (Abingdon: Routledge).
Cairns, D. A. (1998) *Advocacy and the Making of the Adversarial Criminal Trial. 1800–1865* (Oxford: Clarendon Press).
Campbell, L. (2002) *Tourism Victim Support Services: Victim Impact Survey Report* (Dublin: Tourism Research Centre, Dublin Institute of Technology).
Campbell, L., S. Kilcommins and C. O'Sullivan (2010) *Criminal Law in Ireland: Cases and Commentary* (Dublin: Clarus Press).
Carey, G. (1999) 'Summary trial and judicial criticism: an educational response', *Irish Law Times*, 17:18, 278.
CARI (2015) *Annual Report 2013 and 2014* (Dublin: CARI).
Carrabine, E., Inganski, P., Lee, M., Plummer, K. and South, N. (2004) *Criminology: A Sociological Introduction* (London: Routledge).
Carroll Burke, P. (2000) *Colonial Discipline: The Making of the Irish Convict System* (Dublin: Four Courts Press).
Central Statistics Office (1999) *Quarterly National Household Survey Crime and Victims* (Dublin: Central Statistics Office).
Central Statistics Office (2003) *Quarterly National Household Survey Crime and Victimisation* (Dublin: Central Statistics Office).
Central Statistics Office (2006) *Quarterly National Household Survey Crime and Victimisation* (Dublin: Central Statistics Office).
Central Statistics Office (2011) *Quarterly National Household Survey Crime and Victimisation* (Dublin: Central Statistics Office).
Central Statistics Office (2015) *Review of the Quality of Crime Statistics* (Dublin: Central Statistics Office).
Central Statistics Office (2016) *Review of the Quality of Crime Statistics 2016* (Dublin: Central Statistics Office).

Charleton, P. (1990) 'The victim in Irish constitutional law: a new departure', *Irish Law Times*, 8, 140–143.

Charleton, P. and S. Byrne (2010) 'Sexual violence: witnesses and suspects – a debating document', *Irish Journal of Legal Studies*, 1:1, 1–83.

Christie, N. (1977) 'Conflicts as property', *British Journal of Criminology*, 17, 1–15.

Christie, N. (1986) 'The Ideal Victim' in E. A. Fattah (ed.) *From Crime Policy to Victim Policy* (Basingstoke: Macmillan), pp. 17–30.

Christie, N. (2010) 'Victim movements at a crossroads', *Punishment and Society*, 12:2, 115–22.

Chubb, B. (1991) *The Politics of the Irish Constitution* (Dublin: Institute of Public Administration).

Chubb, B. (1982) *The Government and Politics of Ireland* (London: Longman, 2nd edn).

Coakley, J. (1996) 'Society and Political Culture' in J. Coakley and M. Gallagher (eds) *Politics in the Republic of Ireland* (Limerick: Political Science Association of Ireland, 2nd edn), pp. 25–48.

Coen, R. (2006) 'The rise of the victim, a path to punitiveness?', *Irish Criminal Law Journal*, 16:3, 10–14.

Coen, R. (2014) *Garda Powers: Law and Practice* (Dublin: Clarus Press).

Collins, M. L. and C. Menton (2006) 'Evidence-Based Social Policy Making' in S. Healy, G. Reynolds and M. Collins (eds) *Social Policy in Ireland: Principles Practice and Problems* (Dublin: Liffey Press), pp. 65–87.

Committee for Judicial Studies (2011) *The Equal Treatment of Persons in Court: Guidance for the Judiciary* (Dublin: Committee for Judicial Studies).

Commission for the Support of Victims of Crime (2013) *Summary of 2012 Evaluation and Financial Reports* (Dublin: Commission for the Support of Victims of Crime).

Commission for the Support of Victims of Crime (2014) *Summary of 2013 Evaluation and Financial Reports* (Dublin: Commission for the Support of Victims of Crime).

Commission to Inquire in to Child Abuse (2009) *Report – Commission to Inquire into Child Abuse* (Dublin: Stationery Office).

Connolly, B. (2015) 'Confronting witnesses in court: a right to confrontation in Irish courts, Part II.', *Irish Law Times*, 33:2, 24–7.

Conway, V. (2010) *The Blue Wall of Silence: The Morris Tribunal and Police Accountability Ireland* (Dublin/Portland: Irish Academic Press).

Conway, V. (2013) *Policing Twentieth Century Ireland: A History of An Garda Síochána* (Abingdon: Routledge).

Cook, D., M. Burton, A. Robinson and C. Vallely (2004) *Evaluation of Specialist Domestic Violence Courts/Fast Track Systems* (London: Crown Prosecution Service).

Cook, K. (2011) 'Rape investigations and prosecution: stuck in the mud?', *Journal of Sexual Aggression*, 17:3, 250–262.

Cooper, J. (2008) *The Emotional Effects and Subsequent Needs of Families Bereaved by Homicide: A Study Commissioned by AdVic and Support after Homicide* (Dublin: Commission for the Support of Victims of Crime).

Cornish, W. R. and G. de N. Clark (1989) *Law and Society in England 1750–1950* (London: Sweet and Maxwell).

Corr, M., P. O'Mahony, L. Lovett and L. Kelly (2009) *Different Systems, Similar Outcomes: Tracking Attrition in Reported Rape Cases in Eleven Countries, Country Briefing: Ireland* (London: Child and Woman Abuse Studies Unit).
COSC (2010) *National Strategy on Domestic, Sexual and Gender-based Violence 2010–2014* (Dublin: COSC).
Cotter, A. (1999) 'The Criminal Justice System in Ireland: Towards Change and Transformation' in S. Quinn, P. Kennedy and A. Mathews (eds) *Contemporary Irish Social Policy* (Dublin: University College Dublin Press), pp. 286–305.
Cotter, A. (2005) 'The Criminal Justice System' in S. Quin, P. Kennedy, A. Matthews and G. Kiely (eds.), *Contemporary Irish Social Policy* (Dublin: UCD Press), pp. 277–298.
Council of Europe (1953) *European Convention for the Protection of Human Rights and Fundamental Freedoms* (ETS5; 213 UNTS 221 as amended by CETS 194 of 1 June 2010).
Council of Europe (1983) *European Convention on the Compensation of Victims of Violent Crimes* (ETS n. 116) (Strasbourg: 24 November 1983).
Council of Europe (2000) *Recommendation (2000)11 on Action Against Trafficking in Human Beings for the Purpose of Sexual Exploitation* (19 May 2000).
Council of Europe (2005a) *Convention on the Prevention of Terrorism* (CETS no. 196) (Warsaw: 16 May 2005).
Council of Europe (2005b) *Convention on Action Against Trafficking in Human Beings* (CETS no. 197) (Warsaw: 16 May 2005).
Council of Europe (2006) *Recommendation (2006)8 on Assistance to Crime Victims* (14 June 2006).
Counihan, C. (2013) 'Rape crisis network perspectives on sexual violence and the criminal justice system', *Irish Criminal Law Journal*, 23:4, 115–23.
Courts Service (2015) *Annual Report 2014* (Dublin: Courts Service).
Courts Service (2016) *Annual Report 2015* (Dublin: Courts Service).
Cowburn, M., P. Senior, M. Duggan and A. Robinson (2015) *Values in Criminology and Community Justice* (Bristol: Policy Press).
Crawford, A. (2000) 'Salient Themes Towards a Victim Perspective and the Limitations of Restorative Justice' in A. Crawford and J. Goodey (eds) *Integrating a Victim Perspective Within Criminal Justice* (Burlington, VT: Ashgate), pp. 285–310.
Crown Prosecution Service (2015) *Victim and Witness Satisfaction Survey* (London: Crown Prosecution Service).
CVH (Crime Victims Helpline) (2015) *Annual Report 2014* (Dublin: Crime Victims Helpline).
CVH (Crime Victims Helpline) (2016) *Annual Report 2015* (Dublin: Crime Victims Helpline).
Curry, J. (2003) *Irish Social Services* (Dublin: Institute of Public Administration, 4th edn).
Damaska, M. (1986) *The Faces of Justice and State Authority* (New Haven: Yale University Press).
Data Protection Commission (2001) *Victim Support: Liaison with An Garda Síochána* (Case Study 8/01: 2001) (Dublin: Data Protection Commission).
Davies, P., P. Francis and V. Jupp (eds) (2004) *Victimisation Theory, Research and Policy* (Basingstoke: Palgrave).

Davies, P., P. Francis and C. Greer (eds) (2007) *Victims Crime and Society* (Sage: London).
Davies, P., P. Francis and C. Greer (2007) 'Victims, Crime and Society' in P. Davies, P. Francis and C. Greer (eds) *Victims Crime and Society* (Sage: London).
Delahunt, M. (2011) 'Video evidence and s. 16(1)(b) of the Criminal Evidence Act 1992', *Bar Review*, 16:1, 2–6.
Delahunt. M. (2015) 'Recorded evidence for vulnerable witnesses', *Bar Review*, 20:3, 46–49.
Delaney, V. T. H. (1979) *The Administration of Justice in Ireland* (Dublin: Institute of Public Administration, 4th edn).
Department of Justice (2006) 'Rebalancing Criminal Justice – Remarks by Tániste in Limerick', 20 October 2006, available at www.justice.ie/en/JELR/Pages/Speech-rebalancing-criminal-justice (last viewed 20 June 2016).
Department of Justice and Equality (2015) '*Istanbul Convention Action Plan: Actions required for ratification of Istanbul Convention (as included in the Draft Second National Strategy on Domestic, Sexual and Gender-based Violence*' (Dublin: Department of Justice and Equality).
Department of Justice and Equality (2016) '*CEDAW Response of Ireland to List of Issues and Questions prior to Reporting*' (Dublin: Department of Justice).
Department of Social, Community and Family Affairs (2000) *White Paper on a Framework for Supporting Voluntary Activity and Developing a Relationship Between the State and the Community and the Voluntary Sector*, available at www.volunteer.ie.download/WhitePaper2000.pdf (last viewed 20 June 2016).
De Than, C. (2003) 'Positive obligations under the European Convention on Human Rights: towards the human rights of victims and vulnerable witnesses', *Journal of Criminal Law*, 67, 165–182.
van Dijk, J. J. M. (1999) 'Introducing Victimology' in J. J. M. van Dijk, R. G. H. van Kaam and J. Wemmers (eds), *Caring for Crime Victims* (Mosney, NY: Justice Press), pp. 1–12.
Doak, J. (2003) 'The victim and the criminal process: an analysis of recent trends in regional and international tribunals', *Legal Studies*, 23:1, 1–32.
Doak, J. (2005) 'Victims' rights in criminal trials: prospects for participation', *Journal of Law and Society*, 32:2, 294–316.
Doak, J. (2008) *Victims' Rights, Human Rights and Criminal Justice: Reconceiving the Role of Third Parties* (Portland: Hart).
Doak, J. (2009) *Victims' Rights, Human Rights and Criminal Justice: Reconceiving the Role of Third Parties* (Oxford: Hart).
Doak, J. (2015) 'Enriching trial justice for crime victims in common law systems: lessons from transitional environments', *International Review of Victimology*, 21:2, 139–160.
Dobson, M. J. (1987) *A Chronology of Epidemic Disease and Morality in South East England, 1601–1800*, Historical Geography Research Series, No. 19, (London: Institute of British Geographers).
Doerner, W. and S. Lab (2002) *Victimology* (Cincinnati, OH: Anderson, 3rd edn).
Domenech, J. (2003) 'Main Instruments in Developing Victim Services in Europe', 11th International Symposium on Victimology, Stellenbasch, S. Africa: World Society of Victimology, available at www.eurowrc.org/06.contributions/European%20%20for%20%victim%20services.doc (last viewed 20 June 2016).

Donagh, S. (2014) 'Section 16 of the Criminal Justice Act 2006 and the judges' charge', *Bar Review*, 19:6, 118–121.

Dowd, M. (1992) 'Dispelling the myths about the "battered woman's defence" towards a new understanding', *Fordham URB Law Journal*, 19, 567.

Downes, D. and R. Morgan (2002) 'The Skeletons in the Cupboard: The Politics or Law and Order at the Turn of the Millennium' in M. Maguire, R. Morgan and R. Reiner (eds), *The Oxford Handbook of Criminology* (Oxford: Oxford University Press, 3rd edn), pp. 286–321.

Drapkin, I. and E. Viano (eds) (1974) *Victimology* (Lexington, MS: Heath).

Driver, A. (1993) *Power and Pauperism: The Workhouse System, 1834–1884*. (Cambridge: Cambridge University Press).

Dublin Rape Crisis Centre (2016) *Annual Report 2015* (Dublin: Rape Crisis Centre).

Duffy, D. (2008) *A Better Deal: The Human Rights of Victims in the Criminal Justice System* (Dublin: Irish Council of Civil Liberties).

Dundon, M. (2004) 'Nine Victim Support Board members quit over alleged bullying', *Irish Examiner* (9 September 2004).

Dussich, J. (2006) '*Victimology: Past, Present and Future*' (Resource Material no. 70) Tokyo: UNAFEI, available at www.unafei.orijpunafei@moj/go.jp (last viewed 20 June 2016).

Dworkin, R. (1985) *A Matter of Principle* (Cambridge, MA: Harvard University Press).

Dworkin, R. (1998 repr.) *Law's Empire* (Oxford: Hart Publishing).

Dworkin, R. (2005 repr.) *Taking Rights Seriously* (London: Duckworth).

Dwyer, R. (2008) 'If the decision seems strange, then the DPP should explain himself', *Irish Examiner* (19 January 2008).

Edelstein, L. (1998) 'An accusation easily to be made? rape and malicious prosecution in eighteenth-century England', *The American Journal of Legal History*, 42:4, 351–390.

Edwards, C. and G. Harold, S. Kilcommins (2012) *Access to Justice for People With Disabilities as Victims of Crime in Ireland* (Dublin: National Disability Authority).

EIGE (2012) *Review of the Implementation of the Beijing Platform for Action in the EU Member States: Violence against women – victim support* (Luxembourg: Publications Office of the European Union).

Elias, R. (1986) *The Politics of Victimization: Victims, Victimology and Human Rights* (New York: Oxford University Press).

Elias, R. (1993) *Victims Still: The Political Manipulation of Crime Victims* (Newbury Park, CA: Sage).

Emmerson, B., A. Ashworth and A. MacDonald (2007) *Human Rights and Criminal Justice* (London: Sweet and Maxwell, 2nd edn).

Eogan, M. (2016) *National Sexual Assault Treatment Unit (SATU) Annual Key Service Activity Report: Annual Report For Year Ending December 2015* (Dublin: Sexual Assault Treatment Unit).

EU (COM/99/0359) *Communication to the Council, the European Parliament, and the Economic and Social Committee – Crime Victims in the EU – Reflections on Standards and Actions*. Commission: 14 July 1999.

EU (2001/220/JHA) *Framework Decision on the Standing of Victims in Criminal Proceedings*. Council of Ministers: 15 March 2001.

EU (2002/29/JHA) *Framework Decision on Preventing and Combatting Trafficking in Human Being and Protecting Victims.* Council of Ministers: 19 July 2002.

EU (2004/68/JHA) *Framework Decision on Combatting Sexual Abuse, Sexual Exploitation of Children and Child Pornography.* Council of Ministers: 24 March 2004.

European Commission DG Justice (2013) '*DG Justice Guidance Document on the transposition and implementation of Directive 2012/29/EU of the European Parliament and of the Council of 25 October 2012 establishing minimum standards on the rights, support and protection of victims of Crime, and replacing Council Framework Decision 2001/220/JHA5*' (Brussels: European Commission DG Justice).

Fallot, J. D. (2011) 'Trauma Informed Care: A Values-Based Context for Psychosocial Empowerment' in Institute of Medicine (IMO) *Preventing Violence Against Women and Children: Workshop Summary* (Washington, DC: National Academies Press).

Fallot, R. D. and M. Harris (2008a) 'Trauma-informed Services' in *The Encyclopedia of Psychological Trauma*, G., Reyes, J. D., Elhai and J. D. Ford (eds.) (Hoboken, NJ: John Wiley), pp. 660–662.

Fallot, R. D. and M. Harris (2008b) 'Trauma-informed approaches to systems of care', *Trauma Psychology Newsletter, Division 56 of the American Psychological Association*, 3:1, 6–7.

Farmer, L. (1996) 'The obsession with definition: the nature of crime and critical legal theory', *Social and Legal Studies*, 5, 57–73.

Farrell, Grant and Sparks (2002) *Final Report: Policy Research Victim Support* (Dublin: Department of Justice and Victim Support Ireland).

Fattah, E. (2000) '*The Vital Role of Victimology in the Rehabilitation of Offenders and Their Re-intergration into Society*', 112th UNAFEI International Training Course (Resource Material no. 56) Tokyo: UNAFEI, available at www.unafei.or.jp/english/pdf/RS_No56/N056_10VE_Fattah3.pdf (last viewed 20 June 2016).

Fennell, C. (1993) *Crime and Crisis: Justice by Illusion* (Cork: Cork University Press).

Fennell, C. (2001) 'The culture of decision-making: a case for judicial defiance through evidence and fact finding', *Judicial Studies Institute Journal*, 2:1, 25–68.

Fennell, C. (2010) *The Law of Evidence in Ireland* (Dublin: Bloomsbury Professional, 3rd edn).

Fenwick, H. (2000) *Civil Rights: New Labour, Freedom and the Human Rights Act* (Essex: Pearson).

Finnegan, F. (2001) *Penance or Perish: A Study of Magdalen Asylums in Ireland* (Kilkenny: Cosgrove Press).

Fitzgerald, L. (1995) 'Victim Support Bill 1995', *Dáil Debates*, vol. 458, no. 5, c. 1141 (21 November 1995).

Fitzgerald, J. (2008) 'Reluctant witnesses and section 16 of the Criminal Justice Act 2006', *Bar Review*, 13:6, 126–129.

Fisher, E. (2011) 'Hidden crimes: efforts to reduce domestic and sexual violence in Ireland', *The Bar Review*, 16:5, 101–102.

Fletcher, A. J. and J. Stevenson (eds) (1985) *Order and Disorder in Early Modern England* (Cambridge: Cambridge University Press).

Flynn, P. (1992) 'Criminal Evidence Bill 1992', *Dáil Debates* vol. 416, no. 6, c. 1284 *et seq* (3 March 1992).

Foucault, M. (1972) *The Archaeology of Knowledge* (London: Tavistock).
Foucault, M. (1979) *The History of Sexuality* (Penguin: Harmondsworth).
Foucault, M. (1991 repr.) *Discipline and Punish: The Birth of the Prison* (Harmondsworth: Penguin).
Foucault, M. (2007 repr.) *The Order of Things* (London: Routledge).
FRA (European Union Agency for Fundamental Rights) (2009) *EU-MIDIS – European Union minorities and discrimination survey – Main results* (Luxembourg: Publications Office).
FRA (European Union Agency for Fundamental Rights) (2012) *EU-MIDIS – Data in Focus 6: Minorities as Victims of Crime* (Luxembourg: Publications Office).
FRA (European Union Agency for Fundamental Rights) (2013a), *EU LGBT Survey – European Union lesbian, gay, bisexual and transgender survey* (Luxembourg: Publications Office).
FRA (European Union Agency for Fundamental Rights) (2013b) *Discrimination and hate crime against Jews in EU Member States: experiences and perceptions of antisemitism* (Luxembourg: Publications Office).
FRA (European Union Agency for Fundamental Rights) (2014a) *Victims of Crime in the EU: the extent and nature of support for victims* (Luxembourg: Publications Office).
FRA (European Union Agency for Fundamental Rights) (2014b) *Violence against Women: an EU-wide survey; Main results* (Luxembourg: Publications Office).
Friedman, L. M. (1993) *Crime and Punishment in American History* (New York: Basic Books).
Friedman, L. M. (2002) *American Law in the Twentieth Century* (New Haven, CT: Yale University Press).
Garda Inspectorate (2014) *Report of the Garda Síochána Inspectorate: Crime Investigation* (Dublin: Garda Inspectorate).
Garda Inspectorate (2015) *Changing Policing in Ireland Delivering a Visible, Accessible and Responsive Service* (Dublin: Garda Inspectorate).
Garland, D. (1981) 'The birth of the welfare sanction', *British Journal of Law and Society*, 8:1, 19–45.
Garland, D. (1985) *Punishment and Welfare: A History of Penal Strategies* (Aldershot: Gower).
Garland, D. (1988) 'British criminology before 1935', *British Journal of Criminology*, 28:2, 1–17.
Garland, D. (2001) *The Culture of Control: Crime and Social Order in Contemporary Society* (Oxford: Oxford University Press).
Gatrell, V. A. C. (1994) *The Hanging Tree: Execution and the English People, 1770–1868* (Oxford: Oxford University Press).
Geoghegan-Quinn, M. (1993) 'Victims of crime', *Dáil Debates*, vol. 426, no. 7, c. 96 (16 February 1993).
Geoghegan-Quinn, M. (1996) 'The Kelly Fitzgerald Child Abuse Case', *Dáil Debates*, vol. 462, no. 7, c. 1997 (7 March 1996).
Gest, T. (2001) *Crime and Politics: Big Government's Erratic Campaign for Law and Order* (New York: Oxford University Press).
Goodey, J. (2005) *Victim and Victimology: Research, Policy and Practice* (London: Pearson).

Goodpaster, G. (1987) 'On the theory of the American adversary criminal trial', *Journal of Criminal Law and Criminology*, 78: 1, 118–154.

Gray, J. (1986) *Liberalism* (Milton Keynes: Open University Press).

Green, T. A. (1987) 'The English Criminal Trial Jury and the Law Finding Traditions on the Eve of the French Revolution' in A.P Schioppa (ed.) *The Trial Jury in England, France, Germany, 1700–1900* (Berlin: Duncker and Humblot), pp. 13–39.

Green, T. A. (1988) *Verdict According to Conscience: Perspectives on the English Criminal Trial Jury 1200–1800* (Chicago: University of Chicago Press).

Greer, C. (2004) 'Crime, Media and Community: Grief and Virtual Engagement in Late Modernity' in J. Ferrell, K. Hayward, W. Morrison and M. Presclee (eds), *Cultural Criminology Unleashed* (London: Cavendish), pp. 109–121.

Greer, C. (2005) 'Crime and Media: Understanding the Connections' in C. Hale, K. Hayward, A. Wahidin and E Wincup (eds) *Criminology* (Oxford: Oxford University Press), pp. 20–50.

Greer, C. (2007) 'News Media, Victims and Crime' in P. Davies, P. Francis and C. Greer (eds) *Victims Crime and Society* (Sage: London), pp. 20–50.

GRETA (2013) '*Report concerning the implementation of the Council of Europe Convention on Action against Trafficking in Human Beings by Ireland: First Evaluation Round*' (Strasbourg: Council of Europe).

Griffin, D. (2007) 'Will the Ombudsman build confidence in Gardaí?', *Law Society Gazette*, 101:5, 14–15.

Griffin, S. (2014) 'Criminal injuries spend triples in just 12 months', *Irish Independent*, 12 January.

Groehuijsen, M. S. and A. Pembertono (2009) 'The EU Framework Decision for Victims of Crime: does hard law make a difference?', *European Journal of Crime, Criminal Law and Criminal Justice*, 17:1, 43–59.

Grozdanova, R. and de Londras, F. (2014) *Protecting Victims' Rights in the EU: National Report: Ireland* (London: Institute of Advanced Legal Studies).

Guiry, R. (2006) 'Who is the victim – the use of victim impact statements in murder and manslaughter cases', *Irish Criminal Law Journal*, 16:3, 1–9.

Habermas, J. (1996) 'Postscript to Between Facts and Norms' in M. Deflem (ed.), *Habermas, Modernity and Law* (London: Sage), pp. 135–150.

Habermas, J. (2004 repr.) *The Theory of Communicative Action: Reason and the Rationalisation of Society* (London: Polity Press).

Habermas, J. (2006 repr.) *The Theory of Communicative Action: The Critique of Functionalist Reason* (Oxford: Blackwell).

Habermas, J. (2008 repr.) *Between Facts and Norms* (Cambridge: Polity Press).

Habermas, J. (2010 repr.) *The Structural Transformations of the Public Sphere: An Inquiry into a Category of Bourgeois Society* (London: Polity Press).

Hall, M. (2010) *Victims and Policy Making: A Comparative Perspective* (Cullompton: Willan Publishing).

Hamilton, C. (2014) *Reconceptualising Penality* (Farnham: Ashgate).

Hamilton, J. (2011) 'Sexual Offences and Capacity to Consent: A Prosecution Perspective' *Annual Conference of the Law Reform Commission*, 7 November 2011.

Hamilton, P. and P. Williams (1995) *Secret Love: My Life with Father Michael Cleary* (Dublin: Mainstream).

Hanly, C., D. Healy and S. Scrivner (2009) *Rape and Justice in Ireland: A National Study Survivor, Prosecutor and Court Responses to Rape* (Dublin: Liffey Press).
Hart, H. L. A. (1961) *The Concept of Law* (Oxford: Oxford University Press).
Haughey, S. (1995) 'Victim Support Bill 1995', *Dáil Debates*, vol. 458, no. 5, c. 1144 (21 November 1995).
Hay, D. (1977) 'Property, Authority and the Criminal Law' in D. Hay et al. (eds) *Albion's Fatal Tree: Crime and Society in Eighteenth Century England* (London: Allen and Unwin), pp. 5–23.
Hay, D. (1983) 'Controlling the English prosecutor', *Osgoode Hall Law Journal*, 21:2, 165–186.
Haynes, A., J. Schweppe, J. Carr, N. Carmody and S. Enright (2015) '*Out of the Shadows: Legislating for Hate Crime in Ireland – Preliminary Findings* (Limerick: HHRG/ICCL).
Haynes, S. (2007) 'The statutory rape crisis: a judgment too far, or a judgment that could have gone further?', *Cork Online Law Review*, 6, 99.
Healy, J. (2004) *Irish Laws of Evidence* (Dublin: Thomson Round Hall).
Heber, A. (2014) 'Good versus bad? Victims, offenders and victim-offenders in Swedish crime policy', *European Journal of Criminology*, 11:4, 410–428.
Heffernan, L. (2013) 'Hearsay in criminal trials: the Strasbourg perspective', *Irish Jurist*, 49:1, 132–160.
Heffernan, L. and Ni Raifeartaigh, U. (2014) *Evidence in Criminal Trials* (Dublin: Bloomsbury).
Henderson, L. (1985) 'The wrongs of victims' rights', *Stanford Law Review*, 37, 937–1021.
Henry, B. (1994) *Dublin Hanged: Crime, Law Enforcement and Punishment in the Eighteenth Century* (Dublin: Irish Academic Press).
Henry, M. (2006) 'Unnecessary symphysiotomy surgeries', *Seanad Debates*, vol. 182, no. 25, c. 2011 (9 March 2006).
Hentig, H. von (1948) *The Criminal and His Victim: Studies in the Sociology of Crime* (New Haven, CT: Yale University Press).
Herman, J. L. (1992) *Trauma and Recovery: The Aftermath of Violence-From Domestic Abuse to Political Terror* (New York: Basic Books)
Herman, J. L. (2003) 'The mental health of crime victims: impact of legal intervention', *Journal of Traumatic Stress*, 16:2, 159–166
Herrup, C. (1989) *The Common Peace: Participation in the Criminal Law in Seventeenth Century England* (Cambridge: Cambridge University Press).
von Hentig, H. (1948) *The Criminal and His Victim: Studies in the Sociology of Crime* (New Haven, CT: Yale University Press).
Hobsbawm, E. (1968) *Industry and Empire: An Economic History of Britain since 1750* (London: Weidenfeld and Nicolson).
Hoffman, H. (1988) 'What Did Mendelsohn Really Say?' in S. David and G. Kirchoff (eds), *International Faces of Victimology* (Jerusalem: World Society of Victimology), pp. 89–104.
Hohl, K. and E. A. Stanko (2015) 'Complaints of rape and the criminal justice system: fresh evidence on the attrition problem in England and Wales', *European Journal of Criminology*, 12:3, 324–341.
Holdsworth, W. (1908 repr.) *A History of English Criminal Law*, Vol III (London: Methuen).

Holt, S. and J. Devaney (2016) 'Understanding Domestic Abuse and Sexual Violence' in D. Healy et al. (eds.), *The Routledge Handbook of Irish Criminology* (Abingdon: Routledge), pp. 70–89.

Home Office (UK) (2006) *Rebalancing the Criminal Justice System in Favour of the Law Abiding Majority: Cutting Crime, Reducing Reoffending and Protecting the Public* (London: Home Office).

Home Office, Her Majesty's Court Service and Crown Prosecution Service (2008) *Specialist Domestic Violence Courts Review 2007–08; Justice With Safety* (London: HM, HMCS, CPS).

Hough, J. and P. Mayhew (1983) *The British Crime Survey: First Report* (Home Office Research Series no. 76) (London: Her Majesty's Stationery Office).

Hoyle, C. (1999) *Evaluation of the 'One Stop Shop' and Victim Statements Pilot Projects* (London: Home Office).

Hoyle, C. (2012) 'Victims, The Criminal Process and Restorative Justice' in M. Maguire et al. (eds), *The Oxford Handbook of Criminology* (Oxford: Oxford University Press, 5th edn), pp. 398–425.

Hoyle, C. and L. Zedner (2007) 'Victims, Victimization and Criminal Justice' in M. Maguire, R. Morgan and R. Reiner (eds), *The Oxford Handbook of Criminology* (Oxford: Oxford University Press, 4th edn), pp. 461–495).

Hunt, D. (2001) 'Background and history of Rape Crisis Centres' *Irish Association of Victim Support Newsletter* (Christmas 2001) (Dublin: Irish Association of Victim Support).

ICCL (Irish Council for Civil Liberties) (2008) *A Better Deal: The Human Rights of Victims in the Criminal Justice System* (Dublin: Irish Council for Civil Liberties).

Ignatieff, M. (1978) *A Just Measure of Pain: The Penitentiary in the Industrial Revolution, 1750–1850* (London: Macmillan).

IILE (2011) 'Rathmines women's refuge: 25th anniversary', *The Brief: Journal of the Irish Institute of Legal Executives*, https://www.iilex.ie/images/pdfs/briefs/2011journal.pdf, 24–26.

Immigrant Council of Ireland (2016) *Exploitive Sham Marriages and Human Trafficking in Ireland: Irish National Report* (Dublin: Immigrant Council of Ireland, 2016).

Inglis, T. (2003) *Truth, Power and Lies: Irish Society and the Case of Kerry Babies* (Dublin: University College Dublin Press).

Institute of Public Administration (2011) *White Paper on Crime: Report of Proceedings of Regional Consultation Meetings on the Community and the Criminal Justice System* (Dublin: Institute of Public Administration).

Irish Human Rights and Equality Commission (2015) *Report: Ireland and the International Covenant on Economic, Social and Cultural Rights* (Dublin: IHREC).

ITAS (Irish Tourist Assistance Service) (2016) *Annual Report 2015* (Dublin: Irish Tourist Assistance Service).

Irons, P. (1999) *A People's History of the Supreme Court* (New York: Penguin).

Jackson, J. (1993) 'Competence and compellability of spouses to give evidence', *Dublin University Law Journal*, 15, 202.

Jones, T. and T. Newburn (2007) *Policy Transfer and Criminal Justice: Exploring the US Influence over British Crime Control Policy* (Maidenhead, Berkshire: Open University Press).

Joyce, N. and M. Keenan (2013) *Restorative Justice and Sexual Violence: Ireland Joins the International Debate* (Dublin: UCD Working Paper Series)

Karmen, A. (2004) *Crime Victims: An Introduction to Victimology* (Belmount, CA: Thomson, 5th edn).

Keenan, M. (2016) 'Hindsight, Foresight and Historical Judgement: Child and Sexual Abuse and the Catholic Church' in D. Healy et al. (eds), *The Routledge Handbook of Irish Criminology* (Abingdon: Routledge), pp. 525–540.

Kehoe, I. (2005) 'Victim support files sit in disused office', *Sunday Business Post* (10 July 2005).

Kelleher and Associates with M. O'Connor (1995) *Making the Links: Towards an Integrated Strategy for the Elimination of Violence Against Women in Intimate Relationships with Men* (Dublin: Women's Aid).

Kelleher and Associates with M. O'Connor (1999) *Safety and Sanctions: Domestic Violence and the Enforcement of the Law in Ireland* (Dublin: Women's Aid).

Kelly, L. (2000) 'Republican mothers, bastards' fathers and good victims: discarding citizens and equal protection through the failures of legal images', *Hastings Law Journal*, 51, 557–597.

Keniry, S. (2016) 'Judicial review of the decisions of the Director of Public Prosecutions', *Trinity College Law Review*, 19:1, 196–212.

Kennedy, H. (2004) *Just Law: The Changing Face of Justice and Why It Matters to Us All* (London: Vintage).

Kennedy, K.M., A. McHugh and E. Eogan (2016) 'The forensic medical examination of adults who report sexual violence in Ireland: a practical overview for the legal practitioner', *Irish Criminal Law Journal*, 26:1, 3.

Kennedy, L. (2015) 'The Tourist Victim', presentation delivered at Victims' Rights: An Agenda for Change conference, University of Limerick, 11 September 2015.

Kilcommins, S. (1998) 'Context and contingency in the historical penal process: the revision of revisionist analysis using the twelve judges' notebooks as one tool of analysis', *Holdsworth Law Journal*, 19:1, 1–54.

Kilcommins, S. (2004) 'Historical Jurisprudence' in T. Murphy (ed.), *Western Jurisprudence* (Dublin: Round Hall, Sweet and Maxwell), pp. 144–167.

Kilcommins S. (2014) 'Victims of Crime with Disabilities in Ireland' in I. Bacik and D. Prendergast (eds), *Criminal Law and Practice Review* (Dublin: Clarus Press), pp. 107–128.

Kilcommins, S. (2016) 'Crime control, the security state and constitutional justice in Ireland: discounting liberal legalism and deontological principles', *International Journal of Evidence and Proof*, 20:4, 326–341.

Kilcommins S. and L. Moffett (2015) 'Victims of Crime in Ireland' in D. Healy, C. Hamilton, Y. Daly and M. Butler (eds), *Irish Handbook of Criminology* (London: Routledge), pp. 379–399.

Kilcommins S., C. Edwards and T. O'Sullivan (2013) *An International Review of Legal Provisions and Supports for People with Disabilities as Victims of Crime* (Dublin: Irish Council for Civil Liberties).

Kilcommins, S., I. O'Donnell, E. O'Sullivan and B. Vaughan (2004) *Crime, Punishment and the Search for Order in Ireland* (Dublin: Institute of Public Administration).

Kilcommins, S., M. Leane, F. Dodson, C. Fennell and A. Kingston (2010) *The Needs and Concerns of Victims of Crime in Ireland* (Dublin: Commission for the Support of Victims of Crime).

Kilpatrick, D. G. and Acierno, R. (2003) 'Mental health needs of crime victims: epidemiology and outcomes', *Journal of Traumatic Stress*, 16:2, 119–132.

King, P. (1984) 'Decision-makers and decision-making in the English criminal law, 1750–1800', *The Historical Journal*, 27:1, 25–58.

King, P. (2000) *Crime, Justice, and Discretion in England, 1740–1820* (Oxford: Oxford University Press).

Kirwan, G and M. O'Connell (2001) 'Crime victimisation in Dublin revisited, *Irish Criminal Law Journal*, 11:2, 10–13.

Kool, R. (2016) 'RJ, Victims' Rights within a Human Rights Perspective: A Plea towards Diversion', 9th International Conference of the European Union for Restorative Justice, 22–24 June 2016.

Lacey, N. (1998) 'Contingency, Coherency and Conceptualism: Reflections on the Encounter between Critique and the Philosophy of the Criminal Law' in P. Duff (ed.), *Philosophy of the Criminal Law* (Cambridge: Cambridge University Press), pp. 9–59.

Lacey, N. (2001) 'In search of the responsible subject: history, philosophy and social sciences in criminal law', *Modern Law Review*, 64:3, 350–571.

Lacquer, T. W. (1989) 'Crowds, Carnival and the State in English Executions, 1604–1868' in A. L. Beier et al. (eds.), *The First Modern Society: Essays in English History in Honour of Lawrence Stone* (Cambridge: Cambridge University Press), pp. 305–356.

Landsman, S. (1990) 'The rise of the contentious spirit: adversary procedure in eighteenth century England', *Cornell Law Review*, 75, 498–609.

Langbein, J. H. (1973) 'The origins of public prosecution at common law', *The American Journal of Legal History*, 17:4, 313–335.

Langbein, J. H. (1983) 'Shaping the eighteenth century criminal trial: a view from the Ryder sources', *The University of Chicago Law Review*, 50:1, 1–135.

Langbein, J. H. (1994) 'The historical origins of the privilege against self incrimination at common law', *Michigan Law Review*, 92:5, 1047–1085.

Langbein, J. H. (1999) 'The prosecutorial origins of defence counsel in the eighteenth century: the appearance of solicitors', *Cambridge Law Journal*, 58:2, 314–165.

Langbein, J. H. (2003) *The Origins of Adversary Criminal Trial* (Oxford: Oxford University Press).

Law Reform Commission (1989) *Consultation Paper on Child Sexual Abuse* (Dublin: Law Reform Commission).

Law Reform Commission (LRC 33 -1990) *Report on Sexual Offences against the Mentally Handicapped* (Dublin, LRC).

Law Reform Commission (LRC CP 63 -2011), *Consultation Paper on Sexual Offences and Capacity to Consent* (Dublin: Law Reform Commission).

Law Reform Commission (LRC 112 -2014) *Report on Disclosure and Discovery in Criminal Cases* (Dublin: Law Reform Commission).

Law Society Gazette (2003) 'Hardiman blames the media', *Law Society Gazette*, 97:3, 6.

Lea, J. (2002) *Crime and Modernity* (London: Sage).

Lea, J. (2004) 'Law, Ideology and the Gallows in 18th and 19th Century England', available at http://www.bunker8.pwp.blueyonder.co.uk/hisotry/36804.htm

Leahy, S. (2008) 'In a woman's voice: a feminist analysis of Irish rape law', *Irish Law Times*, 26, 203–12.
Leahy, S. (2012) 'The defendant's right or a bridge too far? Regulating defence access to complainants' counselling records in trials for sexual offences', *Irish Criminal Law Journal*, 22:2, 34–39.
Leahy, S. (2013) 'Summing up in rape trials: the challenge of guiding effectively and without prejudice', *Irish Criminal Law Journal*, 23:4, 102–107.
Leahy, S. (2014) 'The corroboration warning in sexual offence trials: final vestige of the historic suspicion of sexual offence complainants or a necessary protection for defendants?', *The International Journal of Evidence and Proof*, 18:1, 41–64.
Leane, M., S. Ryan, C. Fennell and E. Egan (2001) *Attrition in Sexual Assault Offence Cases in Ireland: A qualitative Analysis* (Dublin: Stationery Office).
Lee, J. J. (1989) *Ireland 1912–1985: Politics and Society* (Cambridge: Cambridge University Press).
Loftus, C. (2015) 'Address to Association for Criminal Justice Research and Development Annual Conference: Victims in Focus', Association for Criminal Justice Research and Development Annual Conference, 2 October 2015.
Longford, Lord (F. Pakenham) (1991) *Punishment and the Punished* (London: Chapman).
Lovett, J. and L. Kelly (2009) *Different Systems, Similar Outcomes: Tracking Attrition in Reported Rape Cases in Eleven Countries* (London: Child and Woman Abuse Studies Unit).
Maguire, M. (1991) 'The needs and rights of victims of crime', *Crime and Justice*, 14, 363–433.
Mahon, E. (1996) 'Women's Rights and Catholicism in Ireland' in M. Threlfall (ed.), *Mapping the Women's Movement in Ireland: Feminist Politics and Change* (London: Verso), pp. 184–215.
Maine, H. (1927 repr.) *Ancient Law* (London: Dent).
Mastrocinque, J. M. (2010) 'An overview of the victims' rights movement: historical, legislative, and research developments', *Sociology Compass*, 4:2, 95–110.
Mawby, R. I. (2007) 'Public Sector Services and the Victim of Crime' in S. Walklate (ed.), *Handbook of Victims and Victimology* (Devon: Willan Publishing).
Mawby, R. I. and M. Gill (1987) *Crime Victims, Needs, Services and the Voluntary Sector* (London: Tavistock).
Mawby, R. I. and S. Walklate (1994) *Critical Victimology: International Perspectives* (London: Sage).
May, A. (2003) *The Bar and the Old Bailey, 1750–1850* (London: University of North Carolina Press).
Mayock, P. and S. Sheridan (2012) *Women's 'Journeys' to Homelessness: Key Findings from a Biographical Study of Homeless Women in Ireland. Women and Homelessness in Ireland, Research Paper 1.* (Dublin: School of Social Work and Social Policy and Children's Research Centre, Trinity College Dublin).
McAlinden, A. M. (2014) 'Deconstructing victim and offender identites in discourses on child sexual abuse hierarchies, blame and the good/evil dialectic', *British Journal of Criminology*, 54:2, 180–198.
McAuley, F. and J. P. McCutcheon (2000) *Criminal Liability: A Grammar* (Dublin: Round Hall, Sweet and Maxwell).

McCormack, R. (1999) 'United States Crime Victims Assistance: History, Organization, and Evaluation' in P. Tobolosky (ed.), *Understanding Victimology: Selected Readings* (New York: Matthew Bender), pp. 247–258.

McCullagh, C. (1986) 'Crime in Ireland: facts, figures and interpretations', *Studies: An Irish Quarterly Review*, 75:297, 11–20.

McCullagh, C. (1999) 'Rural Crime in the Republic of Ireland' in G. Dingwall and S. R. Moody (eds), *Crime and Conflict in the Countryside* (Cardiff: University of Wales Press), pp. 18–35.

McCullagh, C. (2014) 'From offender to scumbag: changing understandings of crime and criminals in contemporary Ireland', *Irish Journal of Sociology*, 22:1, 8–27.

McDowell, M. (2004) 'Victim support funding', *Dáil Debates*, vol. 584, no. 16, c. 491 (5 May 2004).

McEldowney, J. (1989) 'Crown Prosecution in Nineteenth Century Ireland' in D. Hay and F. Snyder (eds), *Policing and Prosecution in Britain, 1750–1850* (Oxford: Clarendon), pp. 427–458.

McEldowney, J. (1980) 'Policing and the Administration of Justice in Nineteenth Century Ireland' in C. Emsley and B. Weinberger (eds.), *Policing Western Europe: Politics, Professionalism and Public Order, 1850–1940*. (London: Greenwood Press), pp. 18–35.

McEvoy K. and K. McConnachie (2012) 'Victimology in transitional justice: victimhood, innocence and hierarchy', *European Journal of Criminology*, 9, 527–38.

McGee, H., R. Garavan, M. deBarra, J. Byrne and R. Conroy (2002) *The SAVI Report: Sexual Abuse and Violence in Ireland: A National Study of Irish Experiences, Beliefs and Attitudes Concerning Sexual Violence* (Dublin: Liffey Press).

McGovern, L. (2002) 'The Victim and the Criminal Justice System' in P. OMahony (ed.), *Criminal Justice in Ireland* (Dublin: Institute of Public Administration), pp. 393–406.

McGowen, R. (1983) 'The image of justice and reform of the criminal law in early nineteenth century England', *Buffalo Law Review*, 32, 89–125.

McGowen, R. (1986) 'A powerful sympathy: terror, the prison and humanitarian reform in early nineteenth century Britain', *Journal of British Studies*, 25, 312–334.

McGowen, R. (1988) 'The changing face of God's justice: the debates over divine and human punishment in eighteenth century England', *Criminal Justice History*, IX, 63–98.

McGrath, A. (2008) 'Is anybody listening, and why do they hear? The use of victim impact statements in Ireland', *Dublin University Law Journal*, 15:1, 71–99.

McGrath, A. (2009) '*The Living Victims of Homicide: What Place for the Families of Homicide Victims in the Criminal Justice System?*' (unpublished PhD thesis) (Cork: University College Cork).

McGrath, D. (2014) *Evidence* (Dublin: Round Hall, 2nd edn).

McGuiness, C. (1993) *Report of the Kilkenny Incest Investigation* (Dublin: Stationary Office).

McHugh, R. (2013) 'Tracking the Needs and Service Provision for Women Ex-prisoners', Association for Criminal Justice Research and Development, July 2013.

McKendrick, N. (1961) 'Josiah Wedgwood and factory discipline', *The Historical Journal*, IV, 40–52.

McMahon, A. M. (2015) 'Putting Victims at the Heart of Garda Service', presentation delivered at Association for Criminal Justice Research and Development Annual Conference, Dublin, 2 October 2015.

Meade, J. (2000) 'Organised crime, moral panic and law reform: the Irish adoption of civil forfeiture', *Irish Criminal Law Journal*, 10:1, 11.

Meese, E. (1986) 'The Supreme Court of the United States: bulwark of a limited constitution', *South Texas Law Review*, 27:1, 455–470.

Mendelsohn, B. (1937) 'Methods to be used by counsel for the defence in the researches made into the personality of the criminal' *Revue de Droit Penal et de Criminologie*, France (August–October) 877–883.

Minow, M. (1993) 'Surviving victim talk', *UCLA Law Review*, 40, 1411.

Moore Walsh, K. (2013) *'Victims' Rights in Ireland: Influences, Illusions and Impacts'* (unpublished PhD thesis) (Cork: University College Cork).

Morris Tribunal (2008) *Reports of the Morris Tribunal, 2002–2008* (Dublin: Government Publications Office).

Mulcahy, A. (2016) 'Trajectories of Policing in Ireland: Similarities, Differences, Convergences' in D. Healy et al. (eds), *The Routledge Handbook of Irish Criminology* (Abingdon: Routledge), pp. 261–280.

Mulcahy, A. and E. O'Mahony (2005) *Policing and Social Marginalisation in Ireland* (Paper 05.02) (Dublin: Combat Poverty Ireland).

Mulkerrins, K. (2003) 'Trial venue: the victim and the accused', *Judicial Studies Institute Journal*, 3:1, 120–129.

Muller-Rappard, E. (1990) 'Perspectives on the Council of Europe's approach to the issue of basic principles of justice for victims of crime', *Human Rights Quarterly*, 12:2, 231–245.

Murphy, A. and P. de Rosa (1993) *Forbidden Fruit: The True Story of My Secret Love With Ireland's Most Powerful Bishop* (New York: Little, Brown).

Murray, E. (2008) 'Criminal Injuries Compensation Tribunal still going strong', *Law Society Gazette*, April, 17.

National Coalition for the Homeless (2010) *Hate Crimes Against The Homeless America's Growing Tide of Violence* Washington, DC: NCH).

National Commission on Restorative Justice (2009) *Final Report* (Dublin: National Commission on Restorative Justice).

Newburn, T. (2003) *Crime and Criminal Justice Policy* (London: Pearson, 2nd edn).

Newmann, J. P. and J. Sallmann (2004) 'Women, trauma histories, and co-occurring disorders: assessing the scope of the problem', *Social Service Review*, 78:3, 466–499.

Norrie, A. (2001) *Crime, History and Reason: A Critical Introduction to Criminal Law* (London: Butterworths, 2nd edn).

Office of the Data Protection Commissioner (2001) *'Case Study 8/01: Victim Support-liaison with An Garda Síochána-disclosure of victims' details-issue of consent'* (Laois: Office of the Data Protection Commissioner)

Office of the DPP (Director of Public Prosecutions) (2013) *Going to Court as a Witness* (Dublin: Office of the Director of Public Prosecutions).

Office of the DPP (Director of Public Prosecutions) (2015) *How to Request Reasons and Reviews* (Dublin: Office of the Director of Public Prosecutions).

Office of the DPP (Director of Public Prosecutions) (2016a) *Annual Report 2015* (Dublin: Office of Director of Public Prosecutions).

Office of the DPP (Director of Public Prosecutions) (2016b) *Guidelines for Prosecutors* (Dublin: Office of the Director of Public Prosecutions, 4th edn).

O'Brien, B. (2006) 'Miscarriages of justice: Paul McCabe and Nora Wall', *Studies: An Irish Quarterly Review*, 95:380, 355–364.

O'Connell, M. (2002) 'Assessment of the Crime Rate in Ireland: Issues and Considerations' in P. O'Mahoney (ed.) *Criminal Justice in Ireland* (Dublin: Institute of Public Administration), pp. 116–133.

O'Connell, M. and A. Whelan (1994) 'Crime victimisation in Dublin', *Irish Criminal Law Journal*, 4:1, 85–112.

O'Donnell, I. (2011) 'Crime and punishment in the Republic of Ireland: a country profile', *International Journal of Comparative and Applied Criminal Justice*, 35:1, 69–84.

O'Hara, E. (2005) 'Victim participation in the criminal process', *Journal of Law and Policy*, 13, 229–47.

O'Flaherty, H. (2002) 'Punishment and the Popular Mind: How Much Is Enough?' in P O'Mahony (ed.), *Criminal Justice in Ireland* (Dublin: IPA), pp. 371–383.

O'Donnell, I. (2005) 'Crime and justice in the Republic of Ireland', *European Journal of Criminology*, 2:1, 99–131.

O'Donnell, I. and K. Edgar (1996) *The Extent and Dynamics of Victimisation in Prison* (Oxford: Centre for Criminological Research).

O'Donnell, I. and E. O'Sullivan (2001) *Crime Control in Ireland: Notes From the Irish Front* (Cork: Cork University Press).

O'Donoghue, J. (1999) 'Sentencing of Garda killers', *Dáil Debates*, vol. 500, no. 1, c. 49–53 (9 February 1999).

O'Higgins, K.C. (2016) *Commission of Investigation (Certain Matters Relative to the Cavan/Monaghan Division of an Garda Síochána)* (Dublin: Department of Justice and Equality).

O'Mahony, P. (1999) 'Modern criminality: a response', *Studies: An Irish Quarterly Review*, 88:350, 120–5.

O'Mahoney, P., M. L. Corr, J. Lovett and L. Kelly (2009) *Ireland Country Report* (London: CWASU, London Metropolitan University)

O'Malley, T. (1993) 'Punishment and moral luck: the role of the victim in sentencing decisions', *Irish Criminal Law Journal*, 3:1, 40–60.

O'Malley, T. (2009) *The Irish Criminal Process* (Dublin: Thomson Round Hall).

O'Malley, T. (2016) *Sentencing Law and Practice* (Dublin: Roundhall).

O'Malley-Dunlop, E. (2015) *Press Release: The EU Directive on Victims Rights*, 16 November 2015, available at http://www.drcc.ie/2015/11/press-release-the-eu-directive-on-victims-rights/ (last viewed 9 October 2016).

O Siocháin, C. and M. Dunphy (2005) 'All victim support funding withdrawn', *Village-Politics Media and Current Affairs* (7 April 2005), available at www.villageie/index (last viewed 3 November 2008).

O'Sullivan, C. (2008) 'The nun, the rape charge, and the miscarriage of justice: the case of Nora Wall', *Northern Ireland Law Quarterly*, 59:3, 305–325.

Owen, N. (1996) 'Victims Charter', *Dáil Debates*, vol. 470, no. 1, c. 29–30 (15 October 1996).

Owen, N. (1997a) 'Victims Charter', *Dáil Debates*, vol. 476, no. 4, c. 872 (13 March 1997).

Owen, N. (1997b) 'Victim Support Ireland', *Dáil Debates*, vol. 478, no. 6, c. 1333 (1 May 1997).

Packer, H. (1968) *The Limits of the Criminal Sanction* (Stanford, CA: Stanford University Press).

Paley, R. (1989) 'Thieftakers in London in the Age of the MacDaniel Gang, c. 1745–1754' in D. Hay and F. Snyder (eds), *Policing and Prosecution in Britain, 1750–1850* (Oxford: Clarendon Press), pp. 301–341.

Paley, W. (1833) *The Works of William Paley DD Archdeacon of Carlisle, With A Life of the Author* (London: Thoemmes Continuum).

Palmer, S. (1988) *Police and Protest in England and Ireland, 1780–1850* (Cambridge: Cambridge University Press).

Palmer, S. (2003) 'The Irish Police Experiment: The Beginnings of Modern Police in the British Isles, 1785–1795' in I. O'Donnell and F. McAuley (eds), *Criminal Justice History: Themes and Controversies from Pre-Independence Ireland* (Dublin: Four Courts Press), pp. 98–112.

Parkinson, D. (2010) 'Supporting victims through the legal process: the role of sexual assault service providers', *Australian Institute of Family Studies*, 8, 1–16.

Parole Board (2016) *Annual Report 2015* (Dublin: Parole Board).

Parsons, S. (2016) 'Crime Trends' in D. Healy et al. (eds), *The Routledge Handbook of Irish Criminology* (Abingdon: Routledge), pp. 15–48.

Pearson, G. (1987) 'Short Memories: Street Violence in the Past and Present' in E. Moonman (ed.), *The Violent Society* (London: Frank Cass), pp. 13–46.

Philips, D. (1983) 'A New Engine of Power and Authority: The Institutionalisation of Law Enforcement in England 1780–1830' in V. Gatrell, B. Lenman and G. Parker (eds), *Crime and the Law: The Social History of Crime in Western Europe since 1500* (London: Europa Publications), pp. 115–189.

Philips. D. (1989) 'Good Men to Associate and Bad Men to Conspire: Associations for the Prosecution of Felons in England, 1760–1860' in D. Hay and F. Snyder (eds), *Policing and Prosecution in Britain, 1750–1850* (Oxford: Clarendon).

Peele, G. (1988) 'The State and Civil Liberties' in H. Drucker et al. (eds), *Developments in British Politics* (London: Palgrave Macmillan, 2nd edn), pp. 144–175.

Peers, S. (2013) 'Guidelines for Transposition: The EU Directive on Victims' Rights (2012/29/EU) and homophobic and transphobic crime victims' [online] Essex: ILG Europe, available at http://www.ilgaeurope.org/sites/default/files/Attachments/guidlines_transportation_2014–5_0.pdf (last viewed 8 December 2016)

Philips, D. (1983) 'A New Engine of Power and Authority: The Institutionalisation of Law Enforcement in England 1780–1830' in V. Gatrell, B. Lenman and G. Parker (eds), *Crime and the Law: The Social History of Crime in Western Europe since 1500* (London: Europa Publications), pp. 155–189.

Philips, D. (1989) 'Good Men to Associate and Bad Men to Conspire: Associations for the Prosecution of Felons in England, 1760–1860' in D. Hay and F. Snyder (eds), *Policing and Prosecution in Britain, 1750–1850* (Oxford: Clarendon), pp. 113–170.

PICUM (2013) *Guide to the EU Victims' Directive: Advancing Access to Protection, Services and Justice for Undocumented Migrants* (Brussels: PICUM 2013), available at http://

picum.org/picum.org/uploads/publication/VictimsDirective_EN.pdf (last viewed 8 December 2016)

Polat, A. (2010) 'The role and importance of victim surveys in criminal research', *Journal of Human Sciences*, 7:1, 1290–1310.

Probation Service (2013) *Restorative Justice Strategy: Repairing the Harm: A Victim Sensitive Response to Offending* (Dublin: Probation Service).

Probation Service (2016) *Annual Report 2015* (Dublin: The Probation Service).

Quigley, M., A. Martynowicz and C. Gardner (2014) *Building Bridges: An Evaluation and Social Return on Investment Study of the Le Chéile Restorative Justice Project in Limerick* (Limerick: Le Chéile).

Quill, E. (2014) *Torts in Ireland* (Dublin: Gill and Macmillan, 4th edn).

Quinn O'Flaherty, L. (2016) 'An argument for advocates for victims of crime in light of Ireland's obligations under Directive 2012/29/EU', *Hibernian Law Journal*, 15:1, 114–129.

Radzinowicz, L. (1956) *A History of English Criminal Law and Its Administration from 1750*. Vol. II (London: Stevens).

Radzinowicz, L. (1994) 'Reflections on the state of criminology', *British Journal of Criminology*, 34:2, 99–104.

Raftery, M. and E. O'Sullivan (1999) *Suffer Little Children: The Inside Story of Ireland's Industrial Schools* (Dublin: Continuum).

Rawlings, P. (1999) *Crime and Power: A History of Criminal Justice, 1688–1998* (London: Longman).

RCNI (Rape Crisis Network of Ireland) (2012) *Position Paper on Previous Sexual History Evidence in Criminal Trials* (Galway: RCNI).

RCNI (2014) *RCNI National Rape Crisis Statistics* (Dublin: Rape Crisis Network Ireland).

Redress (2013) *Explanatory Working Paper Related to the Implementation of the Directive 2012/29/EC establishing Minimum Standards on the Rights, Support and Protection of Victims of Crime* (London: Redress, 2013).

Ring, S. (2009) 'Beyond the reach of justice? Complainant delay in historic child sexual abuse cases and the right to a fair trial', *Judicial Studies Institute Journal*, 2: 162–203.

Ring, S. (2013) 'Analysing fairness in context in historic child sexual abuse prohibition applications', *Irish Criminal Law Journal*, 23:4, 132–140.

Rock, P. (1990) *Helping Victims of Crime: The Home Office and the Rise of Victim Support in England and Wales* (Oxford: Clarendon).

Rock, P. (1994) *Victimology* (Dartmouth, UK: Aldersot).

Rock, P. (2004a) *Constructing Victims' Rights: The Home Office, New Labour, and Victims* (Oxford: Oxford University Press).

Rock, P. (2004b) 'Victims, prosecutors and the state in nineteenth century England and Wales', *Criminal Justice*, 4:4, 331–354.

Rogan, M. (2006a) 'Victims' rights: theory and practice – Part I', *Irish Law Times*, 24:9, 140–144.

Rogan, M. (2006b) 'Victims' rights: theory and practice – Part II', *Irish Law Times*, 24:10, 151–155.

Rogan, M. (2006c) 'The role of victims in sentencing – the case of compensation orders', *Irish Law Times*, 24:2, 202–208.

Rogers, S. (2016) 'Forensic unit can keep samples for year as rape victim decides on reporting crime', *Irish Times*, 6 September 2016.
Rose, N. (2008 repr.) *Powers of Freedom: Reframing Political Thought* (Cambridge: Cambridge University Press).
Ryan, A. and C. Hamilton (2016) 'Criminal Justice Policy and the European Union', in D. Healy et al. (eds), *The Routledge Handbook of Irish Criminology* (Abingdon: Routledge), pp. 467–486.
Safe Ireland (2016) *The State We Are in 2016: Towards a Safe Ireland for Women and Children* (Dublin: Safe Ireland).
Saleilles, R. (1968 repr.) *The Individualisation of Punishment* (New Jersey: Patterson Smith).
Schafer, S. (1968) *The Victim and His Criminal: A Study in Functional Responsibility* (Englewood Cliffs, NJ: Prentice Hall).
Schafer, S. (1974) 'The Beginnings of Victimology', in I. Drapkin and E. Viano (eds), *Victimology* (Lexington, MS: Heath).
Schwartz, B. (1993) *A History of the Supreme Court* (New York: Oxford University Press).
Schweppe, J. and A. Haynes (2015) '*Submission on the Heads of the Criminal Justice (Victims of Crime) Bill 2015*' (Limerick: HHRG).
Schweppe, J., A. Haynes and J. Carr (2014) *A Life Free From Fear: Legislating for Hate Crime in Ireland: An NGO perspective* (Limerick: HHRG).
SATU (Sexual Assault Treatment Unit) (2014) *Recent Rape/Sexual Assault: National Guidelines on Remuferral and Forensic Clinical Examination in Ireland* (Dublin: Sexual Assault Treatment Unit, 3rd edn).
Shapiro, B. (2014) ' "Beyond reasonable doubt": the neglected eighteenth century context', *Law and Humanities*, 8:1, 19–52.
Shapiro, I. (1986) *The Evolution of Rights in Liberal Theory* (Cambridge: Cambridge University Press).
Shapland, J. (1986) 'Victim Assistance and the Criminal Justice System: The Victim's Perspective' in E. A. Fattah (ed.), *From Crime Policy To Victim Policy* (Basingstoke: Macmillan), pp. 218–233.
Shoemaker, R. (1987) 'The London mob in the early eighteenth century', *Journal of British Studies*, 26:3, 273–304.
Shubert, A. (1981) 'Private Initiative in Law Enforcement: Associations for the Prosecutions of Felons, 1744–1856' in V. Bailey (ed.), *Policing and Punishment in Nineteenth Century Britain* (London: Croom Helm), pp. 25–41.
Silver, A. (1967) 'The Demand for Order in a Civil Society: A Review of Some Themes in the History of Urban Crime, Police and Riot' in D. Bordua (ed.), *The Police: six sociological issues* (New York: John Wiley), pp. 1–24.
Sked, A. and C. Cook (1984) *Post-War Britain: A Political History* (London: Penguin, 2nd edn).
Smyth, A. (1993) 'The Women's Movement in the Republic of Ireland 1970–1990' in A. Smyth (ed.), *Irish Women's Studies Reader* (Dublin: Attic), pp. 245–269.
Smyth, S. (2004) 'The increasingly puzzling case of Judge Brian Curtin', *Irish Independent* (24 July 2004).

Spain, E., S. Gibbons and S. Kilcommins (2014) *Analysis of Text for the Final Review of the National Strategy on Domestic, Sexual and Gender Based Violence, 2010–2014* (Dublin: COSC).

Spalek, B. (2006) *Crime Victims: Theory, Policy and Practice* (Basingstoke: Palgrave Macmillan).

Srikantiah, J. (2007) 'Perfect victims and real survivors: the iconic victim in domestic human trafficking law', *Boston University Law Review*, 87, 157–211.

Steiker, C. S. (1997) 'Counter-revolution in constitutional criminal procedure', *Harvard Journal of Law and Public Policy*, 20:2, 435–442.

Stephen, J. F. (1883) *A History of the Criminal Law of England*, Vol I. (London: Routledge/Thoemmes Press).

Stone, L. (1987) *The Past and Present Revisited* (London: Routledge).

Storch, R. D. (1975) 'The plague of the blue locusts: police reform and popular resistance in northern England, 1840–1857', *International Review of Social History*, 20:1, 61–90.

Storch, R. D. (1980) 'Crime and punishment in nineteenth century England', *History Today*, 30, 32–37.

Street, H. (1982) *Freedom, the Individual and the Law* (Middlesex: Penguin, 5th edn).

Thompson, E. P. (1963) *The Making of the English Working Class* (London: Gollancz).

Thompson, E. P. (1967) 'Time, work discipline and industrial capitalism', *Past and Present*, 38, 56–97.

Thompson, E. P. (1971) 'The moral economy of the English crowd in the eighteenth century', *Past and Present*, 50, 76–136.

Thompson, F. M. L. (1981) 'Social control in Victorian Britain', *The Economic History Review*, 34, 189–208.

Tilly, C. (2008) *Credit and Blame* (Princeton: Princeton University Press).

Todino, I. (2013) 'Next Steps in Progressing Victims' rights – Future plans', Victim Support Europe Conference. [online] Scotland: Victims Support Europe, available at http://victimsupport.eu/activeapp/wp-content/files_mf/1371554211P311IngridBellanderTodino.pdf (last viewed 8 December 2016)

Tulkens, F. (2011) 'The paradoxical relationship between criminal law and human rights', *Journal of International Criminal Justice*, 9:3, 577–595.

UN Manual (1985) *Declaration of Basic Principles of Justice for Victims of Crime and Abuse of Power* (UN Doc. GA/RES/40/34) (29 November 1985).

UN, Office on Drugs and Crime and Economic Commission for Europe Task Force (2010) *Manual on Victimization Surveys* (ECE/CES/4) (Geneva: UN).

USI (Union of Students of Ireland) (2013) *Say Something: A Study of Students' Experiences of Harassment, Stalking, Violence and Sexual Assault* (Dublin, Union of Students of Ireland).

Valier, C. (2004) *Crime and Punishment in Contemporary Culture* (London: Routledge).

Van Dijk, J. (2005) 'Benchmarking Legislation on Crime Victims: The UN Declaration of 1985' in E. Vetere and P. David (eds), *Victims of Crime and Abuse of Power: festschrift in honour of Irene Melup* (New York: United Nations), pp. 202–208.

Van Kesteren, J., P. Mayhew and J. van Dijk (2013) 'The international crime victims surveys: a retrospective', *International Review of Victimology*, 20:1, 49–69.

Vaughan, B. and S. Kilcommins (2008) *Terrorism, Rights and the Rule of Law: negotiating justice in Ireland* (Devon: Willan Publishing).

Vaughan, B. and S. Kilcommins (2010) 'The governance of crime and the negotiation of justice', *Criminology and Criminal Justice*, 10, 59–75.
Viano, E. (1992) *Critical Issues in Victimology: International Perspectives* (New York: Springer).
Victims of Crime Office (2010) *Victims Charter* (Dublin: Department of Justice, Equality and Law Reform).
Victims of Crime Office (2015) *Summary of 2014 Evaluation and Financial Reports* (Dublin: Victims of Crime Office).
Victims' Rights Alliance (2014) *The Implementation and Enforcement of the Victims' Rights Directive in Ireland: Ensuring the Consistency of Victims' Rights for all Victims of Crime* (Dublin: VRA).
Waldron, J. (1999) *Law and Disagreement* (Oxford: Oxford University Press).
Walklate, S. (2000) 'Researching Victims of Crime' in R. D. King and E. Wincup (eds), *Doing Research on Crime and Justice* (Oxford: Oxford University Press), pp. 183–201.
Walklate, S. (2007) 'Comparative Perspectives, Introduction' in S. Walklate (ed.), *Handbook of Victims and Victimlogy* (Cullompton, Devon: Willan), pp. 333–337.
Walklate, S. (2011) 'Reframing criminal victimization: finding a place for vulnerability and resilience', *Theoretical Criminology*, 15: 179–194.
Walsh, D. (1999) 'Crime and society: an Irish response', *Studies: An Irish Quarterly Review*, 88:350, 110–114.
Walsh, D. (2002a) *Criminal Procedure* (Dublin: Thomson Round Hall).
Walsh, D. (2002b) 'The democratic deficit in criminal law and criminal justice in Title VI of the Treaty on European Union', *Irish Criminal Law Journal*, 12:4, 7–16.
Walsh, D. (2005) *Juvenile Justice* (Dublin: Thomson Round Hall).
Walsh, D. (2013) 'Liability for Garda negligence in the prevention and investigation of crime', *Irish Jurist*, XLIX, 1–28.
Watson, D. (2000) *Victims of Recorded Crime in Ireland: Results from the 1996 Survey* (Dublin: Oak Tree Press).
Weber, M. (1978 repr.) *Economy and Society* (Vol II), G. Roth and C. Wittich (eds) (London: University of California Press).
Weed, F. (1995) *Certainty of Justice: Reform in the Crime Victim Movement. Hawthorn* (New York: Aldine de Gruter).
Wemmers, J. (1998) 'In memory of Benjamin Mendelsohn, founder of victimology', *The Victimologist: Newsletter of the World Society of Victimology*, 2:1, 5.
Wemmers, J. (2005) 'Victim policy transfer: learning from each other', *European Journal on Criminal Policy and Research*, 11:1, 121–133.
Whyte, G. (2002) *Social Inclusion and the Legal System: Public Interest Law in Ireland* (Dublin: Institute of Public Administration).
Whyte, D. (2007) 'Victims of Corporate Crime' in S. Walklate (ed.), *Handbook of Victims and Victimology* (Cullompton, Devon: Willan), pp. 446–483.
Wiener, M. J. (1990) *Reconstructing the Criminal: Culture, Law, and Policy in England: 1830–1914* (Cambridge: Cambridge University Press).
Wiener, M. J. (1999) 'Judges v jurors: courtroom tensions in murder trials and the law of criminal responsibility in nineteenth century England', *Law and History Review*, 17:3, 467–506.

Williams, B. (1999) 'The Victims' Charter: citizens as consumers of criminal justice services', *Howard Journal of Criminal Justice*, 38, 384.

Williams, B. and H. Goodman (2007) 'The Role of the Voluntary Sector' in S. Walklate (ed.), *Handbook of Victims and Victimology* (Cullompton, Devon: Willan), pp. 240–254.

Willis, J. (2008) 'Punishment and the cultural limits to state power in late eighteenth century Britain', *Punishment and Society*, 10:4, 401–428.

Wolfgang, M. (1958) *Patterns of Criminal Homicide* (Philadelphia: University of Pennsylvania Press).

Wolhuter, L., N. Wolhuter and D. D. Olley (2008) *Victimology, Victimisation and Victims' Rights* (UK: Routledge-Cavendish).

Women's Aid (2010) *Submission to the White Paper on Crime: Discussion Document 2: Criminal Sanctions* (Dublin: Women's Aid).

Women's Aid (2016) *Impact Report 2015* (Dublin: Women's Aid).

Wood, M., K. Lepanjuuri, C. Paskell, J. Thompson, L. Adams and S. Coburn (2015) *Crown Prosecution Service Victim and Witness Satisfaction Survey* (London: CPS).

Young, M. (1997) 'Victim's Rights and Services: A Modern Saga' in R. Davis, A. Lurigio and W. Skogan (eds), *Victims of Crime* (Thousand Oaks, CA: Sage, 2nd edn), pp. 194–210.

Young, M. (2006) 'History of the Victims Movement in the US', available at http://www.iovahelp.org/About/MarleneAYoung/USHistory.pdf (last viewed 2 January 2017).

Young, P., I. O'Donnell and E. Clare (2001) *Crime in Ireland: Trends and Patterns, 1950–1998* (Dublin: National Crime Council).

Zedner, L. (1994) 'Victims' in M. Maguire, R. Morgan and R. Reiner (eds) *The Oxford Handbook of Criminology* (Oxford: Oxford University Press), pp. 1207–1246.

Zedner, L. (2002) 'Victims' in M. Maguire, R. Morgan and R. Reiner (eds) *The Oxford Handbook of Criminology* (Oxford: Oxford University Press, 3rd edn), pp. 419–456.

Zedner, L. (2004) *Criminal Justice* (Oxford: Oxford University Press).

Index

accomplices 10, 18
adversarialism 5, 21, 22, 52
An Garda Síochána
  decision to prosecute 97
  Ethnic Liaison officers 129
  Family Liaison officers 92, 93, 129
  front-line experience 124–125, 129
  Garda Strategic Transformation Office 125
  LGBT officers 129
  reporting 120–123
  service provision 90–95
  specialist interviewers 93, 129
  statistics 118–119
  Victim Service Offices 93, 125, 129, 143
attrition rates 6, 123–124, 144

Balance in the Criminal Law Review Group (Ireland) 28, 32, 41, 43, 49

Catholic Church 34, 46
Celtic Tiger economy 46
centralised police force, emergence of 17–18, 27
Commission for the Support of Victims of Crime (Ireland) 32, 38, 48, 86, 88, 131
Coroner's Service 102–103

Council of Europe 4, 37, 40–43, 45, 49, 68
  Convention on Action against Trafficking in Human Beings (2005) 42
  Convention on Compensation (1983) 43, 104
  Convention on the Prevention of Terrorism (2005) 42
  European Convention for the Protection of Human Rights and Fundamental Freedoms (1953) 4, 41, 42, 45, 53, 55, 68–71, 78, 114
crime as a political issue
  1964 US presidential campaign 44
  1968 US presidential election 44
  1979 British elections 45
  1997 Irish general election 47
Crime Council (Ireland) 29, 37
crime rates 3, 44, 45, 47, 48, 118–123, 143
crime victimisation surveys 2, 29, 31–32, 89, 92, 119–122, 142
Crime Victims Helpline 3, 88–90
Criminal Justice (Victims of Crime) Act 2017 86, 94, 99, 101, 103–104, 109, 112–115
criminal law 15, 25, 26, 54
criminal trials 12, 14, 20, 21
criminology
  British 29
  Irish 30

European Court of Human Rights 4, 41, 43, 45, 46, 53, 69, 70, 78, 114
European Court of Justice 45, 46
European Union 4, 40, 42, 43, 49, 71
  cross-border victims 43
  Directive 2004/80/EC relating to compensation to crime victims 43, 74, 104
  Directive 2011/36/EU on preventing and combating trafficking in human beings and protecting its victims 74, 83
  Directive 2011/92/EU on combating the sexual abuse and sexual exploitation of children and child pornography 74, 84
  Directive 2011/99 EU on the European Protection Order 74, 84
  Directive 2012/29/EU establishing minimum standards on the rights, support and protection of victims of crime *see* European Union Directive on Victims' Rights
  Framework Decision on Preventing and Combating Trafficking in Human Beings and Protecting Victims 43, 74, 83
  Framework Decision on Preventing and Combating the Sexual Abuse and Exploitation of Children and Child Pornography (2004) 43, 74
  Framework Decision on the Standing of Victims in Criminal Proceedings (2001) 4, 37, 41
  Maastricht Treaty 42
European Union Directive on Victims' Rights 43, 124, 128, 71–74, 143
  information and support 87, 90, 108–109, 113, 114, 128
  monitoring effectiveness 117–120, 130–132
  participation 97, 103, 104, 107
  protection 101, 127
  training 128–130
  transposition 112–114
evidence 13, 18, 20, 21, 52
  background evidence 67
  competence to testify 62, 63, 64
  corroboration 64
  cross-examination 81
  disclosure 76
  doctrine of recent complaint 52, 66
  identification 60
  intermediaries 57
  opinion evidence 66
  pre-trial statements 58
  presumption of innocence 76
  video-link 56, 57, 75
exculpatory justice 1, 8 14
expenses 103–104

fear of crime 6, 108, 142
funding 114–117

health care providers 125–126, 128–130, 136

ideal victim 132–133
inculpatory justice 7, 9, 12, 27

judiciary 13, 26, 37, 40, 44, 48–49, 55, 115, 128, 130
juries 11, 22

law and order 45, 46, 47
lawyerisation 18, 21
legal aid 67–68, 90, 94
lobbying 35, 36, 37, 38

media 132–133, 142
moral panic 46

non-reporting 120–123
  information on services 87–90
  reasons for 122–123

Index

pardons 10
prosecution of crime 23, 123–124, 120, 127, 129, 130
  decision to prosecute 123
  private prosecutors 9, 19
  reasons for decisions 97–98, 143
  review of decisions 98–99
public interest 1, 3, 4, 8, 19, 24, 27, 53, 54, 141–143
punishment 16, 17, 26, 108, 137–138
punitiveness 55, 144

research 117–120
Rule of Law 16, 17, 20, 22, 25

secondary victimisation 41, 124–127
sentencing 11–12, 20, 23, 41, 61, 67, 76, 109–110
Sexual Assault Treatment Units (SATUs) 95–96, 117
social contract 16, 17
social movements
  civil rights movements 34
  feminist victims' movement 33, 34
  human rights approach for crime victims 39, 43
  human rights movement 33
  international victims' movement 33
  Irish women's liberation movement 34
  victims' rights movement (US) 33, 45
stakeholder training 127–130
state compensation 2, 40, 43, 67, 72, 73, 88, 90, 103–107

thieftakers 9, 18
trauma 124–127
trial
  cross-examination 123–124
  counselling notes 123, 136

court accompaniment 101–102, 114
court facilities 126–127
delay 123, 126
prosecution pre-trial meeting 100, 124, 125
support 99–102, 124

United Nations 37, 39, 40, 43, 49
  Declaration of Basic Principles of Justice for Victims of Crime and Abuse of Power (1985) 4, 40, 41, 85, 87
  low profile in Ireland 40
  Universal Declaration of Human Rights (1948) 39

victim impact statements 35, 37, 61, 75, 86, 137
victim precipitation 30, 31
victimology
  dark figures of crime 31
  earliest studies 2, 30, 49
  examining experiences of crime victims 31, 32, 33, 142
  international symposium 31
  review of legislation on victim support (Ireland) 33
  sub-discipline of criminology 30
Victims Charter and Guide to the Criminal Justice System 2, 3, 33, 37, 38, 86, 90, 91, 92, 97, 100, 101, 102, 103, 106, 109, 143
volunteers 116, 129
vulnerable persons 6, 68–71, 92–93, 120–121, 134–136

war on crime 44, 143
Women's Movement 2, 142

EU authorised representative for GPSR:
Easy Access System Europe, Mustamäe tee 50,
10621 Tallinn, Estonia
gpsr.requests@easproject.com

www.ingramcontent.com/pod-product-compliance
Ingram Content Group UK Ltd.
Pitfield, Milton Keynes, MK11 3LW, UK
UKHW021848140426
5217IPUK00022B/1663